# ENCOUNTERING THE OTHER

# Religious Pluralism and Public Life
## SERIES FOREWORD

WELCOME TO YOU, AS you join us in exploring religious pluralism—a topic both simple and complex.

Simply put, North America, like much of the world, is home to many different religious traditions. Though our traditions have different histories and philosophies, we share a common life. Thus, we must work together to navigate questions about politics, ethics, education, environment, possible futures, and more. Naturally, our different perspectives come into conversation and, sometimes, conflict. Conversation helps us discover new facets of problems and solutions. Conflict challenges us to learn skills of resolution: listening, waiting, translating, compromising, collaborating.

But living into religious pluralism can be complex. How exactly do we bring theologies into conversation? Can we face historical hurts and ruptures? When we honestly encounter one another, what happens to our traditions? Do we remain distinct? Teach one another new ideas and practices? Adopt a unifying spirituality that holds a place for all? And in its light creatively re-interpret our own sacred texts and rituals? Answers to these questions are likely situational, emerging out of our collaborations, conversations, and conflicts over specific issues.

Thus, this book series, Religious Pluralism and Public Life, begins with issues-oriented discussions. These exchanges uncover deeper theological and cultural challenges for scholars and activists of different traditions to explore together. By reading, discussing, and even writing to series contributors, you, the readers, become part of the discussion.

Thank you for joining us.

Laura Duhan-Kaplan
Harry O. Maier

# ENCOUNTERING THE OTHER

*Christian and Multifaith Perspectives*

EDITED BY Laura Duhan-Kaplan
AND Harry O. Maier

☙PICKWICK *Publications* • Eugene, Oregon

ENCOUNTERING THE OTHER
Christian and Multifaith Perspectives

Religious Pluralism and Public Life 1

Copyright © 2020 Wipf and Stock Publishers. All rights reserved. Except for brief quotations in critical publications or reviews, no part of this book may be reproduced in any manner without prior written permission from the publisher. Write: Permissions, Wipf and Stock Publishers, 199 W. 8th Ave., Suite 3, Eugene, OR 97401.

Pickwick Publications
An Imprint of Wipf and Stock Publishers
199 W. 8th Ave., Suite 3
Eugene, OR 97401

www.wipfandstock.com

PAPERBACK ISBN: 978-1-5326-3328-7
HARDCOVER ISBN: 978-1-5326-3330-0
EBOOK ISBN: 978-1-5326-3329-4

*Cataloguing-in-Publication data:*

Names: Duhan-Kaplan, Laura, editor. | Maier, Harry O., 1959–, editor.

Title: Encountering the other : Christian and multifaith perspectives / edited by Laura Duhan-Kaplan and Harry O. Maier.

Description: Eugene, OR : Pickwick Publications, 2020 | Series : Religious Pluralism and Public Life 1 | Includes bibliographical references.

Identifiers: ISBN 978-1-5326-3328-7 (paperback) | ISBN 978-1-5326-3330-0 (hardcover) | ISBN 978-1-5326-3329-4 (ebook)

Subjects: LCSH: Religions—Relations. | Religious Studies—Religion and Society.

Classification: BL695 .E53 2020 (print) | BL695 .E53 (ebook)

Manufactured in the U.S.A. APRIL 13, 2020

Images "Guru Nanak Converses with Muslim Clerics" and "Guru Nanak meets Nath Siddhas at the village of Achal Batala" reprinted with permission of the Asian Art Museum of San Francisco.

TO A MORE COMPASSIONATE WORLD

# Contents

*Contributors* | xi
*Acknowledgments* | xiii
*Abbreviations* | xiv
*Introduction* by Laura Duhan-Kaplan and Harry O. Maier | xv

## I. Constructions of the Religious Other

1   Esau My (Br)other: The Esau Narrative in Multiple Traditions | 3
    *Jay Eidelman*

2   "I Consider Them Shit": Paul, the Abject, and the Religious Construction of the Other | 12
    *Harry O. Maier*

3   Friendship between Muslims, Christians, and Jews: A Qur'anic View | 27
    *Syed Nasir Zaidi*

4   Encountering Difference and Identity in South Asian Religions | 39
    *Anne Murphy*

5   Religious Courts on Trial | 49
    *Terry S. Neiman*

6   We Are All Outsiders: Negotiating Imaginary Territory in Pakistan | 59
    *Patricia Gruben*

7   Dogs as the Other in St. Augustine's *City of God:* Exploring the Limits of Human Social Relations | 70
    *Midori E. Hartman*

8   "Is This Your God . . . Killer of Children?": Israel's "Childish" Deity and the Other(s) in *Exodus: Gods and Kings* | 82
    *James Magee Jr.*

## II. Theology and Practice of Encounter

9   Encountering the Other: Positive Lessons from Contemporary Science | 107
    *Marc Gopin*

10  Vibration of the Other: A Kabbalistic Ecumenism | 118
    *Laura Duhan-Kaplan*

11  "Unitive Being" in the Face of Atrocity: North American Contemplative Christian Responses to Terrorism | 127
    *Paula Pryce*

12  Searching for the Sacred Other in the Palestinian/Israeli Conflict | 141
    *Lynn E. Mills*

13  For the Love of Strangers: A Theology of Hospitality in Colonial Canada | 153
    *Anita Fast*

14  Hindu Traditions: A Positive Approach to the Other | 168
    *Acharya Shrinath Prasad Dwivedi*

## III. Responsibility to the Other in Christian Mission

15  Indigenous People as the Other: Bartolomé de las Casas in Conversation with Tzvetan Todorov | 177
    *Ray Aldred*

16  The Constructive Iconoclasm of Lamin Sanneh | 191
    *Robert S. Paul*

17  Light from a Dark Horse: Karl Barth on Approaching the Religious Other | 212
    *Roger Revell*

18  From Other to Brother: Re-interpreting the Canadian Christians' Call as We Stand with the Syrian Muslim Refugee | 226
    *Alisha Fung*

19  Christianity without Enemies | 237
    *Jason Byassee*

# Contributors

Rev. **Ray Aldred**, PhD, a member of the Cree Nation from Alberta (Treaty 8), Director of Indigenous Studies at the Vancouver School of Theology, and a communications trainer.

Rev. **Jason Byassee**, PhD, Butler Chair of Homiletics and Biblical Hermeneutics at the Vancouver School of Theology and former Pastor at Boone United Methodist Church in North Carolina.

Rabbi **Laura Duhan-Kaplan**, PhD, Director of Inter-religious Studies and Professor of Jewish Studies at Vancouver School of Theology.

**Acharya Shrinath Prasad Dwivedi**, MA, author of six books of poetry, is actively involved in interfaith work in Canada as a teacher and an organizer.

**Jay Eidelman**, PhD, historian, writer, and lecturer, teaching history of the Holocaust at the University of British Columbia.

**Anita Fast**, MATS, Registrar at Vancouver School of Theology and member of Mennonite Church Canada.

**Alisha Fung**, student at the Vancouver School of Theology, completing her MDiv degree, and volunteer for the Uniting Church of Australia.

**Marc Gopin**, PhD, Director of the Center for World Religions, Diplomacy, and Conflict Resolution and James H. Laue Professor at the School of Conflict Analysis and Resolution at George Mason University.

**Patricia Gruben**, PhD, Director of Praxis Centre for Screenwriters, recently retired as Associate Professor of Film in Simon Fraser University's School for the Contemporary Arts.

**Midori E. Hartman**, PhD, MATS, Visiting Assistant Professor of Religious Studies at Albright College.

**James Magee Jr.**, MATS, MA, recently completed the thesis "Cinematic Childhood(s) and Imag(in)ing the Boy Jesus: Adaptations of Luke 2:41–52 in Late Twentieth-Century Film."

**Harry O. Maier**, PhD, Professor of New Testament and Early Christian Studies at Vancouver School of Theology and Research Fellow at the Max Weber Center for Advanced Cultural and Social Studies at the University of Erfurt, Germany.

**Lynn E. Mills**, MATS, PhD student at Trinity College Dublin in the School of Religion.

**Anne Murphy**, PhD, Associate Professor in the Department of Asian Studies at the University of British Columbia.

**Terry S. Neiman**, PhD, conflict intervention professional, faculty member at Douglas College, and Research Associate at the Vancouver School of Theology.

**Robert S. Paul**, PhD, Associate Professor of Mission Theology at the Vancouver School of Theology and Dean of St. Andrew's Hall.

**Paula Pryce**, PhD, lecturer and research fellow at the Department of Anthropology at the University of British Columbia and research associate at Vancouver School of Theology.

Rev. **Roger Revell**, ThM, PhD student in Theology and Religious Studies at Cambridge University.

**Syed Nasir Zaidi**, PhD, Muslim Spiritual Care Professional, Vancouver General Hospital; Research Associate, Vancouver School of Theology; Religious Consultant, Al-Zahraa Islamic Center; Research scholar, Al-Mustafa Academy Society of BC.

# Acknowledgments

WE THANK ALL WHO helped this volume move from concept to completion.

We thank the Vancouver School of Theology and Principal Richard Topping for their enthusiastic support. VST hosted the conference where first drafts of chapters were shared and discussed. We are also grateful to conference funders, the Victoria Foundation and Hugh and Helen Mogenson.

Of course, the volume's contributors did much of the creative work. We thank our dedicated student assistant of four years, Hillary Kaplan, for staying in touch with authors and helping to format their work. We also thank graduate assistant Eloecea for helping us organize information in recent months.

Thanks go to the Asian Art Museum for permission to reproduce images. Our editors at Wipf and Stock provided guidance and advice. We thank editors Charlie Collier, Matthew Wimer, and Daniel Lanning.

And, last but not least, we thank our family and friends for their patience as we pored over the book's many details.

LAURA DUHAN-KAPLAN and HARRY O. MAIER
Vancouver School of Theology, British Columbia, Canada
Traditional, ancestral, and unceded territories of the Musqueam people

# Abbreviations

ASV — *American Standard Version.* New York: Thomas Nelson, 1901.

CD — Barth, Karl. *Church Dogmatics.* Translated by G. T. Thomson, et al. Edinburgh: T&T Clark, 1936–77.

ESV — *The English Standard Version.* Wheaton, IL: Crossway, 2002.

GNT — *Good News Bible.* Philadelphia: American Bible Society, 1992.

ISV — *The Holy Bible: International Standard Version.* Bradenton, FL: ISV Foundation, 1996–2012.

KJV — *King James Version.* 1611. Rev. 1769. New York: American Bible Society, 1975.

NABRE — *The New American Bible.* Rev. ed. Rome: Confraternity of Christian Doctrine, 2011.

NASB — *New American Standard Bible.* New York: Thomas Nelson, 1977.

NET — *The NET Bible/New English Translation.* Richardson, TX: Biblical Studies, 2005.

NIV — *The New International Version.* New York: New York International Bible Society, 1978.

NRSV — *New Revised Standard Version.* New York: National Council of the Churches of Christ, 1989.

RSV — *Revised Standard Version.* New York: National Council of Churches of Christ in the USA, 1952.

TLB — *The Living Bible.* Carol Stream, IL: Tyndale, 1971.

# Introduction

## Laura Duhan-Kaplan
## and Harry O. Maier

In May 2016, a multi-faith group of one hundred scholars, students, and activists gathered at the Vancouver School of Theology to talk together about "Encountering the Other." The topic, we felt, was urgent. Canada is working to implement a program of reconciliation with its Indigenous peoples. Our country also hopes to create a multi-cultural, multi-faith society, with a public square welcoming to multiple religious expressions. The Vancouver School of Theology, an ecumenical Christian seminary located on the campus of the University of British Columbia, has embraced both these national projects. All our graduate students—future ministers, scholars, and spiritual care providers—are introduced to Indigenous Studies and Inter-Religious Studies. Given their relevance to current events, these fields are changing faster than our core curriculum can. So, to keep our students and faculty up to date, and to learn from and with the larger community, we convened a conference to discuss religious approaches to encountering the Other.

In its simplest meaning, something "other" is simply something separate, different, or contrasting with something else. In philosophy, sociology, and politics, however, we also speak of the act of "othering." To "other" is to interpret negatively other people who are different from you. Psychologically, those who "other" may enhance their own self-esteem as they compare themselves with devalued others. Socially, they may try to contain, limit, oppress, change, or eliminate those others. This violent othering, said our conference presenters, may be caused by ignorance, anxiety, fear, or greed. These impulses have come between Jews, Christians, Muslims, Sikhs, and Hindus. They have placed Christian missionaries and Indigenous peoples at odds. They have even divided professional groups supposedly working towards the same common good. Still, conference presenters said, the divides caused by othering can be bridged through listening, contemplation, mediation, positive psychology, thoughtful practice, and new theologies.

This book brings a taste of the conference to the larger community, offering a selection of conference papers written by scholars, advanced graduate students, and community activists. Here, we have grouped those papers into three sections. Section One, "Constructions of the Religious Other," focuses on a description of the challenge. How do people use religious texts and social trends to define themselves in opposition to others? Section Two, "Theology and Practice of Encounter," responds to the challenge. What concepts, approaches, and spiritual practices can we cultivate to reach across volatile divisions between people? These two sections draw on multiple faith perspectives, including Jewish, Muslim, Sikh, Hindu, and Indigenous traditions. Section Three, "Responsibility to the Other in Christian Mission," applies the concepts and practices to a key Christian practice. How does one share the gospel in a way that respects the integrity of God working through multiple faith traditions?

## CONSTRUCTIONS OF THE RELIGIOUS "OTHER"

In his essay, "Esau my (Br)other: The Esau Narrative in Multiple Traditions," Jay Eidelman shows how a scriptural story can supply raw materials for talking about a threatening Other. In the biblical book of Genesis, Esau is the twin brother of featured character Jacob, father of the Israelite people. Esau is a neutral character, with good and bad personality traits. But in the hands of later commentators, Esau becomes a negative mirror of his brother. His name is used as a metaphor for Israel's enemies, Amalek and Rome. Eidelman analyzes the biblical text, shows how commentators developed it, and notes how it shapes contemporary Jewish perceptions of self and other.

Harry Maier, in his essay "'I Consider Them Shit': Paul, the Abject, and the Religious Construction of the Other," turns to the New Testament writer Paul. Paul, a master of rhetoric, doubly uses his speech to disrupt social orders. He associates his enemies with socially abject things, such as excrement, mutilation, and feral dogs. At the same time, he describes his own religious creativity as the ability to leave behind social orders that reject what is abject. By first distancing himself from the abject, and then identifying with the suffering of the abject Christ, he proclaims himself founder of a new order. He identifies his enemies with a negative "Other" and himself with a positive "Other."

In "Friendship Between Muslims, Christians, and Jews: A Qur'anic View," Syed Nasir Zaidi looks at Qur'anic passages about Christians and, to a lesser extent, Jews. While both are honored as "People of the Book," they are also criticized. Both communities, says the Qur'an, have fallen away from their own prophets' original teachings. Christians have moved away from strict monotheism. At times, local Christians and Jews have been at odds with the Prophet Muhammad's early community. As non-Muslims, they may not be eligible to enter Paradise. What grounds, then, does the Qur'an provide for friendship with Jews and Christians? Zaidi introduces multiple answers to the question, concluding that the Qur'an favors interreligious friendship.

Anne Murphy discusses "Encountering Difference and Identity in South Asian Religions." She turns to the Punjab, examining early manuscripts depicting Guru Nanak (1469–1539), the founder of Sihki, in dialogue. Without undermining the Guru's originality, Murphy shows that his religious teachings were formed in encounter with other traditions. It is possible, she says, to "embrace . . . multiple modes: to discover commonalities . . . discern distinctions . . . and to reimagine religious self-articulations in new modes."

In "Religious Courts on Trial," Terry Neiman describes another kind of religious tension: between religious courts and secular legal systems in a democratic society. Religious courts, e.g., Jewish and Islamic courts of halacha and sharia, primarily mediate disputes within communities. But their function is not well understood. Lawyers who seek to keep dispute resolution within the legal system consider these courts transgressive. So do secularists who worry that empowering religious bodies abridges the civil rights of participants. Properly understood, however, religious courts enhance the life of the community and remain within the boundaries of law.

Patricia Gruben, a Canadian screenwriter, provides a concrete example of navigating a complex religious society. In her essay, "We Are All Outsiders: Negotiating Imaginary Territory in Pakistan," she tells the story of trying to produce a screen adaptation of the novel *The Pakistani Bride*. The novel is a story of the friendship between two culturally different women, each an outsider in her own community. Gruben's own work on the film illustrates the complexities of inter-cultural encounter. Using Hall's concept of a high context society, in which insiders share a strong background knowledge of cultural norms, she describes her attempt to navigate the Pakistani work environment. She was challenged by her own gender and nationality, as well as her Pakistani colleagues' limited knowledge of religious and class complexities in their own country. Ultimately, the film was not produced; but Gruben learned a great deal about encountering the other.

Midori Hartman moves away from inter-religious tension, to focus on a more general human practice of "othering." Her essay is called "Dogs as the Other in St. Augustine's *City of God*: Exploring the Limits of Human Social Relations." Sometimes, says Hartman, we project onto non-human species the anxieties we feel about our own selves. Early Christian theologian Augustine (354–430) spoke of dogs' pro-social and anti-social behavior as a way of understanding disruptions in human society. He noted that, while dogs do not feel shame, humans do have access to the spiritual gift of shame, an emotion we understand as a punishment for sin. While we are weighed down by original sin, we can be comforted by our superiority over other animals. Hartman's essay reminds us that, even if we let go of religious stereotyping, defining ourselves over against others may be a stubborn human trait.

In his essay, "'Is This Your God . . . Killer of Children?' Israel's 'Childish' Deity and the Other(s) in *Exodus: Gods and Kings*," James Magee speaks about the "othering" of children in popular cinema. In *Exodus: Gods and Kings*, God is portrayed as a boy named Malak. Viewers who expect the child to be innocent are challenged to respond to his maliciousness. Thus, they are led to reflect on their expectations of God. At the same time, filmmakers use Malak's childishness to denigrate God. Finally, the film offers viewers a chance to confront stereotypes of children, some of which block our society's ability to tend to their needs. Magee reminds us of the practical consequences of acting on our own images of the "other."

## THEOLOGY AND PRACTICE OF ENCOUNTER

In his essay about "Encountering the Other: Positive Lessons from Contemporary Science," Marc Gopin acknowledges that people do see the world and one another differently. Sometimes, those competing visions lie at the root of conflict. But contemporary research in physics, psychology, and neuropsychology show that we can change. Physics teaches that how we see affects what we see. Positive psychology reminds us to look not only at the chaos and violence featured daily on the news but also at the reality that the world is actually becoming less violent overall. Neuropsychology affirms the power of neuroplasticity, that is, our ability to change pathways in our nervous system. Gopin calls on us to actively use these potentials in conflict resolution, and to investigate the positive role that religious traditions can play in doing so. The other authors in this section take up Gopin's call.

Laura Duhan-Kaplan draws on the Jewish mystical tradition of Kabbalah to articulate a positive theory of deep inter-religious ecumenism. In her essay, "Vibration of the Other: A Kabbalistic Ecumenism," she explores a sermon about the Exodus story from Rabbi Nachman of Breslov (1772–1810, Ukraine). God, says Reb Nachman, is the universal vibration. Slavery is the addiction to being right. Pharaoh observed this and became an atheist. Moses, who is slow of speech, used his listening skills to bring Pharaoh to belief. If only we all listened, we would hear God behind the different keys of each religious tradition. Duhan-Kaplan notes the different ways this ecumenical view has appeared at different times in Jewish history. She concludes by understanding her own mystical experience in the context of early twenty-first-century Canada.

Paula Pryce shares her anthropological studies of Christian contemplatives in her essay, "'Unitive Being' in the Face of Atrocity: North American Contemplative Christian Responses to Terrorism." These practitioners (both monastic and non-monastic) of silent centering prayer seek to dissolve boundaries between self and other in order to be of service. For them, their moral and spiritual commitment to service is more important than holding particular theological beliefs. They see contemplative prayer as a necessary grounding for both their social justice work and prophetic calls to action against violence.

Lynn Mills applies the philosophies of listening in her essay, "Searching for the Sacred Other in the Palestinian/Israeli Conflict." She presents Martin Buber's (1878–1965) philosophy of "I/Thou" relationship, in which one relates to the other with full presence and without analysis. This philosophy permeated Buber's own political activism, as he called for early Zionists to practice negotiation and partnership with Palestinians. Mills shows how several partnerships for peace active today consciously apply Buber's philosophy in order to resist demonization and seek the sacred in the other.

In her essay, "For the Love of Strangers: A Theology of Hospitality in Colonial Canada," Anita Fast wonders if uncritical theologies of hospitality undermine some Canadian churches' ability to welcome Indigenous people. To Christians of European descent, she offers three exploratory suggestions for re-envisioning those theologies. Churches can re-define hospitality in a way that more fully honors the mores of Indigenous culture, recognizing, for example, a culture of gift rather than exchange. They can reclaim a biblical understanding of hospitality in which welcoming the stranger is also a practice of justice and liberation. Finally, settlers can recognize that they themselves are guests on the land.

In his essay, "Hindu Traditions: A Positive Approach to the Other," inter-faith activist Acharya Shrinath Prasad Dwivedi connects the positive lessons presented by Gopin with a Hindu theology. Spirit and matter, he says, are part of a single metaphysical continuum. All being is interconnected. Therefore, right thinking shapes action and right action shapes thinking. The cultivation of positive attitudes leads to inner calm and to practices of respect and care.

## RESPONSIBILITY TO THE OTHER IN CHRISTIAN MISSION

In his essay, "Indigenous People as the Other: Bartolomé de las Casas in Conversation with Tzvetan Todorov," Ray Aldred compares and contrasts two visions of the conquest of the Americas, those of Bartolomé de las Casas (1484–1566) and Tzvetan Todorov (1939–2017). Las Casas, a missionary whose father sailed with Columbus, believed that the Kingdom of Spain was divinely ordained to bring the gospel to the Indians. However, he also insisted that Christian values require the gospel be taught to free people, without brutality. Todorov, writing from a democratic perspective, criticizes las Casas' mixed motives. He argues for a humanist, non-religious view that respects the Other as equal. Aldred himself prefers the views of las Casas, because they allow for the evolution of Christian ethics and the possibility of a humane, anticolonial Christian practice.

Bob Paul's essay is titled "The Constructive Iconoclasm of Lamin Sanneh." Sanneh (1942–2019), a Christian theologian raised as a Muslim in West Africa, saw Christianity from a unique multicultural perspective. Revelation and faithful living, he said, always take place within specific cultural communities. Respect for those cultures, their communal bonds, and their creativity enables the diversity and vibrancy of world Christianity. Cultural knowledge, a clear separation between evangelism and nationalism, and nuanced use of postcolonial categories are important to the integrity of Christian mission.

Roger Revell takes a close look at the theology of the Swiss theologian Karl Barth (1886–1968) in his essay, "Light from a Dark Horse: Karl Barth on Approaching the Religious Other." First, Revell highlights Barth's distinction between religion and revelation. Revelation is primary, as it comes from God. Religion, on the other hand, is a human construct. Next, Revell notes Barth's discussion of "little lights," that is, parables of grace in which God self-reveals outside of structured Christianity. These two Barthian ideas imply a kind of pluralism that does not diminish Christianity and should bring Christians to the interfaith table.

Alisha Fung's essay, "From 'Other' to 'Brother': Re-interpreting the Canadian Christians' Call as We Stand with the Muslim Refugee," uses Christian

Trinitarian theology to speak to the urgent needs of refugees from Syria's civil war. Evangelism, she says, is the opportunity for Christians to share the divine love they have experienced. In this context, the Trinity represents human relationships created through a self-emptying love. Love, even more than religion, holds the key to salvation. This love calls Christians to accept their Muslim brothers and sisters as they are. Through this mode of spiritual consciousness, Christians see God at work through anything and anyone, and begin to fulfill their responsibility to create peace.

In the closing essay, "Christianity Without Enemies," Jason Byassee argues that Christianity insists on a positive approach to encountering the other. Today, anxieties about identity, materialism, war, politics, and the media polarize people. In a sense, the theology of Manichaeism, i.e., classifying everything in the world as either good or evil, is alive and well. However, as Augustine taught, Manichaeism is a heresy. It distorts reality, leads to scapegoating, and forgets that the biblical God so often takes the side of the marginalized, the forgotten, the young, and the sinners. In fact, the Christian story itself undermines the practice of scapegoating by making God the scapegoat. When salvation unexpectedly comes from the excluded one, Christians should be very careful about living into exclusive categories.

Of course, the essays in this book only begin a conversation. But the conversation operates on multiple levels: critical readings of scripture, thoughtful analyses of culture, helpful techniques of dialogue and self-awareness, and emerging understandings of Christian practice in a multifaith society. We hope that you, too, will find the book a helpful way to start discussion in your own classes, community groups, and research studies. Please do let us know where your discussions lead.

# I.

## CONSTRUCTIONS OF THE RELIGIOUS OTHER

# 1

# Esau My (Br)other
## The Esau Narrative in Multiple Traditions

### Jay Eidelman

Esau is the Rodney Dangerfield of the Hebrew Bible. No respect.

With perhaps the exception of Jezebel, there is no character more execrable than Esau to the early rabbis who lay the foundations for Judaism. Like Jezebel, Esau is the victim of a hatchet job perpetrated by the Bible's redactors and post-biblical commentators who flip the narrative to portray Esau as the villain and his twin brother Jacob as an innocent.

In Hebrew, my name is Ya'akov (Jacob), and though I am not a twin, I am a youngest son, so I think I have some insight into the family dynamic at play here. Yet in reading and rereading this story over many years and looking at the Jewish commentaries on it, I have not come to identify with Esau exactly, but I certainly feel tremendous sympathy for his character. For Esau, though no innocent, is not a villain either. Indeed, even a cursory reading of the Jacob-Esau narrative as presented in Genesis would reveal many admirable qualities in Esau's character. He is rash but also attendant to his father. Learning that Isaac has been deceived into giving the blessing reserved for him to Jacob, he is genuinely hurt, crying out: "Have you but one blessing, father? Bless me too, father" (Gen 27:38).[1] And when the time

---

1. All Hebrew Bible translations are from Cohn, *Modernized Tanakh*.

comes to reconcile with Jacob in Genesis 33, Esau is forgiving to his brother, embracing him with genuine warmth.

While Jewish commentators occasionally recognize these positive qualities, Esau as the negative image of Jacob is the norm. Elsewhere in the Hebrew Bible and throughout Second Temple-era and rabbinic texts, Esau is portrayed as the eternal "other" through his connection to Edom/Amalek and, by extension, to Rome. The origin of this enmity in Jacob's supplanting of Esau, serves to bolster exclusive claims on the part of Jacob's descendants to the promised land.

Descriptions of Esau as the embodiment of negative and despised qualities and his association with Israel's eternal enemies Amalek and later Rome, are closely related to the covenantal drama that plays out between Esau and Jacob. Leaving aside the historicity of the narratives of the matriarchs and patriarchs in the Torah as beyond the scope of this paper, it is interesting to note that some scholars posit a late sixth century BCE origin for these texts.[2] This corresponds roughly to the period between the exile of the Northern Kingdom of Israel by the Assyrians (722 BCE) and the Babylonian exile of the Southern Kingdom and its restoration under the Persians (completed 582 BCE and begun 539 BCE, respectively). The period also includes the religious reforms under King Josiah (641–609 BCE) that sought to purge idolatry and refashion the definition of the covenant.[3]

The depiction of Esau not only as other but as eternal enemy beginning in the Hebrew Bible but taking full form in *midrash* (rabbinic biblical exegesis), fits with the inter-exilic and restoration era worldview much in the same way that the emergence of the Exodus story as a central narrative does. The trauma of loss of the land promised in the covenant necessitates a narrative claim to the land. Esau becomes Edom so that Jacob can be Israel. These themes continue to resonate today.

## ESAU-JACOB IN THE HEBREW BIBLE

The Esau-Jacob narrative has four main components:

- The birth of twins Esau and Jacob and the oracle that the younger will supplant the elder
- Esau's selling of his birthright to Jacob
- Jacob's deception of an aged and blind Isaac to take his blessing intended originally for Esau
- Esau's reconciliation with Jacob

2. For a full discussion, see Moore and Kelle, *Biblical History and Israel's Past*.
3. For examples, see Mendenhall, "Covenant Forms in Israelite Tradition."

The first three of these appear in *Bereshit*/Genesis chapters 25–27 and are read as part of *Parashat Toldot* or the "Generations of Isaac" in the cycle of weekly Torah readings in synagogues. The third part appears in *Parashat Vayishlach*, which comprises Genesis 32:4 to 36:43 and is read in synagogues two weeks after *Toldot*. This paper will focus primarily on early rabbinic interpretations of Esau's character as related to the selling of his birthright.

We first meet Esau in Genesis chapter 25, about half way through the book. Following a summary of the life of Ishmael, Abraham's son by his wife's servant Hagar, the text launches into the generations that followed Yitzhak/Isaac, Abraham's son from his wife Sarah. In Genesis 22, we find Isaac, who has been absent from the text since his near sacrifice on Mount Moriah, 20 years into his marriage with Rebekah. Like the biblical matriarch Sarah, Rebekah is barren. Isaac beseeches God and, about the time that he is 60, Rebekah conceives. Hers is a troubled pregnancy. She inquires and God tells her:

> Two nations are in your womb, Two separate peoples shall issue
> from your body; One people shall be mightier than the other;
> And the older shall serve the younger. (Gen 25:23)

Even *in utero*, the text is setting up for the core event of the Esau-Jacob narrative, the selling of Esau's birthright.

At birth, Esau, the elder twin, is described as "ruddy" and covered in hair. This is the source of Esau's name—*eisav*, as he is called in Hebrew, means hairy. Jacob emerges next, his hand grasped around Esau's heel. Again the text uses an aptronym, as Ya'akov in Hebrew comes from the word for heel (*akev*) or the word for "follow." This grasping at Esau's heel is foreshadowing of the deception that is to come and the text bears this out in Genesis 27:36 when Esau laments how his brother has duped him twice:

> And he said: "Was he, then, named Jacob that he might supplant
> me these two times? First he took away my birthright and now
> he has taken away my blessing." (Gen 27:36)

Esau, we learn in Genesis 25:27, grows up to be a man of the field and a skilled hunter, but Jacob "was a quiet man, dwelling in tents." The actual words used in Hebrew are *ish tam*. The Hebrew adjective *tam* could equally mean perfect, innocent, honest, guileless, or in the case of a beast, tame. This last meaning of the word *tam* presents the reader with a tantalizing contrast of Esau as a wild, dangerous bad boy and Jacob as a domesticated homebody.

The rabbis will seize upon these differences in their negative assessment of Esau. In *Bereshit Rabba*, the classical collection of biblical homilies on Genesis, Rabbi Levi offers a parable. Jacob and Esau "were like a myrtle and a wild rosebush growing side by side; when they matured and blossomed, one yielded its fragrance and the other its thorns." Rabbi Levi continues, "For thirteen years both went to school and came home from school, [but] after this age, one went to the house of study and the other to idolatrous shrines" (*Genesis Rabba* 63:10). This understanding of the brothers' characters is repeated by one of the best-known Jewish biblical and Talmudic commentators, Rabbi Shlomo Yitzchaki or Rashi (1040–1105), who writes that "at the age of thirteen, one went his way to the houses of learning and the other went his way to the idolatrous temples"[4] (Rashi on Gen 25:27).

As the narrative builds, it is revealed that Isaac loves his eldest son, Esau, but Rebekah loves her youngest, Jacob (Gen 25:28). The Hebrew word *ahav* used in the text can translate as love in its most direct sense but rabbinic tradition interprets the use here to mean election. Isaac has chosen Esau as his heir but Rebekah prefers that Jacob be reconfirmed in the covenant. The weekly reading from Prophets that accompanies *Parashat Toldot* picks up this theme, using the words love and hate in this manner. God loves Jacob but hates Esau, and, as a result, Esau's descendants must live in desolation, their "territory a home for *beasts*" (Mal 1:2–3, emphasis mine). They may look out over the neighboring promised land but they may never possess it.

It is at this point that the text transitions from third person omniscient narrator to a dialog between the brothers. Esau returns hungry from hunting game for his father. Jacob is cooking stew of some kind of pulse. Esau says to his younger brother, "Please let me eat [the Hebrew word is closer to gulp down, gorge, or pour it into my mouth as one would do with an animal] some of this red, red stew; for I am faint" (Gen 25:30). Jacob counters that Esau must first sell him his birthright. To which Esau replies, "Now I am going to die; and what good does the birthright do to me?" (Gen 25:32). Then Jacob insists; Esau swears and Jacob gives him bread and lentil stew. Esau eats, drinks, and leaves. The text then says, "So Esau repudiated his birthright" (Gen 25:34). Here the text may be offering a specific interpretation of Esau's motivation to help explain Rebekah's and Jacob's actions later in the narrative.

Starting in the text itself, the repudiation or "scorning of the birthright" presents a treasure trove of material for discerning Esau's "true" nature. First, we learn from the biblical text that Esau is the progenitor of Edom, a neighboring people usually portrayed as a nemesis. The name is a play on the Hebrew word for red, on account of his eating the red, presumably

---

4. Various rabbinic interpretations, including Rashi, suggest that Esau lived a double life of iniquity up until this point.

raw, lentils. The Apocrypha's Book of Jubilees or "Little Genesis" relates the tale almost verbatim, adding, "And Jacob became the elder, and Esau was brought down from his dignity" (*Jub* 24:7).

A Second Temple-era New Testament reading in the Epistle to the Hebrews (12:14–17) offers a more damning critique of Esau. Dated to the middle of the first century CE either before or shortly after the destruction of the Temple in Jerusalem in 70 CE, the passage encourages people to live in peace and holiness, and to avoid falling short of the grace of God or to let bitterness cause trouble. In verse 16 the text warns, "See that no one is sexually immoral, or is godless like Esau, who for a single meal sold his inheritance rights as the oldest son." Then, skipping over Jacob's deception, verse 17 admonishes the reader, "Afterward, as you know, when he wanted to inherit this blessing, he was rejected. Even though he sought the blessing with tears, he could not change what he had done."[5] This is similar to rabbinic readings that likewise connect sexual immorality and godlessness with Esau's repudiation of the birthright.

Esau's act is certainly rash, but Jewish tradition teaches that the twins were fifteen at this point, which might explain Esau "catastrophizing" his hunger—as anyone who has spent enough time in presence of a teenager can attest. The rabbis of the Talmud see it otherwise, however. In Talmud *Baba Bathra* 16b, there is a discussion in which the participants deduce from scripture that Esau did not turn away from a correct path until Abraham's death. "How do we know that Esau did not break away while he [Abraham] was alive?" they ask. "Because it says, 'And Esau came in from the field and he was faint.' It has been taught [in connection with this] that that was the day on which Abraham our father died, and Jacob our father made a broth of lentils to comfort his father Isaac." In the rabbis' reckoning, Esau returns from the hunt while Jacob is dutifully and appropriately preparing the meal of consolation for his grieving father. Then Rabbi Johanan offers a *midrash* [biblical exegesis], claiming that on the day of Abraham's death Esau committed five sins. According to Rabbi Johanan, Esau dishonored a betrothed maiden, committed murder, denied God, denied the resurrection of the dead, and repudiated his birthright (*Baba Bathra* 16b). So by the time of the Talmud, in the sixth century, a tradition had developed in which Esau is not only a brute, but guilty of the worst, most reprehensible transgressions. With Abraham now gone, Esau should have become the heir apparent but, according to the rabbis, the sinful Esau is not worthy of being confirmed in the covenant.

---

5. From Charles, *Apocrypha and Pseudepigrapha of the Old Testament*.

## I. CONSTRUCTIONS OF THE RELIGIOUS OTHER

### ESAU AS EDOM/AMALEK

We do not meet Esau again until near the end of the Genesis 26. The text recounts how a famine descends on the land, the first major famine since Abraham's time. God speaks to Isaac and tells him not to go to Egypt but to dwell in the land that God would show to him. If Isaac dwelt in that land, God would reaffirm the covenant that had been made with Isaac's father Abraham.

> Sojourn in this land, and I will be with you, and will bless you; for to you, and to your seed, I will give all these lands, and I will fulfill the oath which I swore to Abraham thy father; and I will multiply your seed as the stars of heaven, and will give to your seed all these lands; and all the nations of the earth will bless themselves by your see; because Abraham listened to My voice, and kept My guard, My commandments, My statutes, and My laws. (Gen 26:3–5)

Isaac does what God suggests and, following a series of tumultuous interactions with Canaanites and Philistines, God tells Isaac that he has fulfilled his part of the bargain and re-establishes the covenant with him. The confirmation of the covenant with Isaac at this point in the text is very important for later understandings of Esau's character, for we then read that Esau, now forty, chooses to marry two Hittite women, Judith the daughter of Be'eri and Basemath the daughter of Elon (Gen 26:34). Isaac and Rebekah are disappointed in their son's choice and the text reports the women "were a source of bitterness of spirit to Isaac and to Rebekah." The text here is silent about why, but the proximity to the re-making of the covenant is telling. Abraham took his half-sister as his wife and Isaac his first cousin once removed but Esau has chosen wives from outside the clan structure.

As for Jacob, the text offers two different but related reasons for the flight from his parents' home to his uncle Laban's home in Paddan-Aram. The first is Esau's threat to kill Jacob in revenge for the deceit once Isaac dies. Hearing of the threat Rebekah tells Jacob, "Now, my son, listen to my voice; you get up, flee to Laban my brother in Haran; and stay with him a few days, until your brother's fury turns" (Gen 27:43–44). Later, at the start of Genesis 28 the reason for Jacob's departure is more directly tied to marriage. Isaac admonishes Jacob, "You will not take a wife of the daughters of Canaan" (Gen 28:1). With this admonishment comes the blessing:

> And God Almighty bless you, and make you fruitful, and multiply you, that you may be a multitude of peoples; and give the blessing of Abraham, to you, and to your seed with you; that

you may inherit the land of your sojournings, which God gave to Abraham. (Gen 28:3–4)

Still seeking his father's blessing and seeing that marriage to Canaanite women displeases Isaac, Esau marries Mahalat, the daughter of his uncle, Ishmael. Mahalat from the Hebrew *mahal* implies the possibility of pardon or forgiveness for Esau, but the rabbis do not see it that way.[6] *Genesis Rabba* 67:13 offers a teaching from Rabbi Eleazar that Esau, in adding Mahalat to his Canaanite wives, had compounded his transgression. More significantly, Genesis 36:12 reports that Amalek, Israel's eternal enemy, is descended from Esau through his son Eliphaz and the concubine Timna.

The connection to Amalek and other peoples not aligned with the Israelites becomes important in the assessment of Esau/Edom elsewhere in the Hebrew Scriptures.[7] In Numbers 20, Edom blocks Israel's passage into Canaan to protect its territory, while Deuteronomy 2 warns the Israelites to leave Edom unmolested in Seir as they enter into Canaan. In Numbers 24, on the other hand, the seer Balaam, called on by the King of Moab to curse the Israelites, offers the following oracle:

> Edom becomes a possession, Yea, Seir a possession of its enemies; But Israel is triumphant. A victor issues from Jacob to wipe out what is left of it.[8] He saw Amalek and, taking up his theme, he said: A leading nation is Amalek; But its fate is to perish forever. (Num 24:18–20)

Amalek is then singled out in Deuteronomy 25 for eternal enmity and complete destruction. Verse 19 ends with the command "you shalt blot out the remembrance of Amalek from under heaven; do not forget." The text of 1 Samuel 15:3 makes it quite clear that this is meant to be a genocide, as Samuel tells King Saul in the name of God to "attack Amalek, and proscribe all that belongs to him. Spare no one; but kill alike men and women, infants and sucklings, oxen and sheep, camels and asses!"

Obadiah, likely written in the fifth century BCE during the restoration, draws on themes also present in Numbers, Deuteronomy, Ezekiel, and Psalms, which suggest that Esau's descendants, the Edomites, assisted in the destruction of the first Temple in 587 BCE. Another example in Psalm 137,

---

6. Kaufman, *Love, Marriage, and Family*, 161.

7. For a comparison with the Dead Sea Scrolls, see Davis, "Edom as a Polemical Figure."

8. The Hasmonean king, John Hyrcanus, forcibly converted the Edomites/Idumeans to Judaism in 125.

verse 6, invokes God to "remember against the Edomites the day of Jerusalem's fall, how they said 'Strip her, strip her to her very foundations.'"

Taken together, the scriptural sources present a pattern in which Esau's descendants, particularly the Amalekites, are so completely "other" that not only are they capable of heinous transgression, they also act directly to destroy Israel. The rabbis of the Talmud extend this connection by equating Edom with Rome (*Leviticus Rabba* 22) and, later, with Christianity.[9]

Where does this leave us? Constructions of self and other introduced in the Esau-Jacob narrative and its subsequent interpretations continue to shape how individual Jews experience the world, just as they guide Judaism's relationship with other faith traditions. The concepts of election and supersession introduced in the narrative have particular resonance, informing the meaning of Jewish peoplehood and anti-Judaism alike. As religious diversity and acceptance of Jews give way to ethno-nationalism and antisemitism, the us-versus-them dynamic exemplified in the brothers' relationship becomes a cautionary tale that works regardless of one's Jewish outlook. Traditionalists, secularists, Zionists, diaspora integrationists, there's something for everyone. The narrative's enduring relevance rests in this ability to speak meaningfully to the human condition.

## BIBLIOGRAPHY

Bishop, Megan, and Brad E. Kelle. *Biblical History and Israel's Past: The Changing Study of the Bible and History.* Grand Rapids: Eerdmans, 2011.

"Book of Jubilees." In *The Apocrypha and Pseudepigrapha of the Old Testament*, edited by R. H. Charles. Oxford: Clarendon, 1913. Online. http://www.pseudepigrapha.com/jubilees/index.htm.

Davis, Kipp. "Edom as a Polemical Figure: Allusions to the Family History of Esau in the Dead Sea Scrolls." Paper presented at the Manchester, Newton Fellowship, and Nordic Symposium, University of Manchester, Manchester, UK, July 2013.

Feldman, Louis H. *"Remember Amalek!": Vengeance, Zealotry, and Group Destruction in the Bible according to Philo, Pseudo-Philo, and Josephus.* Cincinnati: Hebrew Union College Press, 2004.

"Genesis." In *Modernized Tanakh: Based on the Jewish Publication Society 1917 Edition.* Edited by Adam Cohn. 2013. Online. https://docs.google.com/document/d/1pdNlchu9l2ncCjvQdEgheGGK6k35moiaKBNiaQPMxeU/pub.

"Genesis." In *Tanakh: A New Translation of the Holy Scriptures According to the Traditional Hebrew Text.* Philadelphia: Jewish Publication Society, 1985. Online. https://www.sefaria.org/texts/Tanakh.

"Genesis Rabba" and "Leviticus Rabba." In *Tales and Maxims from the Midrash*, edited by Samuel Rapaport. London: Routledge, 1907. Online. http://sacred-texts.com/jud/tmm/index.htm.

---

9. See Gottheil and Seligsohn, "Edox-Idumea," 41; Feldman, *Remember Amalek!*, 67–69.

Gottheil, Richard, and M. Seligsohn. "Edox-Idumea." In vol. 5 of *The Jewish Encyclopedia*, edited by Isidore Singer, 40–41. New York: Funk and Wagnalls, 1964. Online. http://jewishencyclopedia.com/articles/5434-edox-idumea.

Kaufman, Michael. *Love, Marriage, and Family in Jewish Law and Tradition*. North Vale, NJ: J. Aronson, 1996.

Mendenhall, George. "Covenant Forms in Israelite Tradition." *Biblical Archaeologist* 17 (1954) 50–76.

"Micha." In *Tanakh: A New Translation of the Holy Scriptures According to the Traditional Hebrew Text*. Philadelphia: Jewish Publication Society, 1985. Online. https://www.sefaria.org/texts/Tanakh.

Rosenbaum, M., and A. M. Silberman, trans. *Pentateuch with Targum Onkelos, Haphtaroth, and Prayers for Sabbath and Rashi's Commentary*. London: Shapiro and Valentine, 1929–34. Online. https://www.sefaria.org/texts/Tanakh/Commentary/Rashi.

Simon, Maurice, et al. *Baba Bathra: Translated into English with Notes and Glossary*. London: Soncino, 1976. Online. https://halakhah.com/bababathra/index.html.

Wheeler, Brannon M. *Prophets in the Quran: An Introduction to the Quran and Muslim Exegesis*. New York: Continuum, 2002.

# 2

# "I Consider Them Shit"

## Paul, the Abject, and the Religious Construction of the Other

### Harry O. Maier

> Loathing an item of food, a piece of filth, waste, or dung. The spasms and vomiting that protect me. The repugnance, the retching that thrusts me to the side and turns me away from defilement, sewage, and muck. The shame of compromise, of being in the middle of treachery. The fascinated stare that leads me toward and separates me from them.[1]

## THESIS

THE FOLLOWING DISCUSSION EXPLORES the Apostle Paul's construction of his enemies as a religious other specifically through an exegetical and psycho-social study of disgust. One of the ways ancients sought to "other" opponents or to make fun of them was to evoke feelings of disgust amongst their audiences. Disgust, as Donald Lateiner and Dinos Spatharas argue, is a socially constructed notion which belongs to larger cultural

---

1. Kristeva, *Powers of Horror*, 2.

norms and values.² While disgust may well be a universal human experience, what prompts disgust, the specific affective components associated with it and what threshold must be met to elicit it, differ from culture to culture. People who believe that cleanliness is next to godliness are likely to have a lower disgust threshold than those who live in a society (as the ancient did) without ready access to hot water, toilets, and toilet paper, not to mention funeral homes and crematoria. In the Roman world, people defecated in public, they slaughtered animals on the street, and the only affordance for bathing for the majority was the public bath—without knowledge of germs and effective sanitation a foul space crowded with its dirty patrons. The ancient world was a filthy and smelly place; feces and death were everyday in one's nostrils. This furnished ancients with a great opportunity to draw on the daily experience of filth as a powerful rhetorical tool. Ancients rhetorical theorists argued that speeches should not depart far from the daily experiences of their audiences. It is no accident that references to feces, corpses, bad smells, and so on recur regularly in speeches that vilify or mock others in ancient literature.

The Bible is no exception and in this essay we focus on Paul's uses of disgust to other his opponents. We begin with a passage whose translation has proven troublesome for some, namely Philippians 3:8, and after restoring the verse and surrounding materials to its earthy qualities, we turn to a discussion of abjection and religious identity in Paul. What I hope to show is that Paul both "others" his opponents, and also constructs himself as the religious other. With the help of Julia Kristeva's theory of abjection I seek to show the way the abject becomes a site of religious production and meaning-making in a passage where human excrement becomes the place the apostle creates a new religious identity. My aim is to show how disgust at the abject at once produces cultural strategies for eliminating disorder, but that it also prompts religious identities that are productive of disorder. We can see both aspects of order and disorder in the passage we are taking up for discussion.

The Apostle Paul wrote a letter from prison (Phil 1:7, 23), either in Ephesus or Rome, to Christ believers in the Macedonian city of Philippi in c. 52 or 62 CE. Some have argued the letter is comprised of two or more fragments, a hypothesis that need not concern us here, apart from stating at the outset that what follows assumes a single letter. The particular passage considered here is 3:2–21, specifically verses 2–9, 18–21:

> Beware those dogs, beware those evildoers, beware the mutilation [tēn katatomēn]. For it is we who are the circumcision

2. Lateiner and Spatharas, "Ancient and Modern Modes."

[*peritomē*], we who serve God by his Spirit, who boast in Christ Jesus, and who put no confidence in the flesh—though I myself have reasons for such confidence. If someone else thinks they have reasons to put confidence in the flesh, I have more: circumcised on the eighth day, of the people of Israel, of the tribe of Benjamin, a Hebrew of Hebrews; in regard to the law, a Pharisee; as for zeal, persecuting the church; as for righteousness based on the law, faultless. But whatever were gains [*kerdē*] to me I now consider [*hēgoumai*] loss [*zēmian*] for the sake of Christ. What is more, I consider [*hēgoumai*] everything a loss [*zēmian*] because of the surpassing worth [*hyperechon*] of knowing Christ Jesus my Lord, for whose sake I have lost all things [*ta panta ezēmiōthēn*]. I consider [*hēgoumai*] them shit [*skybala*], that I may gain [*kerdēsō*] Christ and be found in him, not having a righteousness of my own that comes from the law, but that which is through faith in Christ—the righteousness that comes from God on the basis of faith. . . . For, as I have often told you before and now tell you again even with tears [*klaiōn*], many live as enemies of the cross of Christ. Their destiny is destruction, their god is their stomach, and their glory is in their shame [*hōn ho theos hē koilia kai hē doxa en tē aischynē autōn*]. Their mind is set on earthly things [*hoi ta epigeia phronountes*]. But our citizenship is in heaven. And we eagerly await a Savior from there, the Lord Jesus Christ, who, by the power that enables him to bring everything under his control, will transform our lowly bodies so that they will be like his glorious body. (NRSV, slightly emended)

This passage from Philippians offers a potent site for exploration of how religious otherness functions as both slander and self-definition. Identification of those Paul describes as "dogs" and "enemies of the cross of Christ" is by no means simple, indeed fully fifteen different types of opponents have been proposed![3] While many have identified them as Jews who seek to circumcise Gentiles or "Judaizers"—namely Christ believing Jews (or Gentiles)—the text does not offer sufficient warrant for that identification. Another suggestion has been to consider them as "Gnostic libertines," an identification that fails because of a lack of evidence as well as anachronism and precision concerning the term "Gnostic." A further option is to argue that Paul is crafting a "rhetorical other" for the purposes of foregrounding his own Gospel claims, a suggestion difficult to square with Paul's anguish for his made-up unbelievers (verse 18). Still another suggestion is to argue that Paul describes neither Judaioi, nor Christ believing

---

3. For a review, see Williams, *Enemies of the Cross of Christ*, 54–60.

Judaioi/Gentile "Judaizers," but rather Philippian Graeco-Romans, perhaps those who harass the Philippian assembly or from whom Paul seeks otherwise to disassociate the Christ assembly. Finally, they have been identified as apostates from Paul's Gospel.[4] However one decides this matter, it cannot be done on the basis of the highly charged language Paul uses to represent his opponents in the passage in question as clearly he is using strong rhetorical terms to vilify them. Indeed, the apostle draws on traditions of disgust, specifically those involved with defecation and religious castration, traditions that were the currency of popular culture in Paul's social world in order to vilify and mock opponents.[5] In that sense, they qualify as excellent examples of a constructed "religious other" that Paul creates in order to refute. It is on Paul's strategies of "othering" that this essay focuses.

## LOST IN TRANSLATION

Paul is an earthy apostle and to honor that earthiness the term "shit" appears in our title as a translation of Philippians 3:8: "For his [Christ's] sake I have suffered the loss of all things and count them as *skybala*, in order that I may gain Christ." However, the term *skybala* has proven a troublesome term for Bible translators. Renditions fall into four broad camps. One group translates the word as "rubbish" (NRSV; NIV; NASB; ESV; GNT); the New English Bible has "garbage"; and the Darby Bible Translation, "filth." The New Living Translation, moving further in this direction, renders it as "worth less than nothing." A second option, following J. B. Lightfoot, who bases his argument on an association of the term in a Byzantine lexicon where it is translated as "scraps," renders it "dog scraps," which picks up on the start of the chapter: "Beware of the dogs" (verse 2).[6] Eugene Peterson in *The Message* improvises on Lightfoot and translates it as "dog dung." A third camp of translators takes the text in a more scatological direction: "refuse" (RSV; ASV); "dung" (KJV; NET; Lexham English Bible). And finally the fourth group, constituted by the fourteenth-century Bible translator John Wycliffe and, predictably, the sixteenth-century one, Martin Luther, presents the bluntest scatological

---

4. For Gnostic libertines, see Koester, "Purpose of the Polemic." For imaginary opponents, see deSilva, "No Confidence in the Flesh." For further suggestions, including Graeco-Roman opponents, see Oropeza, *Jews, Gentiles, and the Opponents of Paul*. Oropreza considers them apostates.

5. For discussion with an overview, especially with reference to the cult of Cybele, see Rauhala, *Obscena Galli Praesentia*.

6. Lightfoot, *Saint Paul's Epistle to the Philippians*, 147.

rendition: "drit" (Wycliffe Bible, glossed as "deem as turds" by a modern editor) and "Dreck" (Luther translations, 1522–1545).[7]

Sanitation engineers play an important role in society to assure the flow of sewage and they are also ready at hand to remove all refuse from the Bible—motivated in part, no doubt, to avoid upsetting religious sensitivities. In the case of our passage, however, it is important to put the sewage on full view and linger there. The apostle uses highly charged and vivid language centring on excrement and mutilation to construct both opponents and himself as a religious other. Luther and Wycliffe belonged to a culture which, like Paul's, understood scatological humor and vituperative as an important part of a rhetorical repertoire to mock others as well to question stable social order.[8] Scatology engendered a sense of the *carnivalesque*, the inversion of privileged order by obscene gesture, a new sacralisation by way of profanation.[9] Closer to the rhetorical culture of Paul than we are, they recognized the earthy tone of Philippians 3:8 and thus captured it in their translations. In fact not only were they right to do so, but once we recognize that Paul is referring in verse 8 to human excrement we are in a position to recognize its recurrence later in the passage we have quoted, as well as its links with Paul's slander of his opponents as "dogs" and guilty of "mutilation" (verse 2).[10] As a passing aside, it is worth remembering that Paul's Scriptures, the *Tanakh*, use obscene language to discredit opponents and bad religious ideas, no less sanitized by translators anxious not to have a Bible that offends decent company.[11] To give an example: Job says that sinners will "perish forever like their own excrement [*kegayllō*]" (Job 20:7; NET; ISV; "refuse," NASB; "they will be blown away like dust," GNT; "cast away like his own dung," TLB; "like the dung he uses for fuel," NABRE).

---

7. Modern translations are cited from versions furnished by OakTree Software. For Wycliffe, with gloss, see Wycliffe, *Wycliffe's New Testament*, 479.

8. For a discussion of scatology and Luther, see Oberman, "Teufelsdreck: Eschatology and Scatology."

9. For discussion of the role of scatology and obscenity in social inversion in European medieval culture, see Simon, "Carnival Obscenities in German Towns."

10. It is a commonplace to link Paul's vituperative as a reversal of an alleged Jewish slight against Gentiles as dogs (i.e., Paul is applying to Jewish opponents a traditional metaphor Jews use to describe Gentiles). Nanos, "Paul's Reversal of Jews," shows that in fact, apart from Mark 7:27, there are expressly *no* such representations of Gentiles as dogs in Jewish tradition, and that the idea that Jews call Gentiles dogs is a Christian invention. He argues that Paul's concern in Phil 3:8–21 is not with Jewish Christ believers who seek to circumcise Gentile Christ believers but rather with Graeco-Roman outsiders.

11. For an overview, see Hepner, "Scatology in the Bible"; Sherwood, "Prophetic Scatology."

## VIVID LANGUAGE AND PERSUASION

In using such language Paul was fulfilling a chief goal of ancient rhetoric, namely, to use vivid description to turn listeners into observers. Lively language created *phantasia*, or a picture formed in the imagination, to enable audiences to see what a speaker represented in words.[12] Rhetoricians were taught to use graphic description and to rely upon listeners to fill in the gaps from their own lived experience. It is notable that rhetoricians such as Cicero castigated those who used obscene metaphors (expressly excrement) to describe opponents, a complaint that probably indicates how common such practice was.[13] From the perspective of graphic speech it is not difficult to understand the reason for such a commonplace. Human excrement in ancient cities was a much more common sight than what one finds today in the first world where feces are privately deposited into notably white porcelain toilet bowls and flushed away. As most ancient city-dwellers did not have plumbing in their usually meagre and cramped living quarters, they usually relieved themselves in buckets they emptied onto the streets. Alternatively, they could congregate at public toilets where both men and women sat on stalls in full public view of one another. Or they simply squatted on the street to defecate in public. It would not be a stretch to say that excrement was everywhere.[14] Wild city dogs lived, amongst other things, on human waste. The ubiquity of feces prompted lively humor in the Greco-Roman world, whether on the stage, which both urban rich and poor frequented regularly, or in the form of graffiti scribbled on lavatory walls much as it is today and other public places.[15] When Paul talks about his "shit" he is using vivid imagery to connect with this audience; he evokes the sense of sight and probably also of smell.[16]

---

12. For discussion, see Webb, *Ekphrasis, Imagination, and Persuasion*. For a more theological account of the importance of images in Pauline persuasion, see Collins, *Power of Images in Paul*, 40–67 (Philippians), esp. 63–65 (Phil 3:8), but without noticing the way the metaphor is carried through in succeeding verses.

13. Ziolkowski, "Latin Grammatical and Rhetorical Tradition," 58.

14. For discussion of the ubiquity of human and animal excrement in Roman cities and the challenges of removing it from city streets, see van Tilburg, *Traffic and Congestion in the Roman Empire*, 127–35.

15. For theater, see Henderson, *Maculate Muse*, 187–203, specifically on scatological humor. For images of men shitting and scatological imagery at public toilets, see Clarke, *Art in the Lives of Ordinary Romans*, 170–80, in this case in the form of humorous art at a tavern in Pompeii.

16. For rhetoric and smell, see Bradley, "Smell and the Ancient Senses."

## CONSTIPATION, SEX, AND ATHLETIC BODIES

Having introduced excrement in 3:8, Paul continues the theme later in the same chapter. In 3:19 he again turns to bowels, this time to slander his opponents: "Their god is their belly [*koilia*], and their glory is in their shame."[17] The passage here is parallel with verse 8: Paul counts all his achievements (*kerdē*—a term that implies material or monetary gain) as excrement to discard, his opponents' digestive products bring about a different outcome. Their belly produces excrement, but unlike Paul, who will boast of his loss (verse 8—*zēmia*, a commercial term used to describe loss or money or a monetary penalty), they "glory in their shame [*aischynē*]." The passage is parallel with Paul's earlier statement. He renounces his former identity; they magnify it. "Shame" functions here as a metonym for that which Paul has identified as excrement in verse 8. To put it another way, "they are proud of their shit." Further, when Paul goes on to describe them as having their mind on earthly things, one might say that he is putting his opponents' noses in the shit he has accused them of displaying. Of course, they are already there: in 3:2 Paul calls them "dogs [*kynai*]," a slur used widely in ancient culture and in the Tanakh to refer to an unclean animal who scavenges the countryside consuming garbage, vomit, and corpses (Exod 22:31; Prov 26:11; 1 Kgs 21:23; 22:38; 2 Kgs 9:36). In keeping with the metaphor Paul intends slander.[18] They eat excrement like dogs and are proud of it. The point is telling: Paul's achievements are the shit these canines eat, even as they glory in/consume their own.

There is also a sexualized valence to this language. The Greek word for "belly," *koilia*, had a range of meanings in Paul's world. It could refer to a variety of body parts, activities, and attitudes. Thus it could indicate the stomach, but also the seat of desire; it could be associated with gluttony or any excessive practice that involves food, drink or sex.[19] It is surely this broader usage that Paul intends here and when placed within a context of a discussion of circumcision it most probably has a reference to issues

17. *Koilia* has a wide range of meanings amongst which are associations with bowels and excrement. See Liddell and Scott, *Greek-English Lexicon*, s.v. "κοιλία" IIIb, IV.

18. For an overview of connotations and associations, see Michel, "*kyōn, kynarion*,"; and Midori Hartman's essay in this volume, which cites further literature.

19. Behm, "Koilia"; Danker et al., *Greek-English Lexicon*, s.v. "κοιλία" 3. Further, the term contrasts with Paul's own belly as seat of desire, namely his *splagchnon*, as he indicates in Philippians: "For God is my witness, how I long for all of you with the compassion [*splagchnois*] of Christ Jesus" (Phil 1:8). In 2:1 *splagchnon* is used to describe "sharing in the Spirit" associated with fellowship [*splagchnois*] of the spirit. The Greek word *splagchnon* refers to inner parts and as metaphor to the seat of feelings such as anger, anxiety, love, and compassion. See Liddell and Scott, *Greek-English Lexicon*, s.v. "σπλάγχον" I.2, II; Danker et al., *Greek-English Lexicon*, s.v. "σπλάγχον."

relating to male genitalia, although not necessarily associated with Jewish practices. For example, the cult of Cybele was associated with castration: priests were mendicant eunuchs and the cult included rites to her castrated consort, Attis, as well as orgiastic rituals.[20] Even as the opponents like to look at their own "shame," they are also guilty of infractions against genitals. We can see this from the opening of the passage under consideration here. In verse 3 after calling them "dogs," he uses paronomasia to castigate opponents as guilty of *katatomē* (mutilation) whereas Paul and those who follow his Gospel are *hē peritomē* (the circumcision). In fact the term "mutilator" is another sanitized translation as, in its context, it implies a chopping up or shredding of male genitalia.[21] In other words, unlike the true circumcision Paul represents, the association of terms suggests that they butcher penises even as they follow the impulses of sexual desire or the belly.

In contrast to these manglers of genitalia, Paul represents himself and those who follow his example as the true circumcision, that is, those "who serve God by his Spirit, who boast in Christ Jesus, and who put no confidence in the flesh" (verse 2). In his later letter to the Romans he develops what is implicit here by contrasting circumcision of the heart with the physical reality (Rom 2:29; see Deut 30:6; Jer 4:4). In Philippians 3:12–14, he returns to the bodily image by turning attention away from the grotesque toward civic metaphors. The first one is athletic: these opponents are frozen in place inspecting their own feces, but Paul "presses on." "I want to know Christ," he says, "yes, to know the power of his resurrection and participation in his sufferings, becoming like him in his death, and so somehow attaining to the resurrection from the dead." Paul then shifts to the imagery of a runner: "Not that I have already attained all this, or have already arrived at my goal, but I press on to take hold of that for which Christ Jesus took hold of me. Brothers and sisters, I do not consider myself yet to have taken hold of it. But one thing I do: Forgetting what is behind and straining toward what is ahead, I press on toward the goal to win the prize for which God has called me heavenward in Christ Jesus." Unlike the mutilators who "glory in their shame" with minds "set on earthly things," Paul reminds the Philippians, "our citizenship is in heaven. And we eagerly await a Savior from there, the Lord Jesus Christ, who by the power that enables him to bring everything under his control, will transform our lowly bodies so that they will be like his glorious body" (verses

---

20. See Nanos, "Reversal," 47–81, for this as well as other possible identifications. Castration clamps associated with the cult survive. For images, see Pearce, "Castration Clamps." Iconographically, Cybele is often depicted with a dog, which Phil 3:2 possibly references. For priests of Cybele and their castration as a popular object of disgust, see Rauhala, "*Obscena*," 242–48.

21. Koester, "*temnō, ktl.*"

20–21). Paul here is on location, from the shitter, to the race, to the upward heavenly citizenship, from the lowly body to the heavenly one free from all fecal material, even as his opponents, the belly worshipers, remain consumed with their own heap of excrement.

We notice here the oppositions between the heavenly resurrected body that puts the earthly behind, even as Paul has excreted all earthly glory from his rear, "forgetting what is behind" (verse 13); we see the transition from lowly body to glorious body; we notice the ever forward movement of Paul the athlete who contrasts with the stomach worshipers: the gluttonous butchers of genitals. Indeed, there is possibly a medical model here of the regular apostle. Ancient medical writers from Hippocrates onward, linking vice and virtue with physiognomy, theorized that a fat body was the external sign of laziness resulting in bile or phlegm obstructing the passage of feces thereby causing constipation. The healthy body of an athlete, on the other hand, is the one who has no such obstructions, and whose freedom from constipation demonstrates proper self-regulation and is evidence of virtues such as endurance, courage, justice, affection to comrades, a clear mind, and so on.[22] Such is Paul: his forward running, athletic self has successfully evacuated what keeps him from running his race. The apostle is looking forward to a glorious corporeal future with the coming of "a Savior, the Lord Jesus Christ, who will change our lowly body to be like his glorious body, by the power which enables him even to subject all things to himself" (3:20–21). Paul's opponents by contrast are not even running. They are either squatting or hunched over the evidence of their gluttony.

## THE ABJECT AND THE PROPHETIC

In all of this the apostle pillories his opponents as a monstrous religious other. The role of excrement, genital mutilation, and belly shame in our passage is telling as a site of cultural and religious production. The Bulgarian post-structuralist and psychoanalyst Julia Kristeva offers a useful means of recognizing the social construction that comes about through the creation of what she calls "the abject."[23] The abject for Kristeva describes that which is both oneself and other, or that which was once oneself and no longer is, that thus exists in a liminal space between what one simultaneously is and is not. Examples of the abject include things like shed skin, vomit, feces, urine, blood, or any other kind of bodily excretion that is simultaneously

---

22. For the association of gluttony and sex in the ancient world, as well as associations with constipation and its contrast with athletics and virtue, see Hill, *Eating to Excess*, 63–80.

23. Kristeva, *Powers*, 1–32.

both oneself and not—both subject and object. When one sees one's vomit one is looking at what is simultaneously oneself and other from oneself. For Kristeva, the abject horrifies. The disgust it unleashes threatens personal order: it is both inside and thus belongs to oneself, and outside and no longer part of the self. As such it threatens the intactness of the self. Abjection, she argues, gives rise to a horror that is productive of self, culture, and identity. Culture controls and channels abjection by means of suppressive and repressive strategies.[24] The feces are flushed, the wound bandaged, the menses deposited, the cadaver beautified and cremated or buried, and more broadly, the mad are hospitalized and the criminals incarcerated. The abject other that is and is not self thus is classified and organized so that it no longer poses a threat. For Kristeva the other as fantasized or imagined becomes a means of restoring order to an otherwise chaotic situation. This represents the abject as a generator of stability at both a personal and social level.

In our Philippian passage, excrement and cut flesh are the abject. The former terms Paul uses to liken his former achievements and status markers as an abjected or othered part of himself; the latter term he uses to associate his opponents as manglers of the body. In both cases there is a remainder that is simultaneously presence and absence of the erstwhile self, and both are means of cultural production, either of belonging or discarding. They both belong to liminal spaces.

For Kristeva, the abject can also have a kind of prophetic function. The power of scatological humor is to question conventional systems of signification and classification, and to rupture it with adscriptions of the obscene and the perverse.[25] Here the grotesque has an anarchistic function: What you once were I am; what I am you have become. In this aspect classifications that order society are denied any inviolability. For Kristeva, the abject is simultaneously the locus of the production of order and the source of the poetic by which metaphor cracks open a world and tears order apart.

In the case of Paul's toilet rhetoric, we find both a restorative classificatory construction in his abjection of his opponents and himself, and an anarchistic declassification of a traditional religious system. First, as the race metaphor suggests, Paul runs from the abject and he produces a portrait of his opponents with their noses in it: he "forgets what is behind" and does his best to "stretch out to reach what is ahead" [*emprosthen epekteinomenos*]" (3:13). Paul puts behind what he has evacuated. His citizenship is not on the earth, the final depository of the abject, but in heaven: it is not the anarchic

---

24. Kristeva, *Powers*, 56–89.

25. Kristeva, *Powers*, 188–206, with particular reference to the prophets of the *Tanakh* as well as apocalyptic.

indeterminacy of the abject, but it is "the power that enables him [Jesus] to bring everything under his control" and significantly it is an order that is no longer about bodily excretions of the old order, but a transformation of "our lowly bodies so that they will be like his glorious body" (verses 20–21). Taking Kristeva's concept of the abject in a more sociological direction, culture plays an important role in classifying and producing order as a response to and neutralization of the abject. We can see such neutralization here. Paul's desire for a heaven free from excrement, aspired to by the training of the body that assures amongst other things a regulated body in anticipation of the final freedom from the messy defecating flesh produces a new self without the risk of abjection. His lowly body will be glorified like Jesus' resurrected body. Language of defamation creates a profile against which Paul can contrast his listeners as true believers.

## THE CRUCIFIED ABJECT/OTHER

There is however a degree of anarchy that runs alongside Paul's flight from abjection. Even as the abject continues to produce the order and cultural mode of behavior that eliminates it, it is also the site of creativity and artistry that disrupts homeostatic order and harmony. Obscenity breaks social control even as it can have the social role, via the "othering" of enemies, to inscribe it. As such it creates what Bakhtin calls the "carnival" or "carnivalization of the world," namely the inversion of social order and a possibility of new social relations in an upside-down world.[26] In verse 10 Paul expresses his desire: "I want to know Christ—yes, to know the power of his resurrection and participation in his sufferings, becoming like him in his death." Here the abject is not the site of expulsion but of embrace. The body that is raised frees Paul from the abject but the body that was crucified returns him to it.

We may say that for Paul there is abjection on other terms, no longer based in the excrement that is his former identity, but a new identity no less execrable, namely the humiliated and tortured body of Jesus. In 3:8 Paul states that he "considers [*hēgoumai*]" his former achievements and credentials as excrement. The verb is telling: earlier in 2:6 he uses it to describe how Jesus "did not consider [*hēgēsato*] equality with God something to be snatched at." By abjecting himself, Paul joins with the abjected Christ who emptied himself in cruciform humiliation. Like Jesus, he has judged [*hēgoumai*] all things as loss [*ezēmiōthēn*], considered as excrement [*skybala*], in order that he might gain [*kerdēsō*] Christ (verse 8); here the logic is

---

26. Bakhtin, *Problems of Dostoevsky's Poetics*, 107–180.

homologous with Jesus in the Christ hymn, who rejects equality with God, is humiliated on the cross, and is exalted (2:6–11).[27]

## THE TEARS OF SAINT PAUL

On this account, Paul's longing for a citizenship in heaven takes on a reality, not as a religious identity abstracted from the earth, but one centered in the politics of Jesus' death under the Roman Empire. The imperial system of crucifying conquered bodies for the sake of the preservation of an earthly political order is disrupted by the intrusion of a crucified body that makes it possible for an alternative citizenship. As Philippi was an administrative center in Roman Macedonia, the contrast would have been especially noticeable for Paul's Philippian audience. On Paul's imperial view, the lowly body becomes the exalted body, and the old self that Paul has taken his leave from as excrement signifies an imperial mode of production and order that Paul can no longer embrace as a classificatory system of self-definition. It is true that he has reasons to put confidence in the flesh: circumcised on the eighth day, of the people of Israel, of the tribe of Benjamin, a Hebrew of Hebrews; in regard to the law, a Pharisee; as for zeal, persecuting the church; as for righteousness based on the law, blameless" (verses 5–6). All of this is the site of his crucifixion: I have lost all things; Paul has evacuated them and at this site where the suffering body of Jesus disrupts a sacred code, he constructs himself as a new kind of other: losing himself, abjecting himself, with a righteousness that is loss.[28] Such a loss is the negation of not being what one was and is also simultaneously the other.

For all of its language about resurrected bodies and seeking a citizenship in heaven, Paul's representation is not of an incorporeal existence. Paul's defecated past has now been replaced by a new kind secretion, his tears. "I have told you this many times [to pay attention to those who follow the right example], and now repeat it with even with tears [*klaiōn*]: there are many whose lives make them enemies of Christ's death on the cross" (3:18). The NRSV translation "tears" is again too sanitary; the Greek word—as is already indicated by its onomatopoeia—connotes a loud lament or cry of

---

27. Similarly, Williams, *Enemies of the Cross of Christ*, 232–54, where the connection between 2:6–11 and 3:1–21 are similarly explored and recognized, as well as the role of humiliation in making a paradoxical identity. My reading theorizes this more expressly as the site of provocative religious construction of self and other via a doubling "other strategy."

28. For the rhetorical role of negation and contrast in 3:1–16, see Bloomquist, *Function of Suffering*, 129–35.

pain.²⁹ His tears for those he has "othered" represent the creation of an alternative order united with the crucified Jesus. The tears Paul sheds display the suffering Christ and instantiate a new form of abjection. Like *skybala*, they are also a form of natural egress that received medical theorization in antiquity. As with bowel movements where defecation arises as a consequence of nature, so tears are squeezed out even against human will as sadness overcomes a person. In ancient philosophical discussion weeping was a topic of interest because of its involuntary physiological characteristics and hence the evidence of lack of self-control and proper regulation. Epicureans, Stoics, as well as Middle Platonists (for example Plutarch and Philo) contemporary with Paul distinguished between indulgent tears and those properly shed as an expression of virtue and self-containment, in other words, expressly *not* as a sign of excess.³⁰ The wise person sheds tears in the right measure as a right response to situations of joy or grief. In Philippians, Paul's tears are clearly *not* those of the sage, but as a loud cry of lament rather express an excess that contrasts with his former shit as it does with that of those "whose god is the belly, and their glory is their shame; their minds are set on earthly things" (3:19). Belly, shame, and earthly things correspond to Paul's defecated past. Now his loud cries and tears express a new orientation where there is also evacuation, but in a way consistent with a new posture of a believer who mourns over the errors and imminent destruction of others. This suffering self expresses the desire not for self-indulgence, but the salvation of the other.

To conclude: Paul constructs two kinds of religious other on this heap of Drek: the other caught in its own classificatory system that glories in its waste and another lamenting type that is at once resurrection body and suffering body, spirit and flesh. Both contest stable classification schemes. There are two others in this text and two modes of religious construction of the abjected body. In his two constructions of abjection, Paul is a fierce rhetorician who uses the other to his advantage, first to disqualify his opponents' claims to a legitimate religious system and second to qualify himself as the right beneficiary of his upside-down world. Paul's letter to the Philippians reveals the destructive and creative powers of the construction of the religious other.

---

29. Liddell and Scott, *Greek-English Lexicon*, s.v. "κλαίω"; Danker et al., *Greek-English Lexicon*, s.v. "κλαίω."

30. For the discussion of tears in medical and philosophical discourse, see Graver, "Weeping Wise."

# BIBLIOGRAPHY

Accordance Bible Software. *Accordance 10*. Version 10.4.0. Altamonte Springs, FL: OakTree Software, 2014.

Bakhtin, Mikhail. *Problems of Dostoevsky's Poetics*. Translated by Caryl Emerson. Manchester: Manchester University Press, 1984.

Behm, Johannes. "Koilia." In vol. 3 of *Theological Dictionary of the New Testament*, edited by Gerhard Kittel, 786–89 Translated by Geoffrey W. Bromley. Grand Rapids: Eerdmans, 1965.

Bloomquist, Gregory. *The Function of Suffering in Philippians*. Sheffield: JSOT, 1993.

Bradley, Mark. "Introduction: Smell and the Ancient Senses." In *Smell and the Ancient Senses*, edited by Mark Bradley, 1–16. London: Routledge, 2015.

Clarke, John R. *Art in the Lives of Ordinary Romans: Visual Representation and Non-Elite Viewers in Italy, 100 BC–AD 315*. Berkeley: University of California Press, 2003.

Collins, Raymond F. *The Power of Images in Paul*. Collegeville, MN: Liturgical, 2008.

Danker, Frederick W., et al. *A Greek-English Lexicon of the New Testament and Other Early Christian Literature*. 3rd ed. Chicago: University of Chicago Press, 2000.

deSilva, David A. "No Confidence in the Flesh." *Trinity Journal* 15 (1994) 27–54.

Graver, Margaret. "The Weeping Wise: Stoic and Epicurean Consolations in Seneca's 99th Epistle." In *Tears in the Graeco-Roman World*, edited by Thorsten Fögen, 235–52. Berlin: De Gruyter, 2009.

Henderson, Jeffrey. *The Maculate Muse: Obscene Language in Attic Comedy*. 2nd ed. New York: Oxford University Press, 1991.

Hepner, G. "Scatology in the Bible." *Scandinavian Journal of the Old Testament* 18 (2004) 278–95.

Hill, Susan E. *Eating to Excess: The Meaning of Gluttony and the Fat Body in the Ancient World*. Santa Barbara, CA: Praeger, 2011.

Koester, Helmut. "The Purpose of the Polemic of a Pauline Fragment." *New Testament Studies* 8 (1962) 317–32.

———. "temnō, ktl." In vol. 7 of *Theological Dictionary of the New Testament*, edited by Gerhard Kittel, 106–112. Translated by Geoffrey W. Bromley. Grand Rapids: Eerdmans, 1965.

Kristeva, Julia. *Powers of Horror: An Essay on Abjection*. Translated by Leon S. Roudiez. New York: Columbia University Press, 1982.

Lateiner, Donald, and Dimos Spatharas. "Introduction: Ancient and Modern Modes of Understanding and Manipulating Disgust." In *The Ancient Emotion of Disgust*, edited by Donald Lateiner and Dimos Spatharas. Oxford: Oxford University Press, 2017.

Liddell, Henry George, and Robert Scott. *Greek-English Lexicon*. Oxford: Clarendon, 1996.

Lightfoot, J. B. *Saint Paul's Epistle to the Philippians: A Revised Text with Introduction, Notes, and Dissertations*. Cambridge: Cambridge University Press, 1881.

Michel, Otto. "kyōn, kynarion." In vol. 3 of *Theological Dictionary of the New Testament*, edited by Gerhard Kittel, 1101–4. Translated by Geoffrey W. Bromley. Grand Rapids: Eerdmans, 1965.

Nanos, Mark D. "Paul's Reversal of Jews Calling Gentiles 'Dogs' (Philippians 3:2): 1600 Years of an Ideological Tale Wagging an Exegetical Dog?" *Biblical Interpretation* 17 (2009) 448–82.

Oberman, Heiko A. "Teufelsdreck: Eschatology and Scatology in the 'Old' Luther." *Studies in Christian-Jewish Relations* 19 (1988) 435–50.

Oropeza, B. J. *Jews, Gentiles, and the Opponents of Paul: Apostasy in the New Testament.* Eugene, OR: Cascade, 2012.

Pearse, Roger. "Cybele's Castration Clamps—Medical Apparatus of the Magna Mater." *Roger Pearse* (blog), October 1, 2015. Online. http://www.roger-pearse.com/weblog/2015/10/01/cybeles-castration-clamps-medical-apparatus-of-the-magna-mater.

Rauhala, Marika. "*Obscena Galli Praesentia*: Dehumanizing Cybele's Eunuch-Priests through Disgust." In *The Ancient Emotion of Disgust*, edited by Donald Lateiner and Dimos Spatharas, 235–52. Oxford: Oxford University Press, 2016.

Sherwood, Yvonne. "Prophetic Scatology: Prophecy and the Art of Sensation." *Semeia* 82 (1998) 183–224.

Simon, Eckehard. "Carnival Obscenities in German Towns." In *Obscenity: Social Control and Artistic Creation in the European Middle Ages*, edited by Jan M. Ziolkowski, 193–213. Leiden: Brill, 1998.

van Tilburg, C. R. *Traffic and Congestion in the Roman Empire*. London: Routledge, 2007.

Webb, Ruth. *Ekphrasis, Imagination, and Persuasion in Ancient Rhetorical Theory and Practice*. Farnham, Surrey: Ashgate, 2009.

Williams, Demetrius K. *Enemies of the Cross of Christ the Terminology of the Cross and Conflict in Philippians*. London: Sheffield Academic, 2002.

Wycliffe, John. *Wycliffe's New Testament*. Translated by John Wycliffe and John Purvey. Edited by Terence P. Noble. Vancouver: Ward, 2001.

Ziolkowski, Jan M. "Introduction: The Latin Grammatical and Rhetorical Tradition." In *Obscenity: Social Control and Artistic Creation in the European Middle Ages*, edited by Jan. M. Ziolkowski, 3–18. Leiden: Brill, 1998.

# 3

# Friendship between Muslims, Christians, and Jews

A Qur'anic View

SYED NASIR ZAIDI

## INTRODUCTION

THIS ESSAY ATTEMPTS TO show how the Qur'an portrays Christianity and Judaism and how different Qur'anic verses support the importance of friendship between Muslims, Christians, and Jews. The Qur'an suggests the possibility of salvation of Christians and Jews, admires Christian priests and monks because of their moral and ethical soundness, and invites Christians to come close to Islam on similarities and common grounds. The Qur'an also instructs its followers not to dispute with Christians and Jews, except in a moral and intellectual way. The Qur'an's approach to the possibility of friendship with Christians and Jews needs to be understood in the light of the social, cultural, and political context of the time of revelation.

Friendship between Muslims, Christians, and Jews is a very important and interesting question in our social context. There are several reasons that all religious traditions, especially Abrahamic religions, should come close to each other. They share serious challenges from the anti-religious environment at the global level. The role and effectiveness of religion and spirituality in day-to-day matters are being questioned by the non-religious intellectual communities of the world. Religious intolerance among the followers of religious traditions and atrocities committed in the name of religion have left tremendous negative effects in the consciousness of peaceful populations in the world. Among these three major Religious traditions, Islam, specifically, is under intense criticism for promoting intolerance and hatred towards the followers of other religions. This has raised serious questions about some theological principles of Islam and about some Qur'anic verses on the concepts of Jihad and Muslims' relationships with the followers of other religions.

The Qur'an, which is the main focus of this essay, is a prime source of Islamic thought. Islamic law and theological discourse are derived from the Qur'an. If clear guidance is not found in the Qur'an, the sayings and traditions of Prophet Muhammad are considered a source of God's commandments, but only if they do not contradict the Qur'an. According to the majority of Muslim scholars, the Qur'an is a complete word of God and the Prophet Muhammad was only the recipient of the revelation while Gabriel was the intermediary agent. The Qur'an itself says, "Muhammad does not speak out of his own desires. It is a revelation which has been revealed to him" (Qur'an 53:4) and "O Muhammad, do not move quickly your tongue too quickly to recite the Qur'an, We should be responsible for its collection and recitation" (Qur'an 16:19).

A unique aspect of the authenticity of the Qur'an is the oral tradition that established itself as the standard by which the written text was to be judged. Down through the centuries, the complete oral Qur'an has been maintained in an unbroken chain with professional reciters learning the sacred text by memory from their teachers and then passing it on to their students in the same way. However, it is very important to note that understanding of the Qur'an has always been a big issue among Islamic scholars. Thousands of commentaries have been written in order to explain the meaning of the Qur'an, and to understand its message correctly.

Qur'anic commentators and their commentaries are considered highly important by Muslim scholars and Jurists in understanding Islamic teachings and driving Islamic laws. However, despite the commentators' important position in Islamic research, their words are not considered as an authority and final interpretation. Nevertheless, if their interpretation is quoted somewhere, it is given a lot of respect and Muslim scholars avoid challenging it directly. There is an unwritten agreement between Islamic scholars that either (a) they must refer their understanding of the Qur'an to one of the written commentaries; or (b) the researchers must themselves have been renowned commentators on the Qur'an; or (c) the researcher must establish strong academic grounds and adopt an acceptable methodology to interpret any Qur'anic verse.

This essay relies on renowned Sunni and Shia commentators who cannot be easily challenged and this methodology lends validity. However, the views highlighted here mostly favor of inter-religious friendship and opening the door of interfaith harmony.

## COMMON GROUNDS FOR INTER-RELIGIOUS FRIENDSHIP

The Qur'an notes the commonalities between Islam and the People of the Book. Allah instructs the Prophet Muhammad to refer to Christians as "the people of the Book." The Qur'an says: "O People of the book, let us come to an agreement: that we will worship none but God, that we will associate none with Him, and that none of us shall set up mortals as deities besides God" (Qur'an 3:64). By this method of reasoning, the Qur'an teaches every Muslim that if some people do not agree with their point of view, they should invite them to find a common ground. A Muslim scholar and commentator of the Qur'an, Agha Puya, says that the Prophet Muhammad, while preaching the truth, would adhere to the policy of peace and adjustment with the non-Muslims.[1]

The issue of monotheism and polytheism has been very complicated in the history of Christian theology. Christian philosophers and theologians have long been concerned with the question of how to reconcile their belief in three divine Persons with maintaining monotheism.[2] For this reason, the issue of monotheism has been the focus of numerous debates between Christian Trinitarians and other monotheists, particularly Jews and Muslims.[3] However, from the Qur'anic perspective, the invitation to common monotheistic ground is not one-sided. The Qur'an is not inviting Christians to believe in the oneness of God; it assumes they already do. According to some Muslim scholars, Christians claim that their belief in the Father, the Son, and the Holy Spirit is not contradictory to Monotheism.[4] The monotheistic ground can be traced out from the biblical scripture. In the New Testament, Jesus Christ says, "O Israel: The Lord our God is one Lord, and you are to have a love for the Lord your God with all your heart, and with all your soul, and with all your mind, and with all your strength" (Mark 12:29–31).

---

1. Puya, *Noble Qur'an*.
2. Rea, "Polytheism and Christian Belief."
3. McGrath, *Only True God*.
4. Shirazi, *Tafseer-e-Namuna*, 2:594.

## FRIENDSHIPS WITH CHRISTIANS AND JEWS

A common verse, widely quoted from the Qur'an in support of Islam's anti-Christian and anti-Jewish injunction, reads: "O you who believe! Do not take the Jews and the Christians for intimate friends. They are friends with each other. Whoever takes them as intimate friends is one of them. Surely Allah does not take the unjust people to the right path" (Qur'an 5:51).

The apparent message of this verse could be very disturbing for individuals of Christians and Jewish faith traditions. It clearly says that Muslims have to refrain from a deep friendship with Christians and Jews. However, even at a superficial level, this verse does not forbid Muslims to deal with non-Muslims in the spirit of tolerance, sympathy, goodwill, equity, justice, favor, and kindness.[5] The Qur'an also emphasizes at different occasions that the deep, intense and profound friendship of Muslims can only be with Allah, the highest of the high; the Messenger; and those who believe in them.[6]

The question then arises as to why the Qur'an prohibits Muslims from becoming intimate friends with non-Muslims. Should the Qur'an's attitude towards Christians and Jews be considered negative? The answer to this question lies in understanding the Qur'an's approach to this whole issue. We have to examine whether the Qur'an's commandment is related to the faith of Christians or Jews. If this is the case, then it would be very difficult for Muslims to establish a positive relationship with non-Muslims, leading to a serious obstacle along the way of interfaith dialogue. But the historical background of this verse clearly illustrates the fact that this instruction to Muslims was not due to others' religion.

First, it is important to note that when the Qur'an uses the term "Christian or Jew" instead of the "People of the Book," it means to convey that this category of people have deviated from the teachings of their Book and are following their political and national ambitions.[7] Second, at the time of the revelation of this verse, some Muslims were collaborating with Christians and Jews on the assumption that the Christians would come into power and oppress them (Qur'an 5:52). This is why Allah asks them why they don't consider the source of victory or punishment to be Allah, regretting what they hide in their souls (Qur'an 5:52). It should be emphasized that Muslims are not being asked to cut their social and economic relations with Christians and Jews. Rather, they are being told not to rely on their friendship to safeguard against their enemies.[8]

5. Usmani, *Maarif ul Qur'an*.
6. Usmani, *Maarif ul Qur'an*.
7. Shirazi, *Tafseer-e-Namuna*, 4:410.
8. Shirazi, *Tafseer-e-Namuna*, 4:410.

The biggest misconception in understanding this verse is that this verse refers to Christians and Jews of all times. Keeping history and context in mind is extremely important when reading the Qur'an. If we see the context of the verse, we see that it refers to the lifetime of the Prophet Muhammad when Jews and Christians were at war with Muslims. In such a situation, it makes perfect sense to discourage friendship, in the sense of political alliance, with Jews and Christians. In addition, like the Bible, many topics in the Qur'an are continued in other places for clarification.

## CHRISTIANS ARE WORTHY OF FRIENDSHIP

In one Qur'anic verse, a delegation of Christians is admired because of its truth-loving attitude. The Qur'an states: "when they hear what is revealed to the Messenger, you can see their eyes flood with tears, as they learn about the Truth" (Qur'an 5:83). This verse was revealed when the delegation of seventy Christian scholars and priests sent by Negus the king of Ethiopia came to the Prophet Muhammad. The Prophet recited the Surah Yasin chapter 36 of the Qur'an before them. As they listened to it, tears begin flowing from their eyes and all of them remarked how similar the discourse was to the one revealed to Jesus Christ.[9] Although this verse was revealed specifically about the delegation sent by the King of Ethiopia, the verse includes all Christians who are God-fearing and Seekers of Truth similar to the people of Ethiopia.[10]

The Qur'an has itself pointed out this fact at the end of this Surah: "That is because among them, there are priests and monks who are not arrogant." This statement also tells us something crucial about the life of a community of true believers: its spiritual leaders, priests, and monks have a very important role in the community. The monasticism practiced by Christians was predicated on the belief that proximity to God cannot be achieved unless one abstains from all worldly pleasures.[11] The Priests referred to in this verse were overwhelmed because of the recognition of truth in what they heard (Qur'an 5:83).

The recognition of the truth is very important in the view of all sacred scriptures. The Qur'an clearly identifies why people dismiss the truth despite having knowledge. According to the Qur'an, arrogance is one reason people deny the truth. The Qur'an points out that some people deny the truth unjustly and proudly while their soul is convinced of true evidence (Qur'an

---

9. Usmani, *Maarif ul Qur'an*.
10. Usmani, *Tafseer-e-Usmani*.
11. Usmani, *Tafseer-e-Usmani*.

27:14). It explains that the mere perception of truth is not enough to lead to right action. That will not happen unless and until one removes from his or her soul all opposing influences, i.e., the arrogance which prevents him or her from submitting to truth.[12] And if Christians are admired in the Qur'an, this is because they clearly said, "Why should we not believe in God and in the truth, that has come to us" (Qur'an 5:84). One may say here that since this group of Christians converted to Islam, the Qur'an admires them and recommends them for friendship. However, if we look into the historical background of this verse, we will come to know that the Christians are not only being praised because of their acceptance of Islam but, more importantly, due to their understanding of the truth.

Here, Allah has given three reasons for the Christians being the nearest to friendship with the Muslims. According to the Qur'an, these reasons are their exclusive attributes: (a) There are priests among them; (b) and monks and ascetics; and (c) they are not proud. From an inter-religious friendship perspective, the verse reminds us of the importance of removing arrogance, bigotry, and prejudice. This can be a very strong theological criterion for an inter-religious relationship, in which people invite one another to seek the truth while putting aside any arrogance and prejudice towards other faith traditions. It means one has to accept others' understanding of the truth about their own religion even if it is opposite to one's own understanding of truth.

However, in this same verse, the Qur'an uses very unfriendly language about Jews. The Qur'an says that you will certainly find the most violent of people in enmity for those who are Jews (Qur'an 5:82). Jews had the same alternatives as the Christians, but they continued their haughtiness, became harder in their bigotry, and turned to double-dealing and deception. They broke their covenant and eagerly waited for calamities to befall the Muslims. No doubt they had their own scholars, but they behaved proudly, and their arrogance left them unprepared for accepting the truth.[13]

If we look into Islamic history, we will notice that there was a serious clash between Muslims and Jews of that time. However, this was because of other political, social, and moral issues. Hence, all related Qur'anic verses have to be seen in the light of the specific circumstances of that time. As a result, we cannot generalize these verses to the current era and conclude that there is no possibility of friendship between Jews and Muslims. They can be good friends, unless other political and social issues are involved.

---

12. Tabatabai, *Al-Mizan fi Tafsir al-Qur'an*.
13. Tabatabai, *Tafseer al-Qur'an*, 6:118.

## PLACES OF WORSHIP MUST BE PROTECTED

The Qur'an's affirmation of protecting the worship places of Christians and Jews can be an important motivation for Muslims to establish a good relationship with Christians and Jews. Together they can stand against those who want to demolish places of worship. In these places, the name of God is remembered frequently, and thus they are worthy of respect. The Qur'an states: "If Allah had not been repelling some people by means of some others, the monasteries, the churches, the congregations of Jews and the mosques where God's name is abundantly recited would have been demolished. Allah will surely help those who help Him. Indeed, Allah is all-strong, all-mighty" (Qur'an 22:40).

The above verse describes the philosophy behind the permission of physical resistance to the demolition of worship places. It is the duty of every community to defend their places of worship without bias as they all support the common and ultimate goal of "faith" in the community. The verse quoted above also states a divine tradition that Allah does not allow a group of people to exercise its authority over other groups in regard to religious freedom. No individual or community should be allowed to impose their belief system. So, Allah repels or restrains one group by means of another. This principle has also been described in another verse: "If Allah has not pushed back some people by means of another, the earth would have been spoiled" (Qur'an 2:251).

The renowned scholar of the Qur'an, Makarim Shirazi, says that this was the first time in the Qur'an that the sacred fight or *Jihad* for self-defense was justified and permitted. Here, new and small Muslim communities were not only permitted to fight for their existence but also fight to preserve their faith in the true God. Their fight was not for material privileges, but against tyrants and cruel dictators who wanted to eliminate the name of God and wipe out faith from people's hearts.[14] According to Tabatabai, a renowned philosopher and commentator on the Qur'an, this way of opposing is the last resort when there are no options to protect yourself.[15] This intention of fighting is what Allah refers to as "repel some people through other people" in order to protect belief in God from extinction.[16]

---

14. Shirazi, *Tafseer-e-Namuna*, 2:25.
15. Tabatabai, *Tafsir al-Qur'an*.
16. Tabatabai, *Tafsir al-Qur'an*.

## POSSIBILITY OF SALVATION FOR CHRISTIANS AND JEWS IN THE QUR'AN

The concept of salvation is an important theological issue which has widely been discussed by researchers of Abrahamic religions. Research shows that there is no clear-cut answer to the possibility of salvation for all people and also that the grace of God must be available to all. Some verses in the New Testament clearly teach that salvation is by faith only. To gain salvation, one must exercise faith in Jesus and demonstrate that faith by obeying his commands (Acts 4:10; Rom 19:9–10; Heb 5:9). Similarly, the majority of Muslim scholars also claim to have exclusive access to the complete truth. It seems very difficult to believe that by holding the view of exclusivity, one can make a serious initiative to embrace the members of other faith traditions. If we theologically believe that people from other religions will not be saved on the day of judgment, how can we establish a strong friendship with them? Thus, in support of inter-religious friendship, it is important to discuss the issue of salvation in the view of the Qur'an.

The Qur'an says: "Surely those who believe, and those who are Jews, and the Sabians, and the Christians, whoever believes in Allah and the Last Day, and acts righteously, shall have no fear, nor shall such people grieve" (Qur'an 5:69). The basic purpose of this verse is to make it clear that no faith has a monopoly on achieving salvation. This verse explains that Salvation can only be achieved through true faith and belief in God, the Day of Judgment and the performance of good deeds. According to this verse, God will judge people on the quality of their faith rather than by the particular set of religious beliefs to which they adhere, whether they be Muslim, Christian, or Jewish. By means of faith, not affiliation, they can enter paradise. Here, the Qur'an challenges the thought of Christians of that time that none shall enter Paradise unless they are Christians. Ask them, says the Qur'an, to prove that their claim is true (Qur'an 2:111).

Some Muslim scholars debate whether Christians of the pre-Islamic period or Jews of the pre-Christian could have received salvation even if they failed to believe in the prophecy and teachings of the Prophet Muhammad. What if they demonstrated true faith in God, belief in the hereafter, and performed good deeds? Some exegetes note that the Qur'an repeatedly declares that a person who does not believe in the Prophet, angels, and in the books of Allah is not a Muslim and thus could not enter Paradise.[17] The verse quoted above, they say, does not fully spell out the details of true belief, faith, and righteous conduct. These are mentioned in in other places in the Qur'an which say that Allah recognizes no faith or belief which does not

---

17. Usmani, *Maarif ul Qur'an*.

accept the Prophet Muhammad.[18] The Qur'an says: "And whoever desires a religion other than Islam, it shall not be accepted from him, and in the hereafter, he shall be one of the losers" (Qur'an 3:85).

However, the term *Islam* is used in more than one way in the Qur'an. In a general sense, it refers to submission and obedience to God. Literally, a Muslim is "one who submits himself or herself to the will of God." "God named you Muslims before and in this Book, so that the Messenger will witness and will be the witness over mankind" (Qur'an 22:78). According to the Qur'an, Abraham is also called a Muslim in the general sense (Qur'an 3:67). He was an upright person who had submitted himself to the will of God and hence was a "Muslim." On other occasions, the Qur'an uses the word *Islam* specifically to identify the religion of the Prophet Muhammad.

When the Qur'an says that Islam is the only acceptable religion, in what sense does it use the word *Islam*? Generally, Muslim scholars are of the opinion that the application of the term *Islam* is always restricted to a particular community with regards to its own Prophet. When a particular Prophet is replaced by another Prophet, the Islam of the time of the previous Prophet will cease to be operative.[19] The Qur'an also clearly states that it is impossible for God to punish someone to whom the messengers, proofs of the truth, have not been sent (Qur'an 17:15). Thus, Muslim scholars have divided the people of other Books into two categories: (a) those who do not accept the truth due to obstinacy and rejection; and (b) those who are ignorant of or unable to reach the truth.[20] The Qur'an highlights the first category when it states: "And when they said, O' God if this is the truth from You, rain down upon us stones from heaven, or bring us to a painful punishment" (Qur'an 8:32).

So, what is the Qur'an is ultimately telling us about the salvation of Christians and Jews? Can they completely submit to Allah without believing in the Prophet Muhammad? The question is complex. So, to answer this question, we can get help from another Qur'anic verse which says that complex cases have to be submitted to the judgment of God. The most relevant Qur'anic verse illustrates that there is a category of people whose end is not clear enough. Their case must be deferred, and God will decide on the Day of Judgment, whether they will be punished or forgiven (Qur'an 9:106). According to the renowned intellectual and researcher of the Qur'an, Makarim Shirazi, there will be a group of people whose faith and good deeds will not be as strong as they should be. Hence, their faith will not ensure their

---

18. Pirzada, *Dawat ul Qur'an*.
19. Usmani, *Maarif ul Qur'an*.
20. Muthari, *Islam and Religious Pluralism*.

prosperity and salvation. On the other hand, their sinfulness and deviation are not so extreme they should give up any hope for the salvation.[21] The Qur'an also says that those who were not able to find any means of obtaining their freedom or of having the right guidance may receive God's pardon. Allah is All-Merciful and All-Forgiving (Qur'an 4:98–99). In addition, other verses convey that all those who have committed injustice to themselves should not despair. God's Mercy is limitless, and he can forgive all sins (Qur'an 39:53). "And He could have destroyed the people because of their sins but He pardons many sins" (Qur'an 42:34). In the end, it seems, Allah will decide the question of salvation, person by person.

## CODE OF ETHICS FOR THE PROPAGATION OF ISLAM

The Qur'an also describes the universal code of ethics for Islamic propagation. This code of ethics, if followed, can be a very strong ground for interfaith harmony. The Qur'an states, "Invite to the way of your Lord with wisdom and good advice and dispute with them in a manner that is best" (Qur'an 16:125).

In this verse, the Qur'an highlights three very important ethical and intellectual principles for those who are engaged in the propagation of Islam. However, a deeper look indicates that these principles are not confined to Muslims. Rather, they are universal and perhaps the best code of ethics for every religion. Before discussing these principles, it is important to mention that the Qur'an also says that there is no compulsion in religion and no one is allowed to impose his or her religion on another person, especially because the right has become clearly distinct from wrong (Qur'an 2:256).

The first principle mentioned in the Qur'an is the principle of *hikma* (wisdom) which demands that one should keep in view the intelligence and the capability of the addressees and convey the message in accordance to the audience.[22] On different occasions, the Qur'an instructs its followers to use their wisdom and knowledge. It places high regard on the mental nourishment of religious people along with their spiritual enrichment. According to the Qur'an, intellectual growth in religious matters and spiritual refinement should develop side by side. Deficiency in either of these two can cause adverse effects in the area of religious propagation.

The second principle is *mau'izhah* (good advice or admonishment). The Qur'anic term *mau'izhah* is related to a message that appeals to the

---

21. Shirazi, *Tafseer-e-Namuna*, 8:130.
22. Maududi, *Towards Understanding the Qur'an*.

heart of a person. It means, one should not only try to address an audience rationally and intellectually but should also create in them an interest and love for Divine guidance. Admonition should be administered in such a manner that an addressee feels that the invitation is aimed at his or her own prosperity and welfare.

The third principle is *mujadilah*, meaning there is no need to enter into a heated discussion and conflict. The discussion should be approached with rationality and reasoning. Every objection should be answered in a pleasant way, remaining within the limits of decent etiquette to prevent obstinacy, resistance, and violence.[23] The nature of *jadal* (arguing and disputing) is different from the nature of a reasoning and logical environment. In *jadal*, opponents do not give any importance to the truth; rather they misuse the principles which have already been accepted by the opponent.[24] However, one who discusses items in a humble manner, and considers these three principles when inviting conversation, will definitely be able to prevent religious communities from sectarianism and pave the grounds for interfaith harmony.

## CONCLUSION

The essence of every religion is peace, love, and spiritual support for its followers. The universal laws of Islam are beyond time and space. They are applicable to all eras and places. However, Islamic laws made under specific social, political, and cultural circumstances have not always been distinguished from the universal laws of Islam. Sometimes political, social, and cultural circumstances undermine the real message of the Qur'an. They provide the grounds for negative stereotypes of other traditions, leading some to use the most literal meanings of Qur'anic verses against interfaith harmony. Therefore, this essay tried to present the true perspective of the Qur'an in relation to Muslims' relationship with Christians and Jews.

## BIBLIOGRAPHY

Maududi, AbulAala. *Towards Understanding the Qur'an*. London: Kube Publishing, 1980. Online. https://islamicstudies.info/literature/understandingislam.htm

McGrath, James F. *The Only True God: Early Christian Monotheism in Its Jewish Context*. Champaign: University of Illinois Press, 2009.

Mutahari, Murtaza. *Islam and Religious Pluralism*. Translated by Sayyid Sulayman Ali Hasan. Kitchener, ON: 2004. Online. http://www.al-islam.org/islam-and-religious-pluralism-ayatullah-murtadha-mutahhari.

23. Pirzada, *Dawat ul Qur'an*.
24. Tabatabai, *Al-Mizan fi Tafsir al-Qur'an*, 12:534.

Pirzada, Shams. *Dawat ul Qur'an.* Translated by Abdul Karim Sheikh. Mumbai: Idara Dawatul Quran, 1991. Online. http://www.islamicstudies.info/Qur'an/dawat.
Puya, Agha M. *The Noble Qur'an.* Translated by S. V. Mir Ahmed Ali. Elmhurst, NY: PET, 2001. Online. http://quran.al-islam.org.
Rea, Michael C. "Polytheism and Christian Belief." *The Journal of Theological Studies* 57 (2006) 133–48.
Shirazi, Makarim. *Tafseer-e-Namuna.* Qom: Dar al-Kutub al-Islamia, 1996.
Tabatabai, Hussein. *Al-Mizan fi Tafsir al Mizan.* Qom: World Organization of Islamic Studies, 2002.
Usman, Shafi. *Maarif ul Qur'an.* Translated by Muhammad Hasan Askari and Muhammad Shamim. Revised by Muhammad Taqi Usmani. Karachi: Maktaba Darul-Uloom, 2010. Online. http://www.islamicstudies.info/quran/maarif
Usmani, Taqi. *Tafseer-e-Usmani.* 2016. Online. http://www.noorehidayat.org.

# 4

# Encountering Difference and Identity in South Asian Religions

## Anne Murphy

How were difference and identity configured in premodern South Asian religions, and how does this configuration relate to modern forms of religious identity in South Asia? These are complex questions, given the diversity of religious expressions in South Asia and their long and complex histories. This essay will give a partial answer to these questions with reference to how religious difference was imagined in the early modern period at an exemplary moment and location in the cultural and linguistic region of Punjab, now divided between the modern nation-states of India and Pakistan, to suggest how encounters with the "other" could be understood, experienced, and represented in that context (but of course were not always—there is much diversity here). The examples chosen reflect local and particular dynamics, but also indicate broader trends. Examples from the Sikh tradition are our concern, but the focus is on the articulation of relationships with other traditions. At the same time, attention to one tradition allows us also be mindful of particular, tradition-specific concerns.

## I. CONSTRUCTIONS OF THE RELIGIOUS OTHER

## BOUNDARIES AND CROSSINGS OVER

The cultural and linguistic region of Punjab, which is the locus of this exploration, was divided along religious lines between the modern nation-states of India and Pakistan in 1947, at the close of British rule in the subcontinent, with Hindu/Sikh majority areas allocated to India and Muslim-majority sections to Pakistan. The division of this single region into two states dramatically reveals the complexity of what we mean when we call something "Punjabi." How can we imagine the historical dimensions and living connections among the cultural worlds in this once diverse and mixed region, in a time where separation is now a lived reality?

This relates to a larger problem in the historiography of South Asia. It is generally understood that modern definitions of religious identities and communities do not map to pre-colonial religious formations, making any attempt to understand encounters between religious actors difficult to characterize in the terms we use today. A wealth of scholarship has for instance highlighted the recent provenance of the term and idea of "Hinduism."[1] Appearing first in Persian and Arabic sources, the term "Hindu" was ethnic-geographic in its earliest uses, referring to the Indus River and those who lived in the region associated with it.[2] The idea of "Hindu" developed in complex ways in subsequent centuries, expanding slowly to include a cultural and religious sense. Most commonly, before the modern period, "Hindu" was used in a contrastive sense along the lines of "gentile" in Western traditions with reference to non-Jews, in this case designating a group of traditions that were not Muslim and not Christian.[3] Thus, for example, we can see in eighteenth-century Punjabi texts that Sikhs were contained within a sense of "Hindu" in such broad contrastive terms, at the same time that they were portrayed clearly as representing a separate religious/cultural tradition alongside other traditions that were portrayed as similarly distinct, some of which are now included under the umbrella term "Hindu."[4] British colonial administrative technologies accelerated limited existing tendencies to incorporate and simplify religious designations in the region, through colonial administrative technologies like the census and the administration of religious sites.[5] Such designations took on new

---

1. For an overview of debates, see Lorenzen "Who Invented Hinduism?"; Pennington, *Was Hinduism Invented?*

2. Ernst, *Eternal Garden*, 22.

3. This is supported by Lorenzen, "Who Invented Hinduism?," 639–40.

4. Murphy, "*Gurbilas* Literature."

5. On emerging definitions of the category of "Hindu," see, for example, Hare, "Contested Communities"; Hawley, "Four Sampradays"; Horstmann, "Theology and Statecraft"; *Der Zusammenhalt der Welt*; Pinch, *Warrior Ascetics and Indian Empires;* "History, Devotion." On how British administration shaped religious identities in the region, see Jones's classic work, "Religious Identity and the Indian Census." On the management of religious sites, see Murphy, *Materiality of the Past.*

political weight within new Legislative Councils in the beginning decades of the twentieth century and, before that, in committees comprised by appointment rather than election, all of which were configured with reference to religious identity. The establishment of separate electorates for Muslims in 1909 emerged out of this context.

The challenge, then, is to acknowledge, trace, and provide analysis that allows for that which exceeds and subverts the categories we know now, which emerged out of the colonial context; to allow for different understandings of the relationships among and within religions that recently have been seen to be configured in exclusive and agonistic terms, recognizing the historical formation of those very categories; and to allow for interaction among traditions and persons. At the same time, however, it is imperative that we recognize the historical emergence of religious traditions and communities in distinctive terms. One particularly problematic representation of Sikhism, as a religion, is roughly phrased as "Sikhism derives from" or "is a mixture of" Hinduism and Islam. A related but more sophisticated form of this argument is found in discussion of Sikhism solely in terms of its representation of larger devotional (*sant* or *bhakti*) traditions. As Nikky-Guninder Kaur Singh has noted well, such formulations have "implicitly or explicitly . . . questioned the originality and autonomy of [founder] Guru Nanak's message." She rightly asks "to what extent should the existence of 'historical influence' be used to call into question the 'uniqueness' of any religious thinker or religious tradition?"[6] An exclusive concern for context and relationships with other traditions reduces Sikhism to other traditions, disregarding an understanding of its own historical unfolding, and at the same time takes it as given that these other entities, out of which it is derived, are somehow uniquely independent and defined. Just as it would not tell us anything about Christianity if we were to describe it as "just" a combination of Judaism, Greco-Roman religions, and European 'pagan' traditions—because that does not tell us anything about its history, practices and ideas, and the people who have created and reproduced it—this common formulation of Sikhism in relation to other religions with which it was in conversation must be rejected. Thus it is only with recognition of the remarkable endurance of this kind of formulation of the historical underpinnings of Sikhism that we can understand why many who study the Sikh tradition, and many Sikhs, reject the framing of Sikh tradition in relation to its contexts, since that discussion has been engaged as a way of seeing Sikh tradition as an indication of something *else,* other than itself. In similar terms, the argument that encounters among traditions, which often resulted in forms of sharing and collaboration, can be characterized as a form of syncretism or "influence" has thus been rightly critiqued by a range

---

6. Singh, "Myth of the Founder," 342.

of scholars: it provides neither a useful heuristic for understanding *how* religious communities interact in dialogue, nor for examining how religions emerge and develop in their contexts in complex terms.

## A DIALOGICAL NOTION OF RELIGIOUS SELF-FORMATION

So, we must take care in how relationships among traditions are represented. At the same time, we cannot ignore dialogue, because it is central to the constitution of Sikhism as a religion, and it is crucial overall that we allow for discussion of connections across and within traditions, including Sikhism, and examine the ways in which forms of encounter were understood, integrated into traditions, and managed.

Guru Nanak converses with Muslim clerics, from a manuscript of the Janam Sakhi (Life Stories), 1800–1900. India or Pakistan; Punjab region. Opaque watercolors on paper, Asian Art Museum, Kapany Collection.
Photograph © Asian Art Museum, San Francisco.

We can see the centrality of dialogue in this visual portrayal of Guru Nanak seen in a famous illustrated manuscript of a *janamsākhī*, a life story of Guru Nanak, from the early eighteenth century (illustrating a probably late sixteenth, early seventeenth-century text) and related representations (Image 1). Here we see Guru Nanak portrayed in visual terms in debate. In such portrayals, he is often clad in clothing that identified him at the crossroads of Islam and Hinduism; this is typical, and we see many instances of debate and encounter in the text, such as the famous encounter between the descendant of Baba Farid in Pak Pattan, Sheikh Brahm.[7] Philip Wagoner's recent work on dress and the articulation of identity, and Finbarr Flood's work on "cultural cross-dressing" have revealed that "the relationship between dress and identity" in late medieval/early modern South Asia "was not merely metonymic but also constitutive: dress and personal adornment constituted the very categories they signified."[8] At the same time, difference is both encoded and deconstructed through dress and its adaptation.[9] This is visible in such representations where, as Nikky Guninder Kaur Singh shows in a recent essay, Nanak adopts dress that evokes both Muslim and Hindu norms.[10] This positioning with the evocation of multiple traditions draws on these norms, while they are mobilized for a particular message that is not contained within them.

The idea of Sikh practice and thought as an encounter zone is in these ways central to its constitution, although *not* in terms that undermine the idea of being Sikh as an independent thing. Instead we see embrace of a dialogical notion of personhood, experience, and being, and a non-binary sense of religious expression. "There is no Hindu, there is no Musalman" Nanak is represented as saying in the Janamsakhis, expressing a critique of this binary formulation.[11]

We can see this dialogical notion here in a stanza from a central liturgical text, the Jap Ji Sahib which surveys the religious world which Sikhism as a body of thought and practice was in dialogue with (and was responding to) in the sixteenth century:

> He cannot be established, nor can He be made,
> Of Himself He exists, quite free from all stain . . .
> The Guru is Shiv, he is Vishnu and Brahma

---

7. McLeod, *B40 Janam-sakhi*, 60–69.
8. Flood, *Objects of Translation*, 63.
9. Flood, *Objects of Translation*, 61.
10. Singh, "Corporeal Metaphysics."
11. McLeod, *Who Is a Sikh?*

> The Guru is Parvati, known as the Mother.
> If I knew Him, I still could not say what He's like,
> His description is something that cannot be told.
> (JapJi Sahib, Stanza 5)

> The time was not found by the Pandits,
> For it to be in the Puranas.
> The hour was not found by the Qazis,
> For the Koran to record it.
> The date is unknown to the yogis,
> None know the season or month.
> The One who created this world,
> The Creator alone knows the time.
> (JapJi Sahib, Stanza 21)[12]

The Guru Granth Sahib, or sacred scripture of the Sikh tradition, which was first compiled in 1604 (drawing on earlier versions at the close of the sixteenth century) and finalized and canonized in the beginning of the eighteenth century, is itself a compilation of both Sikh self-assertion and a dialogical notion of the religious self. The inclusion in it of the *bhagat bānī*, or compositions of like-minded saints other than the Sikh Gurus, speaks to a larger view of a dialogue in the constitution of the religious community. So too does the dialogic nature of the text, which provides for exchange between the Gurus and these like-minded saints. This can be seen in multiple terms, such as in the way themes resonate. Here we see the Guru responding to the prior words of a Sufi saint (also included in the Guru Granth Sahib):

> People continually talk of the agony of the Beloved's separation but for me, O Love, it is the Lord of life.
> For the body in which such agony does not grow, O Farid, is like a cremation-ground.
> (Shaikh Farid, SGGS 1379)

> The head that bows not to the Lord merits casting off. The body that is not charged with the agony of separation (*biraha*), O Nanak, is worth being burnt.
> (M2 [the Second Guru, Angad], SGGS 89)[13]

We also see the dialogical notion in the way that particular qualifications are made to the message of a *bhagat* by one of the Gurus, in this case by the Third Guru, Guru Amardas:

---

12. Mandair and Shackle, *Teachings of the Sikh Gurus*.
13. See discussion in Singh, *Bhagats*, 50–51.

*Kabīr mahndī kari kai ghāliā āpu pīsāi pīsāi*
*tai sah bāt na puchīā kabahū na lāī pāi*

Kabir, to make henna I have crushed and ground my own self.

Yet, you, O Spouse, never had a word for me and did not bring me to your feet.

(Bhagat Kabir, SGGS 947)

*nānak mahındī kari kai rakhiā so nadari karei*
*āpe pīsai āpe ghasai āpe hī lāi laei*
*ihu piram piāla khasam kā jai bhāvai tai dei*

Having made and kept the henna, Nanak, the Lord may cast a gracious glance

He himself presses [it]. He himself pounds it to powder, and He himself applies it.

This cut of love belongs to the Lord, and He gives it to whom He likes.

(M3 [The third Guru, Amardas], SGGS 947)

Image 2. Guru Nanak meets Nath Siddhas at the village of Achal Batala, from a manuscript of the Janam Sakhi (Life Stories), ca. 1800–1850. India; perhaps Bengal region. Pigments on paper. San Francisco Asian Art Museum, Kapany Collection. Photograph © Asian Art Museum, San Francisco

Then there is the sixteenth-century Siddh Gosht, a debate—by its very nature, a dialogue—where one finds Guru Nanak's patient training of his interlocutors, the *jogīs*. This event is portrayed in this early nineteenth-century *janamsākhī* image. (Image 2) In the text, we see the Guru mobilizing the imagery associated with the Jogis—begging bowl, the mat, the loincloth—and subverting the meaning of these symbols into those that resonate with Sikh thought and practice:

> Make detachment your begging bowl, the five elements (fire, earth, air, water and ether) your cap.
> Let the body be your mat of grass, the mind your loincloth.
> Moderation, contentment and discipline are one's companions,
> Nanak, when through the guru the Name is recollected.
> (Siddh Gosht, M1 [Guru Nanak], SGGS 939)[14]

Here the markers of Jogi identity are reworked to produce a Sikh perspective, drawing on both commonality and difference. Dialogue and encounter: these then are central to the work of the Guru in the world.

At the same time that the Guru Granth Sahib thus embraces and enshrines dialogue within it, its clearly defined structure, which distinguishes work by the Sikh Gurus from that by others, and clearly delineates exact authorship of specific compositions by individual Gurus, works against the treatment of authorship that prevailed in other roughly comparable texts of the period, where subsequent poets would sing in the name of a founding figure and no distinctions were recognized. In the Sikh case, while subsequent Gurus *did*, in fact, write in the name of the founder Nanak, their authorship of verses was noted outside of the content of the poem itself. Thus, Sikhism embraces dialogue in multiple modes: to discover commonalities, to discern distinctions and the distinctiveness of the Gurus' path, and to reimagine religious self-articulations in new modes.

## CONCLUSIONS

Sikh tradition is built through a series of encounters: engagements that function in different modes to define the self, understand the other, find commonality, and distinguish difference. In this, it is not unique, but instead is typical of religious traditions in the early modern period in South Asia (and, I would argue, religious traditions around the world). There is a wide provenance, for example, for Sufi and Jogi synthesis, and the commonalities discerned between these two traditions are based on the perception

---

14. Mandair and Shackle, *Teachings of the Sikh Gurus*.

of allied practices and aims, even when distinctive theological and soteriological programs frame them.[15] The exchange and dialogue that we see present within the Sikh examples provided here, therefore, are indicative of a far broader set of cultural and religious encounters. This does not mean, of course, that there were not moments of conflict. The Mughal state, for example, came into conflict with the Sikh community in the seventeenth century at several points, resulting in the execution of the fifth Guru, Guru Arjan, and the ninth Guru, Guru Tegh Bahadur. Persecution of the Sikh community in the eighteenth century is known today by the terms *choṭā* and *vaḍḍā ghallūgāre*, the small and great carnages. But as I have shown elsewhere, even in the description of violence—such as a late eighteenth-century account of the execution of the ninth Guru—we can see the acknowledgement of commonality between Sikhism and Islam.[16] Encounters do not always bring peace or justice, but the effort to move across and through difference persists.

## BIBLIOGRAPHY

Ernst, Carl. *Eternal Garden: Mysticism, History, and Politics at a South Asian Sufi Center.* 1994. Reprint, Delhi: Oxford University Press, 2004.

Flood, Finbarr B. *Objects of Translation, Material Culture, and Medieval "Hindu-Muslim" Encounter.* Princeton: Princeton University Press, 2009.

Hare, James. "Contested Communities and the Re-imagination of Nābhādās' Bhaktamāl." In *Time, History, and the Religious Imaginary in South Asia*, edited by Anne Murphy, 150–66. London: Routledge, 2011.

Hawley, J. S. "The Four Sampradays: Ordering the Religious Past in Mughal North India." *South Asian History and Culture* 2 (2011) 160–83.

Horstmann, Monika. *Der Zusammenhalt der Welt: Religiöse Herrschaftslegitimation und Religionspolitik Mahārājā Savāī Jaisinghs (1700–1743).* Wiesbaden: Otto Harrassowitz, 2009.

———. "Theology and Statecraft." *South Asian History and Culture* 2 (2011) 184–204.

Jones, Kenneth. "Religious Identity and the Indian Census." In *The Census in British India: New Perspectives*, edited by N. G. Barrier, 73–101. New Delhi: Manohar, 1981.

Lorenzen, David. "Who Invented Hinduism?" *Comparative Studies in Society and History* 41 (1999) 630–59.

McLeod, W. H., ed. *The B40 Janam-sakhi: An English Translation with Introduction and Annotations of the India Office Library Gurmukhi Manuscript Panj B40, a Janam-sakhi of Guru Nanak Compiled in AD 1733 by Daya Ram Abrol.* Amritsar: Guru Nanak Dev University, 1980.

---

15. The definitive work on this relationship is Ernst, *Refractions of Islam in India.* See also Murphy, "Sufis, Jogis."

16. Murphy, "*Gurbilas* Literature."

———. *Who Is a Sikh? The Problem of Sikh Identity.* Oxford: Oxford University Press, 1989.

Murphy, Anne. "The *Gurbilas* Literature and the Idea of 'Religion.'" In *Punjab Reconsidered: History, Culture, and Practice,* edited by Anshu Malhotra and Farina Mir, 93–115. New York: Oxford University Press, 2012.

———. *The Materiality of the Past: History and Representation in Sikh Tradition.* New York: Oxford University Press, 2012.

———. "Sufis, Jogis, and the Question of Religious Difference: Individualization in Early Modern Punjab through Waris Shah's *Hīr*." In *Religious Individualizations: Historical and Comparative Perspectives,* edited by Martin Fuchs, et al., 289–314. Berlin: de Gruyter, 2020.

Pennington, Brian. *Was Hinduism Invented? Britons, Indians, and the Colonial Construction of Religion.* New York: Oxford University Press, 2005.

Pinch, William R. "History, Devotion, and the Search for Nabhadas of Galta." In *Invoking the Past: The Uses of History in South Asia,* edited by Daud Ali, 367–99. Delhi: Oxford University Press, 1999.

———. *Warrior Ascetics and Indian Empires.* Cambridge: Cambridge University Press, 2006.

Shackle, Christopher, and Arvind Mandair, eds. *Teachings of the Sikh Gurus: Selections from the Sikh Scriptures.* New York: Routledge, 2005.

Singh, Nikky-Guninder Kaur. "Corporeal Metaphysics: Guru Nanak in Early Sikh Art." *History of Religions* 53 (2013) 28–65.

———. "Myth of the Founder: The Janamsākhīs and Sikh Tradition." *History of Religions* 31 (1992) 329–43.

Singh, Pashaura. *The Bhagats of the Guru Granth Sahib: Sikh Self-Definition and the Bhagat Bani.* New Delhi: Oxford University Press, 2003.

# 5

# Religious Courts on Trial

## Terry S. Neiman

RELIGIOUS *OTHERNESS* CAN BE understood as a factor in clashes over religious practices. Here, people (actors) who could cooperate to accommodate religious groups choose not to. Instead, they seek to use forceful means to deny others religious accommodation. In these special situations, the conflict is not necessarily religious per se. Rather, such conflicts are essentially political. They are about power and the use of force.

As a practitioner and researcher of conflict intervention, I think that it is fair to say that there are conflicts in every part of the world in which actors opt to use force, even violence, before other options, to assert their claims to truth and justice. Force comes in many forms—small weapons, weapons of mass destruction; police force, military force; civil disobedience, civil unrest; Supreme Court, the court of public opinion. Any and all of these can be processes of conflict.

One can understand conflict as a clash of actors who have interests. As Morton Deutsch has argued in *The Handbook of Conflict Resolution*,[1] conflicts motivate actors to either cooperate or compete. In keeping with Deutsch, I argue that conflicts can be traced to actors' perceptions of *otherness*. In social and political conflict, actors opt to resist, oppose, compete with, or attack those who they see as *other*. They frame the interests of the

---

1. Deutsch, *Handbook of Conflict Resolution*, 21–40.

*other* as either working against their own interests, or as in competition for resources that they want. This has been described by Katz and Block as a *zero-sum game*.[2]

In this chapter, I will draw on communication and conflict theory, and the history of mediation practice to explore how religious courts and traditional justice have become *othered*—targeted by various actors on the basis of differences of identity. First, I will trace how the evolution of mediation in the US and Canada has resulted in a kind of *othering* of mediators who are not lawyers by legal professionals and governmental regulators. Then, I will discuss how that has extended to threaten the existence of religious courts when they use mediation according to their traditions. Finally, I will discuss how the dialogic processes of religious and traditional justice suggest *features* for a framework that respects both secular justice and religious freedom.

## OTHERNESS AND PROFESSIONAL BOUNDARIES

I begin this section with a discussion that is drawn from my review of an emerging conflict between lawyers and non-lawyers.[3] In family law, disputes are resolved through litigation, arbitration, mediation, or negotiation—all of which are facilitated exclusively by lawyers and judges. Out of court, in mediation facilitated by people who are not lawyers, family matters are negotiated privately, often in consultation with lawyers and other professionals, including clergy. Sometimes clergy are involved in resolving family issues through a religious court—e.g., a Jewish *bet din*, or a Muslim sharia court.

I became aware that religious courts in Canada and the US were regarded by some people as a problem through my professional work as a mediator in the 1990s. Later, I learned of the scope of the issue through my field work on relations between lawyers and non-lawyer mediators. I started mediating in 1994, in California, doing mostly family mediation. When I moved my practice to British Columbia in 1996, I found that lawyers and the Law Society there, too, took a strong position against non-lawyer mediation.

The divide between mediation's dominant community of lawyers and the community of *others* was clarified by Bush and Folger's introduction of "transformative" mediation—a concept based on Bush's research in law and Folger's in organizational development.[4] In British Columbia the so-called

---

2. Katz and Block, "Process and Outcomes," 279–88.
3. Neiman, "Communication in Conflict and Problem Solving."
4. Bush and Folger, *Promise of Mediation*.

'evaluative' style of mediation favored by lawyers dominates the practices of labor, employment, and insurance claims mediation. These specialties fall under a broad system of government administration, including court-based programs and mediator rosters.

The literature and my experience indicate that the predominant view frames law-based intervention as the norm. It is seen as something separate from and superior to relationship-oriented "transformative" intervention. However, some lawyer/mediators frame mediation as the same dichotomy but take the position that transformative mediation is better than law-based. In either case, the tendency to favor any orientation or framework can be predictably traced to the professional, occupational, or vocational interests of the person who privileges it.

Bogoch and Halperin-Kaddari[5] found that in family law cases, lawyers and non-lawyers, men and women, use the same mediation processes and get equivalent results. Some lawyers are effective mediators, and some are not. Some non-lawyers are effective mediators, and some are not. Mediator gender is not a factor. This argues strongly that legal credentials and oversight are not essential to assuring that dispute resolution will safeguard the rights and serve the interests of disputants.

Despite the lack of a correlation between both legal training and law society oversight with family mediation outcomes, the perception that there are differences between lawyers and non-lawyers still prevails. This is evident in how mediators describe themselves. For example, most of the mediators I interviewed or observed who have a law background identified themselves according to one of two paradigms: as rights-based lawyer-mediators who practice *alternative dispute resolution* (ADR), or as "recovering" lawyers who no longer practice law and who use an interest-based form of conflict management—i.e., an alternative to ADR.

As the field grew and more cross-disciplinary theory emerged, I noticed an increased tendency for mediators to make distinctions, take sides, and label themselves and *others* according to distinctions of *evaluative*, *transformative*, or *facilitative* mediation. This is still the case in my work on mediation and conflict resolution curriculum design at the Justice Institute of British Columbia. I have found family law to be the specialty of practice that is overall the most entrenched in this regard. However, I have found a few family law practitioners who were among the most flexible of all lawyers in all areas of practice. This is consistent with Bogoch and Halperin-Kaddari's findings.

---

5. Bogoch and Halperin-Kaddari, "Divorce Israeli Style"; "Co-optation, Competition, and Resistance," 115–45; Bogoch, "Adversarial Agreements" 85–105.

In general, a kind of language war over *mediation* became instrumental in the construction of professional boundaries between lawyers and *others* in the field. Here, the word *alternative* frames legal intervention as the norm, and mediation as *other* in a litigation-centric world. Roland Barthes described this kind of linguistic framing as *ex-nomination*.[6] Ex-nomination happens when a group in power names things such that their ideology becomes invisible, and therefore seems to be common sense. That which does not conform to the un-named common sense is framed in language that makes it *other*. For example, in a society where no one is normally referred to as a *male astronaut*, the use of the term *woman astronaut* has buried in it a value that astronauts are normally men. Likewise, *mediation* is ex-nominated in law as *alter(native)/other*.

The "non-lawyer mediator" is thus doubly excluded by ex-nomination: from law, and from mediation.

Underlying this language-based turn of the business of mediation was a professional bias that frames matters of everyday life that *could* fall under the purview of the justice system as falling *necessarily* under the purview of the justice system. First, the resolution of public and private problems was said to fall under a category of procedures denoted as "dispute resolution." Without a clear definition of "dispute resolution," it then became to many a privileged term of the legal profession.

No distinction was made between mediation purely in the context of the institutional practices of justice, and mediation in other practices of everyday life. It was not until 2002 that the American Bar Association took a position that mediation, per se, is not the practice of law. In Canada a similar situation has prevailed, resulting in increased involvement of provincial justice systems in sanctioning mediators (e.g., British Columbia Office of Attorney General's Mediator Roster Society; Saskatchewan Justice Dispute Resolution Office; and Ontario Ministry of the Attorney General's Rosters of Mediators in Toronto, Windsor, and Ottawa).

In 2009, the Law Society of British Columbia began to define regulatory standards and limits of practice for document preparation in mediation. It also recommended aspects of mediation to address next. This process did not set out to claim control of the field of intervention for the Law Society. However, it sought to bring under the Law Society's purview the practices of mediation, and by extension, the mediators themselves. This is complicated by there being no statutory or legal definition of *mediation*, other than being paid to facilitate dispute resolution. There is also no official definition of *dispute resolution*, even though the term is in common use in the field of law.

---

6. Barthes, *Mythologies*, 138.

## OTHERING RELIGIOUS COURTS

The environment of professional *otherness* in law gives crucial context to the issue of religious courts. One argument against non-lawyer mediation is that divorcing couples might seek a judgment from a religious court. Inherent to this line of reasoning is that in acting as a "court," a religious body would abrogate the civil, legal rights of disputants. This fear is more openly expressed by those who believe that sharia-based mediation and arbitration in Canada will come to supplant Canadian law with Islamic law as it happened in the theocratic polity of Iran.

There is no evidence that sharia courts are organized to contravene Canadian or US law. Canadian journalist Douglas Todd—who specializes in religion—reports the following:

> Clearly, shariah gets Canadians worked up. But should it? Researchers are unaware of any official shariah courts in the US or Canada, even though some imams offer voluntary dispute-resolution services based on principles of Islamic law. In addition, shariah is not unique. Most religions maintain their own internal codes of conduct, particularly regarding marriage, divorce, financial wrongdoing, and sexual behaviour. . . . No matter what some Muslims believe in other parts of the world, Canadian Muslims have reassured me they respect this nation's secular laws regarding religious freedom, divorce, sex outside marriage and women's equality.[7]

It might be possible for imams in North America to take direction from religious authorities in Iran. Immigrant communities have close ties to their countries of origin. However, as Todd found, the clergy in North America are not organized to dispense foreign justice. They can, and do, work within the laws of the countries where they live.

The case for Jewish courts is transparent. In Jewish law (*halacha*), *dinah d'malchutah dinah* (Aramaic for "the law of the land is the law"). This can be traced to the *amorah* (third/fourth-century rabbinic authority) Shmuel in what is today Iran.[8] Rabbinic (*bet din*) courts have operated in the Jewish diaspora for centuries according to the *halachic* principle that a rabbinic judgment may not contravene the secular law of the land.

I have observed divorce proceedings in *bet din* courts in Los Angeles and Vancouver. I once served as a judge on a divorce *beit din*. Those courts dealt with scribing and witnessing religious divorce documents (*gets*). In the

---

7. Todd, "'Sharia' Sets Off Alarms."
8. Nedarim 28a; Gittin 10b; Bava Kama 113a; Bava Bathra 54b, 55a (Epstein, *Babylonian Talmud*).

process, rabbis offered spiritual and emotional counselling. Unlike a civil process, the religious process is organized to facilitate emotional and social healing and conflict resolution. Not all Jewish divorces go smoothly. Some husbands try to use the process to extort financial concessions by refusing to give their wife a *get*. There are also rare cases in which a wife refuses to accept a *get* for the same reason. This is not significantly different from how people use coercion in the secular courts. However, a *bet din* has the advantage of being able to generate social pressure on men who do not comply, because a Jewish community is a small town within larger secular society.

The key distinction between secular court and a *bet din* is in the areas of settlement that are not of interest to secular law. A divorce arrangement in secular court will seek fairness and practicality. However, in the so-called separation of Church and State it is not organized to privilege religious considerations that might be vital to the parties. In settling property and debt issues, Orthodox Jews need expertise on Torah law. For example, a loan that would be perfectly legal under Canadian law could be forbidden under Torah law because it involves charging interest. Islamic law has similar concerns about lending.

There is no reason to expect Jews and Muslims to forgo observance of lending laws merely because secular justice is not interested in them. A just settlement that fully complies with both systems is possible—but only if both systems are involved.

Conceptually, secular and religious justice systems have much in common. All are defined by *features*: laws, histories, practices, and beliefs. These features are coherent, rational, and consistent for each local or national system. Torah has formulas and commandments regarding business ethics, clothing, communication, and more. They are particular to Judaism, as the Qur'anic laws of lending are particular to Muslims. A religious justice system safeguards needs that are invisible to, and no consequence to, those who are not members of its religious community.

Religious justice systems have operated under the power and authority of secular justice in Canada, USA, UK, and Israel, to name a few. All of these societies promote multi-culturalism and limit religious particularism. However, there are still concerns that drive popular discourse against religious and traditional justice processes. They stem partly from conflation of religious perspectives and practices including the following.

- A belief that there is a monolithic "Judeo-Christian" value system;
- association of dominant political movements with religious beliefs (e.g., Evangelical Christianity and the US Republican Party; Shiite Islam and the theocratic Iranian government);

- fear that religion—Islam in particular—is by nature misogynist and racist;
- a belief that religious dispute resolution by nature violates a sacrosanct principle of secular justice, because "Church and State" by nature, have zero-sum, mutually exclusive agendas and interests.

The same considerations can be applied to differences between professions and their practitioners. Professions define for themselves their logic, laws, language, and practices. Professional boundaries are legally sanctioned and legislatively protected. This is how Law Societies, family law practitioners, and court-based mediation programs come to assert that privately negotiated agreements violate their authority. It is how their professional bias frames matters of everyday life that *could* fall under the purview of the justice system as falling—necessarily—under the purview of their profession.

By seeking to limit or prevent religious courts from operating, various actors in the legal and justice systems have found common cause with other actors who oppose religion per se, or specific religions. The result is a threat to religious freedom for all.

## JUSTICIABILITY AND THE CASE FOR RELIGIOUS COURTS

This issue of justiciability—who has legal standing—applies to religious and Indigenous justice systems in North America. Longstanding policies have sought to limit traditional justice under the authority of governmental and professional legal administration. From the 1990s to the present, Maryland, New York, and New Jersey supreme courts have ruled that it is unconstitutional for secular courts to be involved in legal disputes about the validity of kosher certifications. In the 2000s, the Canadian federal government asserted federal jurisdiction over Aboriginal justice practices in Canada-First Nations treaty-making. Today there is still discourse and legislative moves to outlaw sharia courts.

However, in practice secular justice can and does accommodate minority ethnic and religious groups. In *Delgamuukw v. British Columbia,* [1997] 3 SCR 1010, the government of Canada accepted that Indigenous peoples in Canada may negotiate in good faith for their rights according to the rationality of their oral traditions.

Kleefeld and Kennedy found that Canadian judicial processes and religious law—often grounded in oral tradition—are commensurable on complex issues.[9] Their research acknowledges that when there is a will to make Canadian justice and religious justice work together, the outcome is better from the minority group perspective and not compromised from the perspective of secular justice.

The cases they cite demonstrate that dialogic court processes work better for a society that seeks to respect those who are *other* than the dominant group. They surveyed resolution of family matters in *bet din* courts. Jewish courts rely on dialogue on two levels: the dialogic nature of its oral tradition, and the use of dialogue in the courtroom process. They also cite the following precedents that support the implementation of *bet din* judgments.

- *Brown v. Notre Dame de Montreal* (Canada, 1869)—religious burial is a right, protected under civil law.
- *Bruker v. Marcovitz* (Canada, 2007)—Supreme Court of Canada ruled that a husband must pay damages to his wife for not granting her a *get*.
- *Melvin Wallace, et al. v ConAgra Foods* (New York, 2013)—in a Hebrew National kosher certification case no laws were compromised.

Other research supports the use of religious legal arbitration in Canada. In 2004, mediator and consultant Marion Boyd—a former Attorney General of Ontario—was commissioned by the Premier of Ontario to review the state of arbitration for alleged violations of Canadian law by sharia-based decisions. Her focus was on a "review of arbitration of family law and inheritance matters and its impact on vulnerable people."[10] She found that sharia in Canada, "is Muslim religious principles within Canadian law," and that it focused on privacy and resolving issues of divorce and inheritance that are ignored by secular courts.

Boyd's report was controversial. She was careful to parse the language to distinguish between *sharia courts*—which the public infers to mean the kind found in theocratic Iran—and "religion-based alternative dispute resolution in family law," or "the use of Muslim personal law." Nonetheless, the public and members of the family law profession rejected the report, incredulous that Boyd—an advocate for women—could find room for Muslim religious principles in family cases. In a blatant rejection of the report, the Ontario government banned sharia courts in 2005.

Fear of *otherness*, and ignorance of the *other* drove Ontario's ban on sharia courts. This conflict has global cross-links from Tehran to Toronto. While there is no justification for any justice system that is not equal for all,

---

9. Kleefeld and Kennedy, "Delicate Necessity."
10. Boyd, *Dispute Resolution in Family Law.*

there is no evidence that such a justice system operates in sharia or *bet din* courts in countries like Canada or the US. The arguments against religious courts were based on the premise that religious orthodoxy is antithetical to secular justice. However, there is ample evidence that a professional trade barrier is the issue. Religious-based and traditional justice systems are serving minority groups better than secular courts alone, and not at the expense of secular justice. Marion Boyd—an advocate for women and justice—understood that, because she talked with people who were involved in those processes. Dialogue—also a key component in religious and Indigenous justice—goes a long way toward dispelling fear and ignorance.

In short, religious courts are *conceptually* acceptable, *de facto* in compliance, and have even enhanced secular justice and the secular State. The intersection of secular and religious justice has promoted the use of contracts and pre-nuptial agreements by religious courts. Independent arbitration and mediation services, including faith-based services, have reduced the caseloads of backlogged, overburdened courts. Still, there is resistance, because the battle against religious courts takes place at the intersection of populist fear and professional protectionism.

## BIBLIOGRAPHY

Barthes, Roland. *Mythologies*. Selected and translated by Annette Lavers. London: Paladin, 1972.
Bogoch, Bryna. "Adversarial Agreements: The Attitudes of Israeli Family Lawyers to Litigation in Divorce Practice." *International Journal of Law, Crime, and Justice* 36 (2008) 85–105.
Bogoch, Bryna, and Ruth Halperin-Kaddari. "Co-optation, Competition, and Resistance: Mediation and Divorce Professionals in Israel." *International Journal of the Legal Profession* 14 (2007) 115–45.
———. "Divorce Israeli Style: Professional Perceptions of Gender and Power in Mediated and Lawyer-Negotiated Divorces." *Law and Policy* 28 (2006) 137–63.
Boyd, Marion. *Dispute Resolution in Family Law: Protecting Choice, Promoting Inclusion*. Boyd Report. Toronto: AG, 2004.
Bush, Robert A. Baruch, and Joseph P. Folger. *The Promise of Mediation: The Transformative Approach to Conflict*. San Francisco: Jossey-Bass, 2005.
Deutsch, Morton. "Cooperation and Competition." In *The Handbook of Conflict Resolution*, edited by Morton Deutsch, et al., 21–40. San Francisco: Jossey-Bass, 2000.
Epstein, Isidore. *The Babylonian Talmud*. London: Soncino, 1977.
Katz, Tal Y., and Caryn Block. "Process and Outcome Goal Orientations in Conflict Situations." In *The Handbook of Conflict Resolution*, edited by Morton Deutsch, et al., 279–88. San Francisco: Jossey-Bass, 2000.
Kleefeld, John C., and Amanda Kennedy. "'A Delicate Necessity': Bruker v. Marcovitz and the Problem of Jewish Divorce." *Canadian Journal of Family Law* 24 (2008) 205–282.

Neiman, Terry S. "Communication in Conflict and Problem Solving: A Study of Dialogue in Everyday Life." PhD diss., Simon Fraser University, 2011.

Todd, Douglas. "'Sharia' Sets Off Alarms in Canada. Here Are the Facts." *Vancouver Sun*, March 27, 2017. Online. http://vancouversun.com/news/staff-blogs/sharia-set-off-alarms-in-canada-check-the-facts.

# 6

# We Are All Outsiders

Negotiating Imaginary Territory in Pakistan

PATRICIA GRUBEN

IN SEPTEMBER 2011 I had come to Pakistan to do research for a screenplay based on a 1961 novel about a young American woman living in Lahore. I was sitting in the basement beauty salon at the Lahore Gymkhana Club, having a manicure in preparation for a fancy dinner party. The manicurists, two undernourished young men, asked me if I was Christian. I knew from prior travels in South Asia that this question was usually more about cultural background than religious beliefs; yet for these Christian young men, who probably came from a Dalit ("untouchable") background, the connection between religious belief and culture was of much more immediate importance than it was to me. When the manicure ended, my host, a secular Muslim who lived in New York and had a law degree from Harvard, was horrified that I had allowed these "untouchable" men to hold my hands.

Religious labels are markers of broader cultural difference in relation to class, ethnicity, colonialism, and gender roles. The status of a particular religious affiliation obviously depends on which group is dominant in a particular society. This can be complicated by layers of colonial history, as with my experience as a high-status white Christian encountering low-status Christian Pakistanis. In my three weeks of travel in Pakistan to research a film about cultural conflict, I had to confront multiple issues of cross-cultural communication, not only to develop the subtext of the screenplay I was writing, but also to understand the subtext of my own communication with Pakistanis from various sectors of society. I came away with the awareness that our cultural identity is an intersection of many components which are always in play. Some are dominant, visible, apparently innate; others are fleeting, perhaps not consciously acknowledged or equally significant to both parties.

## HIGH AND LOW CONTEXT

The American anthropologist Edward Hall (1914–2009) was one of the first to undertake close study of intercultural communication. Hall wrote about high-context and low-context societies in his 1977 book *Beyond Culture*. His observations became popular in business circles, where they were taught in seminars on international negotiation to generate transactional rapport and prevent deal-threatening *faux pas*.

A high-context society is one in which everyone understands the customs and values of the group, and very little explanation is needed in order to communicate. High-context societies tend to be traditional, relatively homogeneous groups; Hall focuses on the example of 1950s-era Japan. A low-context society is what we have in most of North America: people from multi-ethnic origins, unable to assume that all of our attitudes and customs are shared. Here the rules of public behavior need to be clearly defined, regardless of how high-context one's immediate community may be. Low-context societies tend to be legalistic, focusing on the individual, rather than the family or community, as the cultural quantum.

High-context societies, of course, are not entirely homogeneous. In the small Texas town where my father grew up, the white Protestant farmers and the Hispanic Catholic migrant workers were distinctly different in appearance, religion, language, and social status, and had little contact apart from their working relationships. But each group was high-context internally, and each group understood very well the nonverbal rules of their social and personal interactions.

As new groups emerge or arrive to threaten the homogeneity of the dominant culture, the group may deny entry to these outsiders in order to preserve the high-context status quo. The US is a prime example of this, particularly the rural South, which, other than the black/white binary, has historically been less diverse than the cosmopolitan urban centers. As change comes to these areas through media or actual migration, it provokes a low-context response that seeks to preserve dominant values through enforcing their interpretation of fundamental documents such as the Bible or the US Constitution. Much recent political conflict has concentrated around legal issues—whether the Ten Commandments or the Confederate flag can be displayed in front of a state capitol; whether transgendered people are allowed to choose their washroom; whether President Obama intended to impose *sharia* law—all attempts to draw a circle around the privileged group and keep outsiders on the outside. The corollary on the Left is the move toward political correctness, which strives to acknowledge marginalized cultures but, taken to absurd lengths, can mask a similar intolerant tribalism.

Nowadays, through media, globalized economies, migration and tourism, the distinction between high and low context is becoming more and more complex. Globally we are moving toward a low-context culture in which everything must be negotiated rather than implicit. On the one hand we know more about our fellow citizens from other cultures; on the other hand, we don't always like what we see. Within this globalized culture, we are splitting into tribes which communicate through media as well as face-to-face, reinforcing tribal values. To some extent we can choose our tribes; in North America, in particular, many of us leave behind our high school attachments and find new groups to join, based on our developing affinities or circumstances.

When an evolving high-context society represents itself to a global audience, the choice of how to identify and frame its values can be painful and contentious. This is particularly true of a place like Pakistan, which is consistently portrayed by the media as riven by political conflict and fundamentalist violence, primarily against women. How else can the culture be represented? Coming into the country as an outsider to research a screenplay based on a Pakistani novel revealed layers of cultural difference and contradiction which remain unresolved.

## CONTEXT IN PAKISTAN

In 1947, during the transition from British colonial rule to independence, Pakistan split from India over religious lines. India established a secular democracy, and Pakistan became an Islamic republic. This suggests a move to bolster traditional high-context values. The state religion is practiced by 95 percent of the population, 80 percent of them from the Sunni sect. Although other religions are allowed, their political rights are limited. Without the land reform undertaken in India, Pakistan remains somewhat feudalistic in its social hierarchy, with much of its wealth coming from estates owned by the same families for many generations and farmed by indentured laborers. The rural areas are known for their extreme conservatism, in the news for horrific honor killings and for incubating and supporting the Taliban.

Lahore, despite its historical diversity, its important cultural legacy, its century under British rule, its proximity to the border with India, and its rapidly growing population (8.5 million in 2010; 12.2 million in 2019),[1] seems to be relatively homogeneous in its culture, compared to other urban centers of its size. Partition stripped the city of most of its Hindu citizens and many of its Sikhs, along with the departing colonials. For the past few decades, international tourism and business travel have been curtailed by security concerns. The few Westerners to be seen on the streets tend to be agency workers, journalists or private military contractors. As Binah Shah writes, "Seized by a tsunami of religious obscurantism, Pakistan has turned on the very communities that make up its diverse social and cultural fabric."[2] Nevertheless, the mask of homogeneity is inadequate to the complexities of gender, ethnicity, class and the private behavior of the powerful and well-educated.

My research involved three clearly delineated populations: an educated urban culture of considerable privilege; the conservative working class of the old city; and the isolated mountain tribes of Kohistan.[3] Thus, although I was entering a relatively high-context society, I was attempting to cross social boundaries that are extremely stratified, with little cross-communication. Indeed, this was the theme of the novel I was adapting.

## THE BRIDE STRIPPED BARE

*The Pakistani Bride* tells a story of two outsiders and is written by another outsider, all three of them female. The author is Bapsi Sidhwa, one of Pakistan's best-known novelists, who writes in English. Sidhwa comes from a wealthy, well-connected Parsi family in Lahore. The Parsis arrived from Persia more than a thousand years ago, fleeing persecution over their Zoroastrian religion. They prospered in business and banking during the British Raj and were particularly active in the arts. (Two prominent contemporary Canadian novelists, Rohinton Mistry and Anosh Irani, are Parsis.) They have escaped the communal violence that has fractured both India and Pakistan since Partition, which Sidhwa addressed in her 1982 novel *Ice*

---

1. "Lahore Population."
2. Shah, "Literature," 6.
3. We were unable to visit Kohistan for security reasons; we had to settle for the area around Skardu, where the tribal culture is offset by a seasonal invasion of mountain climbers.

*Candy Man*. From her position as a privileged outsider, Sidhwa was a keen observer of the social groups around her.[4]

*The Pakistani Bride* follows the intersecting narratives of two young women in 1961; each marries outside her group and comes to regret it. One is Carol, a California salesgirl who is swept off her feet by a wealthy Pakistani university student. Shortly after they marry, he takes her back to live with his family in Lahore. There she is thrown into an alien language, religion and culture, as well as a social class far above her own. The other is Zaitoon, a motherless girl who grows up in Lahore's old city until the age of sixteen, when her father Qasim takes her back to his mountain village to marry a Kohistani boy.

The two women meet briefly at a remote army base where Carol and her husband are visiting his boyhood friend, and Zaitoon and her father are making their way to the village. Carol's insensitive questioning reveals that Qasim is *not* Zaitoon's birth father; he rescued her as a baby when her family was slaughtered in the communal violence of Partition. Zaitoon is a Punjabi, and the tribe she is about to marry into is not her own. In the village, Zaitoon finds a band of primitive, violent, and misogynistic brutes who torment her doubly as a woman and an outsider. After horrendous abuse she runs away, knowing that even if she survives the mountain journey, her husband's family will likely catch her and cut her throat. When news of Zaitoon's ordeal reaches Carol at the army base, with her own marriage in ruins, she recognizes that she too is subjugated, and is finally able to step up and save Zaitoon.

## A SCREENPLAY NEEDS CONFLICT, BUT . . .

That was the book that I set out to adapt. N. S., the producer who brought me into the project, had grown up in the elite social circles of Lahore and was an old friend of Bapsi Sidhwa, the author of the novel. He had left Pakistan to attend university in England and the US, and had been practicing law in New York for a decade.

A producer must first consider how to lure investors into a highly risky proposition; most films fail to make a profit. An audience must be found, or created. The film industry in Pakistan is overwhelmed by hundreds of better-financed, star-driven Bollywood movies; the market for a domestic art-house drama is virtually nonexistent. N. S. wanted to make a prestigious film that would reach an international audience, the most likely way to gain attention at festivals and return something on the investment. The

---

4. Zaidi, "Glimpses of the New Woman," 64.

few Pakistani or Afghan films that reached this global audience, especially in the years after 9/11, invariably appealed to Western preconceptions about the brutality of Islamic fundamentalism and South Asian misogyny. *Khuda ke Liye (In the Name of God)*, which played in a number of international festivals in 2007, follows a British-Pakistani girl whose father takes her to Karachi and forces her to marry a Talibani who keeps her locked up in a mud-walled village. *Osama* is a film from Afghanistan about a young girl who is disguised as a boy to protect her; she is discovered and forced to marry an old man who keeps her locked up in a mud-walled village. *The Kite Runner*, based on the best-seller by Khaled Hosseini, is about a young man who returns from America to Afghanistan to rescue the son of his boyhood friend, who has been locked up by the Taliban in a mud-walled village. And Deepa Mehta's 1998 film *Earth*, an Indo-Canadian production set in Lahore, is the story of a beautiful Hindu nanny murdered by a Muslim mob during the Partition riots; it is based on Bapsi Sidhwa's 1982 novel, *Ice Candy Man* (published in the US as *Cracking India*).

Thus *The Pakistani Bride*, infused with the patriarchal oppression expected by Western audiences, seemed a likely prospect for a international success. It had the advantage of a built-in hook: the American, Carol, a fish out of water character with whom Westerners could identify as she tries to navigate an alien culture—and who could be played by a recognized American actress. This is why N. S. hired me instead of a Pakistani screenwriter (of which there were few in any case) despite the necessity for extreme cultural cramming on a three-week research trip.

We flew to Lahore during the holy month of Ramadan. As a foreigner I was not expected to fast, and therefore N. S., as a good host, would have to eat when I ate. In fact, we spent much of our time at dinner parties, talking to the people from Carol's world—wealthy and cosmopolitan Pakistanis who travelled frequently to Europe and North America. We dined with the daughter of the judge who had condemned the former Prime Minister Zulfikar Ali Bhutto to death. We had drinks with a correspondent for the *New York Times*. We attended a society wedding with five hundred guests at which I was the only Westerner after the six American bridesmaids were scared off by a Taliban attack on the local women's college.

N. S. was concerned about security, and insisted I wear a Punjabi *salwar kamise* suit and *dupatta* head covering so that I would blend in. This attempt at camouflage had the opposite effect; people stared, bewildered, at my blond hair under the dupatta. I soon found myself playing a subjugated drudge, trailing behind my protector with cast-down eyes. After a few days of unbearable self-consciousness I returned to my Western clothes, at which point everyone immediately stopped staring. Now I was recognizable—probably a journalist, academic or employee of an NGO.

One of the women I interviewed, a wealthy American married to a Pakistani businessman, told me the secret to her success in Lahori society was her total disinterest in adapting. She dressed in men's tailored shirts and designer jeans and drove her own Range Rover when she could well afford a driver. She said that several white women she knew who had married into Pakistani society had tried too hard to fit in and had lost touch with their own identity. The best known of these was the British heiress Jemima Goldsmith, who married the famous cricket player Imran Khan (current prime minister of Pakistan). Goldsmith converted to Islam, exchanged her designer clothes for a *salwar kamise*, and took pains to learn Urdu. After her divorce, she explained that she had "over-conformed in [her] eagerness to be accepted" into the "new and radically different culture" of Pakistan, rather than live with her inescapable other-ness.[5] Although Goldsmith came from a privileged and cosmopolitan background, she seems to have experienced something like what I imagined for Carol, as she struggled to thread her way through a minefield of politics, family histories and cultural difference.

N. S. himself was volatile, prone to starting arguments with strangers. Clearly he had traditional ideas about gender roles, along with anxieties about his financial and social status and postcolonial resentment of white privilege. He liked to say that English women in South Asia reminded him of old carpets, fading in the sunlight. He delighted in quoting the rude remarks of male strangers who could not decipher our relationship. At an isolated mountain resort he started a fistfight with our travelling companion, who had insulted his torso; after his rival left in the only taxi, I began to consider calling the high commission for help getting back to Canada.

I was able to use some of this in the screenplay. N. S. had asked me to smuggle a bottle of prohibited whiskey into the country, insisting that I as a Westerner would not be arrested. That went into the script. At a dinner party, the men started telling dirty jokes. I looked around and realized all the other women had left the room; I laughed politely, but realized I was being tested, and had failed. That went into the script. Carol's anxiety and frustration was becoming more and more my own.

Zaitoon, the sixteen-year old girl, was naturally a greater challenge. N. S. and his friends had virtually no contact with people from the working class except as servants. In the Old City, N. S. accosted young women in hijabs who looked like his idea of Zaitoon, and we had brief, frustrating

---

5. Khan, "My Grandfather's Secret."

chats with them, during which they naturally declined to reveal details of their personal lives.

The Kohistanis from the mountains were completely inaccessible to us. I felt that the novel depicted them as subhuman monsters and I wanted to give them some measure of respect for the hardship and isolation of their lives. However, security concerns made it impossible to travel to the Karakoram region. The best I could gather was a glimpse of one or two fierce-looking Kohistanis in the streets of the old city, or around Skardu, where they crossed the road to avoid us.

One problem with getting the film made was the cultural dissonance between the potential investors and the prospective audience. As noted earlier, the most popular film subject for international audiences was a drama of victimization that made Pakistan look like a fanatical hellhole; yet people with money to invest had a personal and financial interest in making the country seem more progressive and welcoming. As Sidhwa herself wrote:

> I feel if there's one little thing I could do, it's to make people realize: We are not worthless because we inhabit a country which is seen by Western eyes as a primitive, fundamentalist country only. . . . I mean, we are a rich mixture of all sorts of forces as well, and our lives are very much worth living.[6]

For the first draft of the screenplay, N. S. wanted to update the story from 1961 to the present. That made it difficult to avoid mentioning the Taliban, who had infiltrated the Karakoram region and were in the news daily for bombings and kidnappings in the cities. Even if we didn't name them, Zaitoon's ordeal in the mountains with Kohistanis who dressed like Talibani would evoke the negative stereotype of Pakistan as a wild and brutal country.

N. S. dealt with this by commissioning a second draft of the script to be set in 1962, the original time period of the book. This pre-dated the Taliban and eliminated them from our concern, but brought in a whole new set of issues. In 1962, Pakistan was comparatively socially progressive and a strong ally of the US, which needed a bulwark against Soviet influence in Afghanistan and India. That year, First Lady Jackie Kennedy and Princess Lee Radziwill made a spectacular state visit, immortalized by a photo of the two sisters in sleeveless sheath dresses, sitting side-saddle on the back of a camel.

In this society, Carol would have been more readily accepted as an agent of modernity rather than scorned for her naivéte. She would have been less sensitive to post-colonial politics, less aware of her pre-feminist

---

6. Sidhwa, "Third World, Our World," 703–6.

entrapment, less afraid of the fundamentalism that was masked or ignored in the rush toward modernism. She would have entered this world dazzled by the old-world luxury, yet feeling that her white skin and auspicious marriage granted her a higher social status than she had at home. As Sidhwa wrote in the novel:

> Lahore seemed to love Carol. Pakistani men bent over her gallantly, pressing drinks and lighting cigarettes. Beautiful women, graceful in soft flowing garments chattered with her in exquisite English. There was a party every single evening. She felt like someone in *Gone with the Wind*.[7]

In 1961, Carol's culture shock would be more sudden but simpler, without the self-destructive edge that I had given the Carol of 2010. This draft of the script was less dark, more nostalgic, yet still with the irony of hindsight.

Although setting the film in the pre-Taliban era seemed to be more appealing, it was not enough to shake loose any investment. N. S. decided to try Bombay, where film is a multibillion dollar industry. Our timing was unfortunate; our trip to Bombay happened on the first anniversary of the Lashkr-e-Taiba attacks on the city and the burning of the Taj Hotel, which was committed by Pakistanis. It was not an auspicious time to be flogging a project called *The Pakistani Bride*. Muslim producers, directors and actors— of whom there are many in Bollywood—were particularly reluctant to call attention to themselves. In pitching the film, N. S. avoided mentioning that it was set in Pakistan (a challenge, given its title) although he was adamant that it would be shot there.

## UNHAPPY ENDINGS

As earlier noted, Edward T. Hall's 1977 model of high-context/low-context societies became popular in business applications, where people from different cultures could learn the basics of intercultural etiquette. However, the "high context" model typified by 1950s Japan no longer applies in an era of geographic and electronic mobility, where our communication through media greatly exceeds our face-to-face interactions. Even in a relatively high-context Pakistan, with its ancient history, religious homogeneity and highly developed culture, class and language barriers make it difficult for people from different backgrounds to communicate beyond the basics. This was the double narrative of *The Pakistani Bride*: Zaitoon and Carol, each desperate to navigate a fatally alien culture.

7. Sidhwa, *Pakistani Bride*, 107.

The "outsider" story is a popular film trope, connecting with most of us as we nurse our own childhood (or lifelong) sense of not quite belonging in the world. The story of Zaitoon and Carol, both of them unsure of their status and their value in society, seemed reflected on a larger scale in most of the people I met in Pakistan. Even the most privileged were still uncertain of the image that they wanted to project to the outside world. Everyone acknowledged the dysfunction of everyday life and the political problems that seemed unsolvable; social criticism in the novels of Sidhwa, Mohsen Hamid and Salman Rushdie had brought international acclaim to Pakistani literature. Yet people were hypersensitive to exposing these conflicts and failures to the outside world, particularly on film. The high-context behavior that is understood throughout Pakistani society—the *machismo*, the constraints on women, the feudalistic class structure—is precisely what its privileged class does not want to enunciate for the world, because they feed into preexisting stereotypes about the culture. To add to the challenges of financing *The Pakistani Bride*, the ongoing threat of Islamic extremism has become an old story, and so perhaps has the story of the kidnapped innocent who must be rescued by a lady with white skin.

After three years, N. S. finally gave up on the film. He moved from New York back to Lahore, and when last heard from was producing a Pakistani knockoff of *Glee*. I went on to other projects—a short film about an evangelical Christian camp counselor who encounters two fugitives from El Salvador, and a new script in development about a draft dodger from Texas who is taken in by Doukhobors.

There are endless variations on this theme.

## BIBLIOGRAPHY

Chambers, Claire. "'The Heart, Stomach, and Backbone of Pakistan': Lahore in Novels by Bapsi Sidhwa and Mohsin Hamid." *South Asian Diaspora* 6 (2014) 141–59.

Hall, Edward T. *Beyond Culture*. Garden City, NY: Anchor, 1976.

Khan, Jemima. "My Grandfather's Secret." *Times of London*, August 10, 2008. Online. http://web.archive.org/web/20111107021730/http://www.thetimes.co.uk/tto/arts/books.

*Khuda Kay Liye: In the Name of God*. Directed by Shoaib Mansoor. DVD. New Delhi: Eagle Home Entertainment, 2004.

"Lahore Population." *World Population Review*, May 11, 2019. Online. http://worldpopulationreview.com/world-cities/lahore-population.

*Osama*. Directed by Siddiq Barmak. DVD. Beverly Hills, CA: MGM, 2004.

Samovar, Larry A., and Richard E. Porter. *Communication Between Cultures*. 5th ed. Belmont, CA: Thompson and Wadsworth, 2004.

Shah, Bima, "Literature: The Antidote to the Pakistani Identity Crisis." *Journal of Commonwealth Literature* 49 (2014) 3–10.

Sidhwa, Bapsi. *Cracking India*. Minneapolis: Milkweed, 1991.
———. *The Pakistani Bride*. Minneapolis: Milkweed, 2008.
———. "Third World, Our World." *The Massachusetts Review* 29 (1989) 703–6.
Weaver, Mary Ann. *Pakistan: In the Shadow of Jihad and Afghanistan*. New York: Farrar, Strauss & Giroux, 2010.
Zaidi, Najia. "Glimpses of the New Woman in Sidhwa's Novels." *Pakistan Journal of Women's Studies: Alam-e-Niswan* 18 (2011) 63–72.

# 7

# Dogs as the Other in St. Augustine's *City of God*

## Exploring the Limits of Human Social Relations

MIDORI E. HARTMAN

### INTRODUCTION

THE FOLLOWING PAPER EXPLORES Saint Augustine's rhetorical use of dogs within his major treatise, *The City of God*. I argue that while Augustine refers to canine scriptural passages within his other writings, it is within this particular text that he most strategically uses dogs to explore the limits of human social relations. As I will show, Augustine makes use of selective dog tropes to support his examination of how original sin contributes to the breakdown of proper social relations in the post-Eden experience. Specifically, I focus on how he uses canines to examine issues of: A. fidelity and proper order; B. language and issues of disconnection; and C. the limits of human nature concerning shame.

Written from 413 to 426 CE, *The City of God* was Augustine's creative response to the fear and anxiety that the Empire had experienced when the Visigoths sacked Rome in 410 CE. In defending Christianity against accusations that the attack was punishment for Rome's dishonor of the old gods,[1] Augustine was able to reframe this singular event within a larger conversation of how contemporary problems all stem from original sin. For him, dogs can play a key role in this conversation because of their symbolic and practical value as tamed animals that live in close proximity to humans. Notions of order and right relations can be framed through well-behaving and friendly dogs, while disorder and suffering can be expressed with the dog that bites the hand that feeds it. As we shall see in what follows, Augustine imagines the latter to be a striking example of the impact of original sin in the world.

To this end, this paper seeks to offer a small contribution to discussions concerning the role of animality and the non-human *other* in shaping ideology and rhetoric in both antiquity and today. Furthermore, it offers one example of how species particularity sits in tension with the homogeneity that is at the basis of one category of the other, namely the "animal."

## DOGS IN ANTIQUITY

In antiquity, dogs were variously coded—faithful and obedient, yet unclean and shameless—making them particularly useful ciphers to address both attraction to and anxiety over the category of the "other."[2] Within the Greco-Roman context, canines were framed positively with respect to their utility to humanity, while their negative behavior was used to show incorrect human conduct. In other words, people approached dogs in anthropocentric terms, playing with the positive or negative attributes that dogs had in order to frame what they wanted to say about humanity. As we shall see, Augustine used this canine ambiguity to his advantage in his own anthropocentric arguments about the impact of original sin.

As domesticated animals, dogs were praised for their faithfulness and obedience.[3] They were described as affectionate and fawning,[4] faithful and able to hold covenants with humans, and as having a keen sense of smell.[5] Yet it is also true that dogs were eaten, as well as used in sacrifices and medical cures.[6] And as for their occupational roles in society, certain breeds were hunting-dogs, sheepherders, and guardians of doorways and

---

1. Augustine, *City of God* 1.1.

2. For a concise overview of dogs in various societies in the ancient Mediterranean, see Schwartz, "Dogs in Jewish Society," 246–77.

3. For example, Homer, *Odyssey* 17.290–327.

4. Aristotle, *History of Animals* 1.20.

5. Seneca, *Moral Letters* 76.8; Augustine, *City of God* 8.15.

6. Hippocrates, *Regimen* 2.46; *Epidemics* 7.62; Gilhus, *Animals, Gods, and Humans*, 30, 109.

homes, while others were privileged and pampered enough to live the life of lap-dogs.[7]

Yet this sense of canine utility was not merely practical, but also ideological, since it was part of a larger conversation about the human-animal divide and natural hierarchies. Because of rationality and language, philosophers like the Stoics situated humans above animals and below the divine in the natural world order; therefore, dogs and other irrational beasts ought to serve and submit to humanity.[8] Other philosophers were more positive concerning the capabilities of animals, for example arguing that creatures like dogs had their own species-specific language and understanding, thus pushing against the Stoic notion that language was what proved rationality was only for humans, especially when not all humans understood one another.[9] Even in ancient narrative, dogs could be mouthpieces for the divine, for example the talking guard dog in the *Acts of Peter*.[10] This connection and conflict between dogs and communication will be crucial when we come to Augustine's own position on language and communication in what follows.

Now on the flip side of this common assumption that dogs ought to work for and be submissive to humanity is the possibility that this relationship can dissolve, perhaps even infecting humans with negative canine attributes. As I mentioned earlier, these bad traits are brought up as a means to situate what is proper human behavior in relation to what it is not. Dogs are described as eating inappropriate things like improperly slaughtered animals,[11] human corpses,[12] and their own vomit;[13] thus, they are unclean and impure in contrast to what is holy.[14] These are things that humans should not do or be.

More important for our present study, however, is that dogs were connected to a madness and disobedience that signaled a reversal of natural hierarchies. This connection was made especially potent by the fact that rabies was common and understood to be a canine disease that was transmittable

---

7. See Plato, *Laws* 824b; Gilhus, *Animals, Gods, and Humans*, 30.

8. Seneca, *Moral Letters* 76.9; Augustine, *Refutation of the Manichees* 1.17:28; *Literal Meaning of Genesis* 6.12:22; *City of God* 8.15.

9. Porphyry, *On Abstinence from Animal Flesh* 3.2–4. See also Clark "Animal Passions," 88–93.

10. Spittler, *Animals in the Apocryphal Acts*, 130–48, esp. 142–43.

11. Exod 22:31.

12. Homer, *Iliad* 1.5–6; 1 Kgs 14:11; 16:4; 21:24.

13. Prov 26:11; 2 Pet 2:22.

14. See Matt 7:6. For more on the juxtaposition between holiness (food) and dogs, see van de Sandt, "'Do Not Give What Is Holy to the Dogs,'" 223–46.

to humans,[15] even as it was also sometimes considered a sign of demonic possession.[16] Efforts were made not only to find cures for humans, but also for preventative medicine for the dogs themselves.[17] From a rhetorical standpoint, rabies is a threat because of the unnatural and violent behavior it instigates, making it a perfect label to apply to one's opponents, as well as a way to mark the disorder at the core of a community.

Also important for us here is the association between dogs and a lack of control because they engage in behavior that is deemed immodest and immoderate, for example engaging in sex in public[18] or ferociously expressing their distrust of strangers.[19] Dogs were often called shameless for such behavior, although it signaled a shamelessness in contrast to what is expected of human behavior. Again, this relates to reason, which is tied to human virtue.[20] This made it easy and common to refer to one's opponents as dogs, i.e., morally depraved.[21] This is also why Augustine himself was so critical of people who did or thought irrational things about dogs, which reflected their lack of understanding God's design of and power over creation.[22]

As we shall see in what follows, Augustine worked with ancient society's ambivalent understandings of and relationships with dogs to represent how human social relations are imperfect because of original sin, the primal, most broken relationship of all.

## ORIGINAL SIN:
## A BREAKDOWN OF SOCIAL RELATIONS

For Augustine, the impact of original sin can be seen in the breakdown of community.[23] As Catherine Conybeare (2014) persuasively argues, Augustine is invested in unpacking what it means to be in *civitas*, a "dynamic

---

15. Aristotle, *History of Animals* 8.22; Goebel and Peters, "Veterinary Medicine," 601.

16. See Nicolotti, "Cure for Rabies," 513–34.

17. Pliny, *Natural History* 8.152–53; Goebel and Peters, "Veterinary Medicine," 601; Philostratus, *Life of Apollonius* 6.43.

18. The Greek word for public sex was called *kynogamia*, or dog-marriage. Dutsch, "Dog-Love-Dog," 245. For the gendered connections between dogs and sexuality, see Franco, *Shameless*.

19. Philo of Alexandria, *On Animals* 70.

20. Seneca, *Moral Letters* 76.10.

21. Gilhus, *Animals, Gods, and Humans*, 170. See also Phil 3:2; Nanos, "Paul's Reversal," 448–82; Resnick, "Good Dog/Bad Dog," 70–97.

22. See Augustine, *City of God* 5.7, 8.15.

23. Miles, *World Made Flesh*, 98.

community, bound by trans-historical ties, [and] grounded since creation in human sociality."[24] This is true for both the heavenly and the earthly cities he explores in *The City of God*, although the heavenly city is the ideal one to which people should strive for citizenship, while the earthly one is distorted by human desires and the problems that arise from sin.

What we want to emphasize here is how Augustine represents disrupted human sociality as a result of original sin. As the first turning away from God, original sin was Adam and Eve's free will choice to disobey God, forever dividing the human will against itself and God.[25] For Augustine, this broken relationship between humanity and the divine is inherited by all humans through procreation, and the only remedy is the gift of God's grace and future salvation. As such, present human desires are but one effect of the impact of this sin on the world; for example, the desire for power disrupts the ideal goal of community, namely one bound by a common desire for justice and for harmony.[26] In this way, humanity's disordered relationship with God manifests in the injustice and suffering we experience as creation forever tainted by this original sin.

As I stated earlier, dogs provide Augustine with the means to explore this suffering and disorder because they are beings that represent both humanity's control over the natural world, as well as the threat of a lack of control. As we shall see, at their best, dogs are coded as faithful and obedient, while at their worst, they can be used to show humanity's own limitations.

## *Fidelity and Order: Revolt and Rabies*

Concerning our first case-study of his rhetorical use of dogs, namely the issue of fidelity and order, we see Augustine raise up the issue of revolt and rabies. He makes this connection twice, first to make an historical argument of why Christianity is not to blame for the attack on Rome, and the second to meditate on why there is so much suffering in the world.

Now in order to prove that Christianity was not the cause of recent barbarian attacks, Augustine provides historical evidence where the gods had failed to save Rome on various occasions. Important for our present study is that this includes internal social discord like civil war. In book 3, chapter 23 of *The City of God* Augustine uses the example of the Latin Social War against Rome from 91–88 BCE. According to his account, this internal

---

24. Conybeare, "City of Augustine," 139.

25. For a concise overview of the doctrine of original sin, including the historical context from which it arose, see Brown, *Augustine of Hippo*, 388–89.

26. Conybeare, "City of Augustine," 145–46.

war was anticipated by the sign of madness descending upon all domesticated animals—dogs, horses, asses, oxen—causing them to revolt against humanity itself.[27] He engages this line of thought to invite his readers to infer that the present period's problems are far worse: "If such a thing had occurred in our own day, we should find our adversaries more rabid against us than their animals were against them!"[28]

The truthfulness of this historical event is less important than the fact that civil war was imagined in terms of "rabid infection."[29] This is because rabies as madness was viewed as a rejection of natural hierarchies and order. Augustine himself is deeply informed by Genesis 1:28, in which God gives humanity authority over all other living creatures. As such, animal revolt becomes a striking example of the impact of original sin's disordering influence.

Now Augustine continues this line of thought in book 22, chapter 22, arguing that humanity's just punishment for original sin is pain, a miserable condition common to all and which can only be alleviated through the grace of Christ.[30] Rabies is but one of the many ills related to the natural world that Augustine notes, yet it is the following passage that most specifically highlights how this disease represents disorder that is ultimately social:

> Do not innumerable other evils also threaten our bodies from without? . . . Accidents arising out of the fear or malice of domestic animals; from so many poisons in berries, water, air, beasts; from the painful, or even fatal, bites of wild creatures; from the madness which a rabid dog communicates, so that even that animal which is more gentle and affectionate towards its master than any other is feared more vehemently and bitterly than a lion or a dragon, and the man whom it has happened to infect with this dreadful contagion becomes so mad that his parents, wife and children dread him more than any beast.[31]

Here, Augustine taps into the same fear of natural hierarchies being overturned against humans that he introduced with the animal revolt in book 3 and connects it with all natural threats and suffering that are the result of original sin. However, it is the rabid dog that becomes the perfect

---

27. Cf. Orosius, *History Against the Pagans* 5.18.9.

28. Dyson, *Augustine*, 132.

29. Sallust, *Histories*, 1.48(55).19; 1.67(77).9; Hawkins, "Barking Cure," 61–62.

30. See Augustine, *Refutation of the Manichees* 1.16.25–26; *Literal Meaning of Genesis* 3.15.24.

31. Dyson, *Augustine*, 1155.

description of destroyed social order because of its infection of the key social unit, namely the family/household.

As we mentioned previously, the most ideal dog is affectionate and obedient towards its owner, so rabies as a disease turns this relationship on its head. The dog is now made unfamiliar, as signaled by its new affinity with dangerous and wild animals like lions and dragons. The fact that this disease is communicable means that being bit by a rabid dog results in a human's behavior likewise changing, now reflecting social disorder at its most extreme. The fidelity between the dog and master, as well as between the master and his family, is disordered because there is no trusting the madness of either of them. For the human, this is an inability to control property, the dog, or the self, as reflected in the master's unnatural and terrible behavior toward his family.

As such, Augustine views this as one of the most destructive examples of how original sin pollutes social relations and the order of things, resulting in much suffering. Yet for him, it also provides the opportunity to reflect upon humanity's situation and the gift of divine grace. As shown in what follows, Augustine further explores this idea of disorder and its connection to sociality with the issue of language and disconnection, our second case study of his rhetorical use of dogs.

## *Language and Disconnection*

Now just as proper and improper social order is expressed in the hierarchical relationship between the human and the dog, boundaries between humans can be reflected upon with the paradoxical connection between canines and language. Consider the fact that in antiquity one could call someone with poor speech to be as "eloquent as a dog"; in other words, not at all.[32] The varied noises that dogs make—barks, growls, howls, whines—were one means to express moments of failure to speak coherently and rationally.[33] For example, in the *Acts of Peter*, God's power and truth are made manifest through a talking dog, in that the divine overcomes the animal's limitations of speech and irrationality. This point about communication and dogs is important for Augustine, in that it allows him to explore how humanity's fractured existence manifests in the lack of a single, common language across all people.

As Conybeare argues, Augustine sees the human race as bound by a sociality that began with creation of Eve, and is "supported and maintained by

---

32. Jerome, *Letter* 134.1.
33. Hawkins, "Barking Cure," 58.

human communication . . . that may be as much a barrier as a connection."[34] The idea that communication hinders and helps human social relations resonates with the etiology of language variation as represented in the Tower of Babel (Gen 11:1–9). Moreover, in contrast with the imperfect nature of human language as seen in multilingualism, Augustine views God's form of perfect communication to be silent.[35] As such, the reality of language variety itself is seen as a manifestation of a fractured humanity that stems that original break with the order and oneness with God in Eden. Augustine frames this problem in *The City of God*, book 19, chapter 7 as the following:

> For if two men, each ignorant of the other's language, meet, and are compelled by some necessity not to pass on but to remain with one another, it is easier for dumb animals, even of different kinds, to associate together than these men, even though they are both human beings. . . . So true is this that a man would more readily hold a conversation with his dog than with another man who is a foreigner. It is true that the Imperial City [Rome] has imposed on subject nations not only her yoke but also her language [Latin], as a bond of peace and society, so that there should be no lack of interpreters but a great abundance of them. But how many great wars, what slaughter of men, what outpourings of human blood have been necessary to bring this about![36]

For Augustine, it is important to note that Rome, even with an imposed language and an abundance of translators, cannot bring coherence without violence and bloodshed with the foreign peoples. This violent act of forced unity can be seen as a distorted mirror of the original unity of communication that was at the heart of existence in Eden and oneness with God before the original sin. It is reflected even at the personal level, in the strangers who are able to act no better than irrational animals because they are unable and unwilling to communicate their rationality.

However, it is humanity's relationship with the non-speaking dog that allows Augustine to solidify his rhetoric concerning the threat of language preventing human sociality to the extreme. Tapping into the kinship that a person can have with a dog, his point that a person would choose to converse with a dog over another human being ought to be seen as an unfortunate and unnatural result of this linguistic fracturing. It would have been obvious to Augustine's audience that choosing to talk to a familiar dog versus an unfamiliar human shows an irrational approach

---

34. Conybeare, "City of Augustine," 151.
35. See Conybeare, "City of Augustine," 149; Augustine, *City of God* 11.4.
36. Dyson, *Augustine*, 928.

to social relations: the goodness of human relationships is surrendered to either the absence of a relationship, namely the inability or unwillingness to communicate with strangers, or in the creation of an inferior partnership with a non-human, the dog.

In this way, we can see how Augustine uses the idea of kinship between the human and dog to express distorted social relations that arise from issues of communication, just we saw that the disease-broken kinship between master and pet could reveal social turmoil at various levels. Finally, we can now turn our final case study to how Augustine uses canines to explore the limits of human nature through the issue of shame.

## *Shame and Human Nature*

In book 14, chapter 20 of *The City of God*, Augustine locates the root of lust and shame to original sin, namely humanity's disobedient turn away from God:

> Without any doubt, then, human nature is ashamed of its lust, and deservedly ashamed. For the disobedient nature of this lust, which has entirely subdued the organs of generation to its own urges and snatched them from the power of the will, is enough to show what retribution has been visited upon man for that first disobedience.[37]

Now, shame is deeply tied to the fall, as seen in Adam and Eve's reaction upon gaining awareness of their nakedness in Genesis 3:7.[38] Augustine considers lust to be a problem because it directs humans away from simple procreation, thus preventing them from using their free will in alignment with God's intention. For him, sex was a natural part of creation even in Eden, where it had no association with lust or desire.[39] Thus, the punishment for this "first disobedience" was shame. Why does Augustine take for granted that shame would be an appropriate punishment?

The rhetorical force behind understanding why shame is a punishment comes from the fact that lust is tied with the notion of not being in control of oneself. As we have seen earlier in this paper, dogs were considered to be immoderate in their behaviors and sexuality, namely they are shameless. Augustine believes that humans cannot feel shameless as dogs do, and he uses the example of the Cynic[40] philosophers to support this point:

37. Dyson, *Augustine*, 620.
38. Augustine, *City of God* 14.17.
39. Augustine, *City of God* 14; Wetzel, "Augustine on the Will," 344.
40. Note that the word *cynic* was purportedly derived from the Greek word for dog, *kuon*.

> The dog-philosophers, that is, the Cynics ... put forward a view so contrary to human modesty that it can only be called dog-like: that is, unclean and shameless. They believed that since the sexual act is lawful as between husband and wife, no one should be ashamed to perform it in the presence of others, and to have martial intercourse in any street or square.... However, the Cynics subsequently ceased to act in this way, and modesty, which makes men blush in the presence of other men, prevailed over the erroneous belief that men should seek to resemble dogs.
>
> Hence, I believe that Diogenes, and the others who are reputed to have done the same thing, only went through the motions of having intercourse before the eyes of men, who did not know what was going on under the cloak. I do not believe that such pleasure could have been achieved under the gaze of human onlookers.... Anyone who ventured to do so it would be overwhelmed, I do not say with a hail of stones, but certainly with a shower of saliva by the disgusted onlookers.[41]

Cynicism as a movement critiqued societal expectations, exposing them for their constructiveness through the performance of impolite behavior and lifestyle choices.[42] To perform or suggest such actions was intended to cause shock in such a way that would allow viewers (the public) the opportunity to ask why social norms functioned as they did, much like a parable.[43] Yet Augustine's desire to shame the shamelessness of the Cynics depends upon the notion that a human cannot truly act like a dog, which will copulate anywhere.

What is important here is the point that humans as social creatures will limit their behavior in response to others when it comes to virtues and sin, whereas dogs do not recognize such concepts. For Augustine, humans are rational and can comprehend that their suffering is a punishment for falling out of their original relationship with God and can only be fixed by the grace of God through Christ. Thus, Augustine uses canine behavior to mark the limits of human behavior which is always imprinted by and relational to original sin, but yet is always appropriately human.

## CONCLUSIONS

To conclude, in this paper we have seen how Augustine is able to use the dog—a familiar non-human companion—to explore the limits of human

---

41. Dyson, *Augustine*, 619–20.
42. Dutsch, "Dog-Love-Dog," 246–48.
43. For more information on these tropes, see Burrus, *Saving Shame*, 41.

social relations and behavior within the post-Eden existence. As such, he reveals the impact of original sin as it manifests in the reversal of natural hierarchies and relationships through the examples of unnatural infidelity and disorder, improper or lack of communication, and the human nature's limits concerning shame.

While dogs are not the only kind of animal that Augustine thinks with in his large volume of writings, his attention to dogs in *The City of God* does sit in contrast with his focus on animality in very broad and generic terms in number of his works.[44] As such, it is one example of species particularity that shows diversity at the heart of otherness, pushing against the homogeneity that is at the basis of one category of the "other," namely the "animal." We wrestle with this today, as seen in Jacques Derrida's point that we obscure the diversity of animality under the word "animal," as well as in Donna J. Haraway's call to imagine our harmonic multiplicity with the microbes that live within us and with the companion species like the dogs that live and work beside us.[45]

This openness to our interrelationality with animality also helps us think about what we see in the non-human other that reflects our anxieties about ourselves, as humans. In particular, we can begin to ask ourselves what specifically we embrace and resist in our relationships with non-human creatures like dogs, what they represent to us, and what we may represent to them. This also requires us to be open to self-critical analysis of our investments or lack thereof in the non-human other, as well as understanding how we, like Augustine, use them in our rhetorical toolkits today.

## BIBLIOGRAPHY

Brown, Peter. *Augustine of Hippo: A Biography*. Berkeley, CA: University of California Press, 1967.

Burrus, Virginia. *Saving Shame: Martyrs, Saints, and Other Abject Subjects*. Divinations: Rereading Late Ancient Religion. Philadelphia: University of Pennsylvania Press, 2008.

Burton, Philip. "Augustine and Language." In *A Companion to Augustine*, edited by Mark Vessey, 113–24. Oxford: Blackwell, 2012.

Clark, Gillian. "Animal Passions." *Greece & Rome* 47 (2000) 88–93.

Conybeare, Catherine. "The City of Augustine: On the Interpretation of *Civitas*." In *Being Christian in Late Antiquity: A Festschrift for Gillian Clark*, edited by Carol Harrison, et al., 139–54. Oxford: Oxford University Press, 2014.

Derrida, Jacques. "The Animal That Therefore I Am (More to Follow)." Translated by David Wills. *Critical Inquiry* 28 (2002) 369–418.

44. See Augustine, *Unfinished Literal Commentary on Genesis* 15.53; *Literal Meaning of Genesis* 3.11:16.

45. Derrida, "Animal That Therefore I Am," 409; Haraway, *When Species Meet*.

Dutsch, Dorata. "Dog-Love-Dog: *Kynogamia* and Cynic Sexual Ethics." In *Sex in Antiquity: Exploring Gender and Sexuality in the Ancient World*, edited by Mark Masterson, et al., 245–59. New York: Routledge, 2015.

Dyson, R. W., ed. *Augustine: The City of God Against the Pagans*. Translated by R. W. Dyson. Cambridge: Cambridge University Press, 1998.

Franco, Cristiana. *Shameless: The Canine and the Feminine in Ancient Greece*. Translated by Matthew Fox. Oakland, CA: University of California Press, 2014.

Gilhus, Ingvild Saelid. *Animals, Gods, and Humans: Changing Attitudes to Animals in Greek, Roman, and Early Christian Ideas*. New York: Routledge, 2006.

Goebel, Veronica, and Joris Peters. "Veterinary Medicine." In *The Oxford Classical Handbook of Animals in Classical Thought and Life*, edited by Gordon Lindsay Campbell, 589–606. Oxford: Oxford University Press, 2014.

Haraway, Donna J. *When Species Meet*. Minneapolis: University of Minnesota Press, 2008.

Hawkins, Julia Nelson. "The Barking Cure: Horace's 'Anatomy of Rage' in Epodes 1, 6, and 16." *American Journal of Philology* 135 (2014) 57–85.

Miles, Margaret R. *The World Made Flesh: A History of Christian Thought*. Oxford: Blackwell, 2005.

Nanos, Mark D. "Paul's Reversal of Jews Calling Gentiles 'Dogs' (Philippians 3:2): 1,600 Years of an Ideological Tale Wagging an Exegetical Dog?" *Biblical Interpretation* 17 (2009) 448–82.

Nathan, Geoffrey S. *The Family in Late Antiquity: The Rise of Christianity and the Endurance of Tradition*. New York: Routledge, 2000.

Newmyer, Stephen T. *Animals in Greek and Roman Thought: A Sourcebook*. New York: Routledge, 2011.

Nicolotti, Andrea. "A Cure for Rabies or a Remedy for Concupiscence? A Baptism of the Elchasaites." *Journal of Early Christian Studies* 16 (2008) 513–34.

Resnick, Irven M. "Good Dog/Bad Dog: Dogs in Medieval Religious Polemics." *Enarratio* 18 (2013) 70–97.

Schwartz, Joshua. "Dogs in Jewish Society in the Second Temple Period and in the Time of the Mishnah and Talmud." *Journal of Jewish Studies* 55 (2004) 246–77.

Spittler, Janet E. *Animals in the Apocryphal Acts of the Apostles: Early Christianity's Wild Kingdom*. Tübingen: Mohr Siebeck, 2008.

van de Sandt, Huub. "'Do Not Give What Is Holy to the Dogs' (Did 9:5D and Matt 7:6A): The Eucharistic Food of the Didache in its Jewish Purity Setting." *Vigiliae Christianae* 56 (2002) 223–46.

Wetzel, James. "Augustine on the Will." In *A Companion to Augustine*, edited by Mark Vessey, 340–52. Oxford: Blackwell, 2012.

# 8

# "Is This Your God . . . Killer of Children?"
## Israel's "Childish" Deity and the Other(s) in *Exodus: Gods and Kings*

### James Magee Jr.

RAMSES, CARRYING THE CORPSE of his infant son in his arms, his grief-stricken face still marred by boils, confronts Moses with a series of questions the morning after all the children in the city have apparently died: "Is this your god? A killer of children? What kind of fanatics worship such a god?" In what initially appears to be a compassionate grasp of the Egyptian's arm, the deity's reluctant general offers no words of solidarity or comfort, reporting instead that "no *Hebrew* child [has] died." It would seem Moses' god exterminates only *other* people's children. Flustered by the discriminatory violence from on high and tormented by his loss, the pharaoh expels his foreign slaves from the land. The Israelites' four hundred long years of servitude in Egypt have finally come to an end.

This pivotal and pathos-filled scene from the 2014 film *Exodus: Gods and Kings* (hereafter *Exodus*), based on the biblical story of Israel's enslavement and deliverance in the book of Exodus,[1] casts the oppressors in a

---

1. While Jeffrey Caine, one of the scriptwriters, refers to some of the book's conjectured literary sources (Scott and Caine, "Commentary"), there is no attempt in the movie to distinguish between or rely on any one of them to the exclusion of the others. For this reason, I bracket the complicated textual histories of these narratives

sympathetic light.² The pharaoh and his people are ostensibly the victims of a homicidal deity who targets defenseless children. This same god has already battered the Egyptians with a series of natural disasters, initiating the catastrophes with a smirk and showing no concern throughout for the plight of the Egyptian Other. The filmmakers' innovation in embodying the divine drew mixed reviews from critics. One referred to the choice of actor as "bold and . . . genuinely radical,"³ another as "a rather clever idea."⁴ Other critics were less enthralled, one claiming the film's "image of The Almighty [to be] so absurd as to render nearly every scene in which he appears almost satirical."⁵ Similar derisory comments were posted to IMDb with many reviewers of faith referring to the film's representation of Israel's deity as blasphemous, humiliating or insulting. At the center of these polarized interpretations was the character of Malak,⁶ played by eleven-year-old British actor Isaac Andrews. The boy appears to Moses as the divine "I Am" (Exod 3:14) and spars ruthlessly from behind the scenes as a "militant deity"⁷ with the self-proclaimed god Pharaoh.

Situated within a rapidly expanding corpus of critical studies on depictions of children in film,⁸ this essay will focus on the controversial character

---

(Dozeman, *Exodus*, 31–43; Utzschneider and Oswald, *Exodus*, 34–53) and rely for comparisons only on the composite text of the Masoretic tradition, justification for which is provided by Lemmelijn, *Plague*, 209–218.

2. The filmmakers adopt a thirteenth-century date for the exodus event and posit Ramesses II (Ramses) as the pharaoh then oppressing the Israelites. On the difficulties of a historical such event, at least as narrated in the Bible, see the discussions of Dever, *Israelites*, 7–21; Meyers, *Exodus*, 2–12; Dozeman, *Exodus*, 26–31.

3. Scott, "Exodus."

4. Lemire, "Exodus."

5. Berardinelli, "Exodus."

6. Caine notes that *mal'ach* is the Hebrew word for "angel" or "messenger" and the character of Malak is modeled after "the angel from God," whom he describes as a biblical device for expressing how the divine interacts with humans (Scott and Caine, "Commentary"). Since Malak, like his biblical counterpart (Propp, *Exodus*, 198–99; Meyers, *Exodus*, 52–53; Dozeman, *Exodus*, 125), speaks in the first person as Israel's deity (Exod 3:2–4:17), they are treated throughout this essay as interchangeable. See further, Collins, "Divine," 17–25; Walsh, "Child," 312–13.

7. Walsh, "Child," 313.

8. One monograph each in the eighties (Jackson, *Images*) and nineties (Sinyard, *Movies*) have been followed by an explosion of pertinent books and essay collections since the turn of the millennium: Wojcik-Andrews, *Films*; Low, *Kids*; Wilson, *Children*; Schober, *Narratives*; Kapur, *Capital*; Pomerance and Gateward, *Boys*; Cartwright, *Spectatorship*; Lebeau, *Childhood*; Lury, *Film*; Musgrave, *Films*; Wright, *Child*; Olson, *Hitchcock*; Olson and Scahill, *Cinema*; Rocha and Seminet, *Minors*; Olson, *Post-Apocalyptic*; Schober and Olson, *Spielberg*; Donald et al., *Nation*; Olson, *Black*; Randall, *Threshold*; Balanzategui, *Uncanny*; Donald, *Home*; Hogan, *Genre*; McCallum, *Adaptations*; Olson,

of Malak in *Exodus*. I will first ground my exploration in recent theorizing on childhood and film spectatorship, pausing to position my own viewing of the film. I will then look at how Malak is portrayed in his first encounter with Moses and introduce the question of the Other that emerges from their dialogue. The core of the essay will trace the interplay between these two aspects in several key scenes. I will argue that the depiction of Israel's deity as a boy seems to involve an othering of children that is used to negatively characterize religion. I will conclude by drawing the study into conversation with current dialogues on both religiously-motivated violence and the ethics of seeing the Other in film, highlighting the importance of responsible filmic analysis in contemporary culture.

## DECONSTRUCTING THE BOY MALAK AND NEGOTIATING *EXODUS*' CHILDHOODS

The idea for a boy to represent Israel's deity was given to *Exodus*' screenwriters by director Ridley Scott.[9] In an interview with *The Hollywood Reporter*, Scott claimed that "Malak exudes innocence and purity."[10] Children are widely held to possess these two qualities naturally, innocence being paramount.[11] It is difficult, however, to reconcile the violence that Malak unleashes on the Egyptians with Scott's attribution of innocence, the Latin *innocere* meaning "to do no harm."[12] One critic refers to Malak as "so bloody-minded he might have stepped out of William Golding's *Lord of the Flies*,"[13] which 1954 dystopian novel reflects the idea that all humans, children included, are innately evil.[14] While Golding allows for children's innocence in terms of ignorance,[15] Malak's suprahuman knowledge[16] would seem to preclude this sense. Critical examination of *Exodus*' representation of deity will involve deconstructing these naturalized discourses on childhood.

---

*World Cinema*; Castro and Clark, *Agency*; Martin, *Cinema*.
   9. Foundas, "Exodus."
  10. Masters, "Exodus."
  11. Jenks, *Childhood*, 124.
  12. Faulkner, *Innocent*, 7.
  13. Lacey, "Exodus."
  14. Golding, "Fable," 41–42.
  15. Golding, *Pieces*, 89–90.
  16. Collins, "Divine," 18.

Central to contemporary scholarship on childhood[17] is the idea that childhood is a socially-constructed temporal space.[18] While differences between humans variously positioned along the life course may be significant, the meanings and associated restrictions, privileges and responsibilities that are attached to these states of being vary both historically and cross-culturally. Focusing on the temporal spaces inhabited by children,[19] these variables affect experiences of childhood and thus some scholars speak instead of *childhoods*.[20] The dominant image here in the West of the vulnerable, dependent and innocent child is but one historically contingent and contestable construction of childhood.

Children's resistance to constructions of their childhoods is widespread and they often fail to embody the purity imputed to them.[21] Explanations that serve to reinforce the image of childhood innocence typically include children's alleged ignorance of consequences or the assumption their innocence has been lost or corrupted through abuse.[22] When contraventions to the ideal involve extremes of violence or murder, offenders' acceptance within the category of child is sometimes denied in favor of demonization.[23] The cinema is one site where images of children who transgress the boundaries of "normative" Western childhood abound.[24] While some critics see Malak as one such miscreant,[25] directorial assertion of the boy's innocence suggest a more complicated portrayal.

While directors often exert a significant degree of creative control over the films they are involved in, the collaborative efforts of filmmaking complicate singular attribution of authorship and the attendant arbitration of meaning.[26] Furthermore, the notion that meaning comes prepackaged

---

17. Childhood studies emerged as an interdisciplinary focus within the social sciences in the mid-eighties, a brief history of which is provided by Mayall, *History*.

18. Stainton-Rogers, "Child?" 26–29.

19. With Montgomery, *Introduction*, 3, 14, I reject the notion of a universal "child" and acknowledge the difficulties in creating any firm boundary between the categories of "child" and "adult." For the purposes of this essay, "children" are defined as those human beings in the period of the life course before puberty, the visible onset of which here in the contemporary West occurs *around* the age of twelve, as noted in Lancy, *Anthropology*, 294.

20. Jenks, *Childhood*, 5.

21. Faulkner, *Innocent*, 24.

22. Stainton-Rogers, "Child?," 22.

23. Jenks, *Childhood*, 128–29.

24. Olson and Scahill, *Cinema*, ix–xi.

25. Chang, "Review"; Moore, "Review."

26. Watson, "Authorship," 144–45.

in films and is passively consumed by spectators overlooks the active role that viewers take in the meaning-making process.[27] One's life experiences and worldview influence his "reading" of a film and the meaning(s) that he generates in the act of viewing.[28] How one draws meaning from Malak as a representation of the divine depends primarily on the ideas about both childhood and deity that she brings to the viewing experience, as well as her purpose in viewing the film.

I approach *Exodus* as an agnostic, as one who leaves the existence of deities an open question.[29] Since Scott also identifies as an agnostic,[30] my engagement with the film takes up Jacques Berlinerblau's invitation to a study of "secular aesthetics."[31] The spotlight on Malak represents an extension of my research into depictions of juvenile masculinity in film and the cinematic boy Jesus in particular,[32] a focus that aims to fill a void in current Bible-in-film scholarship. Additionally, and with numerous others who conduct research into childhoods, I seek to raise awareness of children's marginalization and to advocate for their flourishing as full and active citizens.[33]

The framework of interpretation I have outlined above positions me to offer what Patrick Phillips calls a "negotiated response" to the movie.[34] What are negotiated in such a "reading" are a film's appealing and unappealing aspects. A skeptical take on Moses' story and a child deity are features of the film that intrigue me. As Berlinerblau points out, however, secular art is "often [in] contentious dialogue with religion."[35] In an interview with *Variety*, Scott remarked with an accompanying gesture how "easy [it is] to (give the finger) to religions."[36] While the director seeks to stifle this impulse and show respect, an underlying (and, for me, unappealing) hostility toward religion seems present in the film.[37] The following examination of how Israel's deity is depicted as a boy will be conducted against the backdrop

---

27. Watson, "Authorship," 153.
28. Phillips, "Spectator," 130.
29. Kenny, "Agnosticism," 117–24; Le Poidevin, *Agnosticism*.
30. Foundas, "Exodus."
31. Berlinerblau, *Bible*, 137.
32. Magee, "Jesus."
33. Bowman and Spencer, "Definition," 12; Alderson, *Childhoods*, 130.
34. Phillips, "Spectator," 131.
35. Berlinerblau, *Bible*, 137.
36. Foundas, "Exodus."
37. Lacey, "Exodus."

of religious skepticism displayed by the film's key protagonist, arguably a projection onto Moses of the filmmakers' secular worldview.[38]

## A MEETING OF THE SKEPTICAL MINDS . . . OR, A MEETING IN THE INJURED MIND?

As with other Bible-to-film adaptations, *Exodus*' filmmakers omit from, add to and contradict the terse biblical source texts in fashioning their narrative.[39] The film opens with a number of sequences that establish Moses' military prowess and his disbelief in the gods of Egypt. When the general's Hebrew ancestry comes to light, Ramses banishes him from Egypt (Exod 2:1–15a). Moses settles in Midian, marries Zipporah and fathers a son, Gershom (2:15b–22). In the shadow of an imposing mountain, the boy explains to his unbelieving father that it is forbidden to climb the mount because it belongs to their god. Moses defiantly ascends the prohibited peak (3:1), but is unexpectedly caught in a rock and mud slide when a storm engulfs the mountain. When he is struck on the back of the head and knocked unconscious, the stage is set for his encounter with Malak.

Moses, trapped in a slurry pit, awakens to the whispered call of his name (Exod 3:4). Off to his left, a bush is ablaze with a blue-white flame, but not burning up (3:2). When he notices a boy approaching, he calls out to him for help. His would-be rescuer is indifferent. When Moses asks who he is, Malak shifts the question back indignantly: "Who are *you*?" Moses identifies himself as a shepherd, but the boy retorts: "I thought you were a general. I need a *general*." Once Moses ascertains the nature of Malak's solicitation, he seeks his interrogator's identity a second time. The boy answers cryptically: "I Am" (3:15). He then disappears, leaving Moses to drown in the mud.

Aspects of filmic narration—*mise en scène*[40] and cinematography[41]—open up sites of meaning-making unavailable to literary narrators.[42] Situated at night, the 'burning' bush casts an eerie blue light over the dark

---

38. Foundas, "Exodus."

39. Reinhartz, *Cinema*, 29.

40. According to Speidel, *mise en scène* refers to everything "staged in front of the camera at the time of filming" and its five key elements are "setting, props, costume and make-up, lighting and performance" (Speidel, "Narrative," 87–88).

41. As Barsam and Monahan say, cinematography is "the process of capturing moving images on film" and this "contribute[s] to a movie's overall meaning . . . [with] the angles, heights, and movements of the camera function[ing] both as a set of techniques and as expressive material" (Barsam and Monahan, *Movies*, 226).

42. Verstraten, *Narratology*, 7.

mountainside setting. Blue is often associated with melancholy, coldness or desolation.[43] The ambiance provides a fitting background for Malak's brooding and irritable disposition, as well as his aloofness. The boy's emotional distance from Moses is expressed visually in one particular shot by positioning them on opposite sides of the frame, a staging technique often used to portray alienation between characters.[44] Camera positions are utilized to visualize other aspects of their relationship. A high-angle shot can emphasize a character's vulnerability[45] or the dominance of one character over another.[46] In the shot over Malak's shoulder the boy stands able and in control over an incapacitated and vulnerable Moses. As Malak delivers his divine self-declaration, a low angle shot is used. This camera position can emphasize a character's power[47] or convey a sense of awe or admiration for him or her.[48]

Typical power dynamics in the West where adults wield authority over children[49] are reversed in this scene, but juxtaposed with props and costuming that reinforce Malak's identity as a child. Throughout the scene, the boy plays with crude dice, common toys in the ancient world.[50] Several close-up shots show Malak stacking the dice in the form of a pyramid, a construction he impulsively destroys moments later. Invoking what are often assumed to be Israel's pastoral origins,[51] the people's deity is imagined and costumed as a shepherd boy. He is distinguished from adult male shepherds in the film by the exposure of his legs from about the knees down. Whatever else such a clothing difference might represent with respect to diminished social status,[52] the boy's bared skin conveys vulnerability in keeping with the dominant contemporary construction of childhood.

Turning from the ways Malak is emphasized as a child to the subject of the Other,[53] a central question the boy leaves with Moses to contemplate

43. Phillips, *Film*, 68.
44. Phillips, *Film*, 43.
45. Phillips, *Film*, 91.
46. Sikov, *Introduction*, 13.
47. Phillips, *Film*, 92.
48. Sikov, *Introduction*, 13.
49. Wyness, *Childhood*, 110.
50. Szpakowska, *Egypt*, 2008; Laird, "Dice," 171–73; Peck, *Egypt*, 178.
51. Dever, *Israelites*, 101–221.
52. King and Stager, *Israel*, 259–60.

53. The construction of an Other is essential to identity formation (Smith, "Equations," 230; Richardson, *Otherness*, 12–15; Cataldo, "Other," 2). While this process can be respectful of difference (Grad and Rojo, "Identities," 12–13), it can also not (Willis, *People*, 6; Leirvik, *Studies*, 54–55). This negative construal of the Other through processes of "othering" is assumed throughout this essay unless otherwise specified.

is whether he considers the Israelites *people*. Implied in the query is an accusation that the Egyptians, Moses included, have dehumanized the Israelites by subjecting them to forced labor. Even though he is an Israelite by birth, Moses' identity is complicated by his early adoption into royal Egyptian life.[54] Malak's distance and callousness during the encounter may reflect trepidation and skepticism based on Moses' current identification with the oppressive Egyptian Other.

Rescued from the mud, Moses wakes under the care of his wife, who tries to convince him the encounter with Malak was all in his head. "God isn't a boy!" Zipporah exclaims. That this and Moses' subsequent meetings with Malak are delusions owing to a brain injury sustained in the mudslide is an interpretative framework the filmmakers subtly suggest rather than impose.[55] However delicately the idea is introduced, it embeds a critical if not insulting view of religious experience. How the filmmakers' depiction of Israel's god as a *boy* might add to this disparaging appraisal will be explored in the following section.

## TYRANTS, TOTS, AND TANTRUMS: REPRISALS OF A "CHILDISH" DEITY

When Moses returns to Egypt (Exod 4:20), without his wife and son, he finds the Israelites being worked to death, their bodies incinerated daily by the cartload. During Moses' initial confrontation with Ramses, the tyrant others and dehumanizes his slave laborers by comparing them to animals.[56] Moses explodes with what appears to be an answer to Malak's question: "Do not call them animals!" At this point in the film, Moses neither identifies with the Hebrews nor views them as a people distinct from the Egyptians. He sees them instead as fellow Egyptians deserving of freedom, rights and to be paid for their work. When Ramses refuses his demands (5:1–2), Malak's general begins the war of attrition for which he was conscripted. Pharaoh's retaliation is swift and merciless. At dawn, Moses finds Malak surveying the carnage he has set in motion. Expecting to report positively on his progress, Moses is instead berated for lack of results. The impatient boy wonders if he even has need of a general and instructs Moses with a smirk: "For now, you can watch."

---

54. Greifenhagen, *Egypt*, 59–63.
55. Collin, "Exodus"; Phipps, "Exodus"; Vishnevetsky, "Bale"; Collins, "Divine," 34.
56. Davis points to such "animalization" as a ubiquitous practice in the history of human slave-holding and its justification (Davis, *Emancipation*, 3–26), but rarely is the underlying othering of (non-human) animals itself critically examined (Borkfelt, "Otherness").

Dismissing his general to the sidelines, Malak dispatches a horde of crocodiles into the Nile. The hungry reptiles, thought by some in ancient Egypt to be agents of divine vengeance,[57] surround a lone fishing boat in the Nile and consume its occupants. The thrashing in the river leads to a series of natural catastrophes (Exod 7:14–10:30), events referred to in 10:2—at least on one interpretation of the underlying Hebrew—as Israel's deity toying with the Egyptians.[58] These disasters culminate in a thick cover of darkness (10:21–29) and Ramses, declaring himself to be *the* god, vows to kill every infant among the Hebrews if one more catastrophe should strike. This sets the stage for the plague Malak unleashes on Egypt's own tots, as well as its older children. When Moses accuses Malak of being motivated by revenge, the boy's hitherto cool and calm demeanor turns to rage: "Revenge? After four hundred years of brutal subjugation? These pharaohs who imagine they're living gods, they're nothing more than flesh and blood. I want to see them on their knees begging for it to stop!" While the boy's desire to see Ramses on his knees begging for mercy never materializes, he does murder the tyrant's infant son and an untold number of other Egyptian children (12:29), a "child killing children."[59]

Later, through the theophany of the storm,[60] Malak drowns several divisions of his nemesis' army in the Red Sea. Prior to the climactic showdown at the sea, Moses' sympathy for the Egyptians' suffering leads Malak to question his general's Israelite identity. The boy insists on a strict separation between Israel and Egypt, the maintenance of boundaries to be evidenced by disregard for the Other. Moses' utopia of the slaves' freedom and absorption into an egalitarian Egyptian society is Malak's dystopia. The boy's mass murder of the Egyptian children achieves his desired result not only of the slaves' emancipation, but their *expulsion* from Egypt (Exod 12:31–36). There is no "mixed multitude" (12:38) among the displaced. Instead, the bereaved Egyptians hurl obscenities at their former slaves, kick dust up into their faces, and spit at them as they leave.

While no prominent character or group emerges in *Exodus* as unquestionably good or irredeemably evil, it is the moral ambiguity attending Malak's actions that interests me here. The awkward shift in the boy's tantrum calls into question his motivations. While indignation and a desire for revenge are understandable reactions to Israel's enslavement

57. Pinch, *Mythology*, 126.
58. Ford, *God*, 102–7.
59. Collins, "Divine," 36.
60. Malak's association with storms and his warmongering are reminiscent of Ba'al, the Canaanite deity of storm and war whose attributes were appropriated by the Israelite god (Smith, *God*, 65–107).

and suffering in Egypt, pharaonic pretenses to divinity seem to be what *really* irk Malak, a lack of humanitarian concern also arguably present in the biblical text.[61] The boy's apparent pettiness, set alongside displays of petulance, impulsivity, impatience, fickleness, showing off and tantrum-throwing, leads numerous critics to claim that Israel's god, so portrayed, is "childish."[62] The adjective is a pejorative one,[63] implying a range of negative qualities that coalesce under the term "immature" and are widely considered endemic to childhood but not adulthood.

Jeffrey Caine, one of *Exodus*' scriptwriters, refers to Malak displaying wisdom a boy would not normally have.[64] Caine here appeals to the dominant view of children's innate "immaturity" and their alleged "progress" toward adulthood,[65] assuming that a deity would exemplify a teleological adult "maturity." Since commercial film audiences are typically comprised of spectators who accept many of the dominant values and ideologies of their society,[66] Malak's less desirable qualities seem likely to be and often were interpreted as "childish," eclipsing his precocious ones. That the filmmakers *intended* this "reading" of *Exodus*' deity as "childish" is more difficult to say. As with the delusion framework, that Israel's god behaves "childishly" implies a critical if not insulting view of Judeo-Christian religion and is subtly rather than explicitly conveyed. In the fourth section of this essay, I will situate this negative characterization of childhood within a number of othering discourses in the film and offer a humanizing "reading" of Malak's character.

## THE MONSTROUS OTHERED CHILD IN CINEMA AND (DE)HUMANIZING MALAK

Stepping back to consider the multiplicity of otherings that have emerged through analysis, each of them involves some form of dehumanization. Nick Haslam argues for two different senses of humanness that may be denied: human *uniqueness* where humans are distinguished from other living beings and human *nature* where humans are distinguished from inanimate

---

61. Eslinger, "Exodus," 43–60; Ford, *God*, 52–53, 66, 142–43, 154.

62. Chang, "Review"; Edwards, "Exodus"; Merry, "Exodus"; Mohan, "Exodus"; Moore, "Review"; Rea, "God"; Collins, "Divine," 37; Walsh, "Child," 314–15.

63. Jones, *Childhood*, 38; Alderson, *Childhoods*, 118.

64. Scott and Caine, "Commentary."

65. This "developmentalism" (Aldgate, "Children," 20) has been critiqued from a variety of perspectives (Stainton Rogers and Stainton Rogers, *Stories*; Woodhead, "Development"; Barnes, "Performance").

66. Phillips, "Spectator," 130.

objects.⁶⁷ Ramses' animalization of the Israelites and Malak's objectification of the Egyptians, playing with them as a boy might with his toys, are reciprocating dehumanizations within the story world that involve denials of human uniqueness and nature respectively. Both fall on the explicit end of Haslam's spectrum of humanness denial.⁶⁸ At the other end of this continuum are subtle dehumanizations, those denials of humanness often not recognized as such by those who employ them.

While the film's examples of explicit dehumanization may be expressed through "less than human" assertions, the subtle examples rely on "less human than" comparisons, where "human" is assumed to be the supposedly rational adult. First, there is the suggestion that Moses' meetings with Malak in the second half of the film are delusions owing to a brain injury. The implication is that encounters with the divine are cognitive distortions of the intellectually disabled, an oft-dehumanized Other⁶⁹ whose experiences and perceptions are portrayed as both different from and inferior to those of the majority "rational" population. This "norm" of rationality is modeled by the skeptical Moses throughout the first half of the film. Second, there is the suggestively "childish" behavior of the Israelite god, children's general conduct often construed as irrational when compared to that of adults.⁷⁰ The ideas of childhood irrationality and immaturity upon which the interpretation of a "childish" Israelite deity rely are rooted in and reinforced by the widespread othering of children in the film's cultural background.⁷¹ The subtle dehumanization at work in such discourses on childhood can be seen in the terminology of "young people" that is sometimes used to describe adolescents and distinguish them from preadolescents, who are, by implication, not yet people⁷² or at best, people in the making,⁷³ not *as* human as *older* humans.

Rejecting and "reading" against this othering of children in Malak's case is complicated by his possession of divine powers, which sets him further apart as a *monstrous* Other.⁷⁴ Deviation from that which is constructed

---

67. Haslam, "Dehumanization," 36.
68. Haslam, "Dehumanization," 37.
69. Hubert, "Introduction," 1, 5.
70. Lee, *Childhood*, 38; Alderson, *Childhoods*, 11.
71. Jones, *Childhood*, 36–41.
72. Montgomery, *Introduction*, 62.

73. An emphasis on children as "being" rather than "becoming" is a key debate in contemporary childhood studies (Prout, *Childhood*, 66). Challenging the static nature of adulthood, Lee reframes the discussion to emphasize the dynamic "becoming" of both children and adults (Lee, *Childhood*, 19, 103).

74. Kearney, *Strangers*, 5–6.

as "human" or considered "normal" human behavior in a given context is common to the various ways in which monstrosity is conceptualized.[75] Israel's god presents as a malevolent supernatural being whose abilities to appear and disappear at will, as well as to influence animals' behavior and control meteorological phenomena, are similar to those possessed by some of cinema's "evil kids."[76] David, the fallen angel kidnapped in *Whisper* (2007), controls wild dogs, moves in and out of locked rooms and creates indoor wind storms. David's adoptive mother, who has orchestrated the abduction in order to rid herself of this "changeling"[77] of sorts, responds to one of the kidnapper's refusal to kill the "little boy": "That is the last thing *it* is. Do you really think he's human?" Barto, the specter who haunts *The Unborn* (2009), is similarly dehumanized by his elderly twin sister: "It's not human anymore. It is an outsider now. It is no longer of this universe." Her brother had long ago been murdered, his reanimated corpse now inhabited by a *dybbuk*[78] who controls animals and the wind, as well as teleports.

Alexa Wright emphasizes the often visual nature of monstrosity[79] and this is most acute in Barto's case, his perpetually youthful body paradoxically showing signs of decomposition. When David refers to eyes as the windows to the soul, his own whitened sclerae turn murky to reflect the inner turmoil and darkness one might associate with a fallen angel.[80] Malak, by comparison, shows no visible signs of monstrosity in his body. The vulnerability suggested by the boy's clothing and concomitant bare skin is reinforced by what appear to be marks of neglect and abuse. Malak's face is dirty and there are lesions on his right temple and on the left of his chin. The boy's patchy buzz-cut hair appears to have been shorn in haste. Malak's appearance bears no resemblance to any of the Hebrew boys depicted elsewhere in the film, but *is* comparable to that of Joshua son of Nun, who is being whipped as a persistent troublemaker when Moses first encounters him. Malak may be a monster, but he seems to be presented as a sympathetic one who bears the scars of Israelite enslavement.

The focus of *Exodus* as a positive story of deliverance from bondage invites a humanizing "reading" of the otherwise monstrous agent of

---

75. Ng, *Monstrosity*, 5; Asma, *Monsters*, 8, 14; Wright, *Monstrosity*, 2–3.

76. Collins, "Divine," 35. As a flourishing contemporary trope at the box office (Renner, *Imagination*, 1), "evil kids" are the focus of several recent monographs: Lennard, *Villains*; Scahill, *Revolting Child*; Kord, *Horrors*.

77. Lancy, *Anthropology*, 13, 51.

78. From a Hebrew root meaning "to adhere," a *dybbuk* refers in Jewish lore to a disembodied soul that takes up residence in another body (Chajes, *Worlds*, 181).

79. Wright, *Monstrosity*, 3.

80. Lennard, *Villains*, 51.

that liberation. This is not to justify the means by which Malak achieves the Israelites' freedom—supernatural powers aside, the boy's actions that lead to the label "killer of children" qualify him as monstrous within the film and its ideological backdrop—but to acknowledge the victimization with which the boy is associated and the ambiguous moral terrain through which pursuits of freedom, justice or revenge are sometimes taken. In this light, Malak's violence may be seen as occupying what Colin Yeo refers to as a liminal space between good and evil,[81] overthrowing tyranny by whatever means one has.

The film's evocation of the Holocaust, particularly through the daily burning of the slaves' bodies, elicits comparison with those children in Nazi-occupied territories who took up armed resistance.[82] One cinematic example of this is Alex in *The Island on Bird Street* (1997). Hiding out in the bombed-out streets and buildings of the cleared Warsaw ghetto, the boy opens fire with a pistol on a German soldier and, with lethal force, stops him from executing two Jewish men found hiding in the rubble. Both Alex and Malak exercise "agency"[83] under harrowing circumstances, choosing to save life while at the same time taking it. Malak's hand is, according to the logic of the story, forced by Ramses' threat against the Hebrews' infants, just as Alex's hand is forced by the Nazi's intent to murder the boy's fellow Jews. In Malak's case, however, mitigation is limited given the boy's supernatural powers and, presumably, far greater range of alternative courses of action. If Malak's choice to respond in kind sounds all too human, perhaps it is because the human and the monster exist along a continuum instead of in binary opposition.

Malak's actions, however one evaluates the extent of their monstrousness, do result in the release of the Hebrew slaves and it is on this positive aspect of the boy's behavior I will conclude. When Malak lifts the cover of darkness during the penultimate plague on the Egyptians—an act that prefigures the Israelites' imminent freedom—he smiles. Journeying to Canaan, Moses peers outside his wagon to see the boy walking alongside and smiling. These frames juxtaposed narrate a theme of liberation. The first is desaturated, a technique used in this scene (and all of Malak's scenes prior

---

81. Yeo, "Monstrous Children," 97.

82. Heberer, *Holocaust*, 324–36; Rosen, *Soldiers*, 83–91.

83. James and James define "agency" as "the capacity of individuals to act independently" and the concept is an important one within the new social studies of childhood, which challenges the dominant construction of children as passive recipients of culture; children are instead seen as and encouraged to be active participants in society, playing a role in all its facets (James and James, *Key Concepts*, 3–6).

to the Hebrews' emancipation) to create a lifeless[84] or dreary[85] ambiance, whereas the second is saturated. The boy has visibly come (in)to life.

## IMAG(IN)ING THE OTHER(S) IN *EXODUS* AND BEYOND

The Exodus story, narrating the liberation of an oppressed people, has been appropriated by a number of contemporary marginalized groups. Exclusive identification with Israel, however, has the potential to close down avenues of interpretation and, at times, foster its own disregard for the Other. From a self-consciously skeptical standpoint, the *Exodus* filmmakers have adapted the biblical narrative for a mixed audience of religious and secular viewers, scripting all the primary characters and groups as occupying ambiguous moral territory. While this may be a deterrent to some viewers, it is an opportunity to adopt a viewing strategy Margaret Miles and Brent Plate call "hospitable vision," a practice of opening up a space for otherness to come into view.[86]

In this essay I have taken up Plate's invitation elsewhere to broaden the categories of otherness beyond race, class, gender and sexuality[87] to include age.[88] The dominant construction of childhood as a time of innocence, vulnerability and dependency is underpinned by the "immature" and "irrational" child, placing those so labeled outside or at the margins of the adult-dominated social-symbolic order.[89] Plate's dualistic term "imag(in)ing" refers first to aesthetics, how others *are* often in derogatory ways imaged in film, and second to ethics, how others *can be* critically, not fancifully, imagined.[90] While my particular "reading" and negotiation of the film has focused on how Malak is negatively imaged and how he might be more positively imagined, numerous others—Gershom, the women pushed to the margins of the story, the animals who are exposed to various forms of cruelty—are all worthy subjects of exploration through the lens of "hospitable vision."

As for Malak, he is not just *any* child, but a *divine* child. This brings his scripted hostile behavior into dialogue with contemporary discussions of

---

84. Phillips, *Film*, 66.
85. Pramaggiore and Wallis, *Film*, 120.
86. Miles and Plate, "Vision," 27–31.
87. Plate, "Introduction," 7.
88. Macnicol, *Discrimination*, 6.
89. Plate, "Introduction," 7.
90. Plate, "Introduction," 3.

religiously-motivated violence.[91] While religion is, for the most part, downplayed in *Exodus*, the Egyptian polytheists are ridiculed and the monotheistic Israelites indicted as fanatics, both within the story world and arguably from without. There are echoes in the film of present conflicts in the Middle East,[92] which are a growing concern, particularly in the post-9/11 world. Even though I am an agnostic, I do not position myself as Other to these debates, nor is violence a uniquely religious phenomenon.[93] With Berlinerblau, I see a need for secularists to engage *thoughtfully* with the religious and their sacred texts[94] (including films based on them), avoiding polarization[95] and working together *with* faith communities for peace.[96]

Filmic images have been used to promote hatred, intolerance and violence[97] and thus urgent and responsible engagement of their contents is needed. In a world rife with conflict and othering, *Exodus'* superficial engagement with the issues is disappointing at best, irresponsible at worst. While the filmmakers' source text and the Hebrew Bible generally offer a number of different voices and complex approaches to identity and the Other,[98] the film draws simple and essentially impervious boundaries between Egyptian and Israelite, with the latter's deity modeling disregard for the Other. While Malak may not be easily (re)imagined as an agent of peace, other cinematic children are, and they are joined by many children in contemporary conflict-ridden circumstances, who have their own aspirations for peace and stories to tell.[99]

---

91. Literature on the topic of religion and violence is voluminous and the following resources are not intended to be an exhaustive list: Schwartz, *Cain*; Ward, *Dangerous*; Steffen, *War*; Juergensmeyer, *Rebellion*; Selengut, *Fury*; Gluck, *Violence*; Teehan, *God*; Eisen, *Judaism*; Murphy, *Companion*; Juergensmeyer et al., *Handbook*; Clarke, *Justification*; Juergensmeyer, *Terror*.

92. Foundas, "Exodus."

93. The boundaries between secular and religious are porous (Göle, "Divide," 41–53) and secular ideologies can be just as prone to violence as those identified as religious (Cavanaugh, *Myth*).

94. Berlinerblau, *Bible*, 2.

95. Such as that found in the writings of those from the so-called "New Atheism" movement (Harris, *Faith*; Dawkins, *Delusion*; Dennett, *Spell*; Hitchens, *Great*), the emergence of which is surveyed in LeDrew, *Atheism*. Thoughtful responses to the "New Atheists" include Johnston, *God*; Reitan, *Delusion*; Amarasingam, *Religion*; Corlett, *Errors*; Markham, *Atheism*; French and Wettstein, *Critics*; Fry, *Rhetoric*.

96. Gopin, *Peacemaking*, 11.

97. Plate, "Introduction," 4.

98. Ben Zvi, "Othering," 20–40.

99. Lee-Koo, "Children," 185–211.

## BIBLIOGRAPHY

Alderson, Priscilla. *An Introduction to Critical Realism and Childhood Studies*. Vol. 1 of *Childhoods Real and Imagined*. New York: Routledge, 2013.

Aldgate, Jane. "Children, Development, and Ecology." In *The Developing World of the Child*, edited by Jane Aldgate, et al., 17–31. Philadelphia: Jessica Kingsley, 2006.

Amarasingam, Amarnath, ed. *Religion and the New Atheism: A Critical Appraisal*. Chicago: Haymarket.

Asma, Stephen T. *On Monsters: An Unnatural History of Our Worst Fears*. New York: Oxford University Press, 2009.

Balanzategui, Jessica. *The Uncanny Child in Transnational Cinema: Ghosts of Futurity at the Turn of the Twenty-First Century*. Amsterdam: Amsterdam University Press, 2018.

Barnes, Ashleigh. "CRC's Performance of the Child as Developing." In *Law and Childhood Studies*, edited by Michael Freeman, 392–418. Oxford: Oxford University Press, 2012.

Barsam, Richard, and Dave Monahan. *Looking at Movies: An Introduction to Film*. 4th ed. New York: Norton, 2013.

Ben Zvi, Ehud. "Othering, Selfing, 'Boundarying' and 'Cross-Boundarying' as Interwoven with Socially Shared Memories: Some Observations." In *Imagining the Other and Constructing Israelite Identity in the Early Second Temple Period*, edited by Ehud Ben Zvi and Diana V. Edelman, 20–40. New York: Bloomsbury, 2014.

Berardinelli, James. "Exodus: Gods and Kings." *Reel Views*, December 12, 2014. Online. http://www.reelviews.net/reelviews/exodus-gods-and-kings.

Berlinerblau, Jacques. *The Secular Bible: Why Nonbelievers Must Take Religion Seriously*. New York: Cambridge University Press, 2005.

Bohlmann, Markus P. J., and Sean Moreland, eds. *Monstrous Children and Childish Monsters: Essays on Cinema's Holy Terrors*. Jefferson, NC: McFarland, 2015.

Borkfelt, Sune. "Non-Human Otherness: Animals as Others and Devices for Othering." In *Otherness: A Multilateral Perspective*, edited by Susan Yi Sencindiver, et al., 137–54. Frankfurt am Main: Peter Lang, 2011.

Bowman, Vibiana, and Laura B. Spencer. "Toward a Definition of Children and Childhood Studies." In *Scholarly Resources for Children and Childhood Studies: A Research Guide and Annotated Bibliography*, edited by Vibiana Bowman, 3–16. Toronto: Scarecrow, 2007.

Cartwright, Lisa. *Moral Spectatorship: Technologies of Voice and Affect in Postwar Representations of the Child*. London: Durham University Press, 2008.

Castro, Ingrid E., and Jessica Clark, eds. *Representing Agency in Popular Culture: Children and Youth on Page, Screen, and In Between*. London: Lexington, 2019.

Cataldo, Jeremiah W. "The Other: Sociological Perspectives in a Postcolonial Age." In *Imagining the Other and Constructing Israelite Identity in the Early Second Temple Period*, edited by Ehud Ben Zvi and Diana V. Edelman, 1–19. New York: Bloomsbury, 2014.

Cavanaugh, William T. *The Myth of Religious Violence: Secular Ideology and the Roots of Modern Conflict*. New York: Oxford University Press, 2009.

Chajes, J. H. *Between Worlds: Dybbuks, Exorcists, and Early Modern Judaism*. Philadelphia: University of Pennsylvania Press, 2003.

Chang, Justin. "Film Review: 'Exodus: Gods and Kings.'" *Variety*, November 29, 2014. Online. http://variety.com/2014/film/reviews/film-review-exodus-gods-and-kings-1201364857.

Clarke, Steve. *The Justification of Religious Violence*. Oxford: Wiley-Blackwell, 2014.

Collin, Robbie. "Exodus: Gods and Kings, Review: 'Bold and Uncompromising.'" *The Telegraph*, December 26, 2014. Online. http://www.telegraph.co.uk/culture/film/filmreviews/11260170/Exodus-Gods-and-Kings-review-bold-and-uncompromising.html.

Collins, Matthew A. "Depicting the Divine: The Ambiguity of Exodus 3 in Exodus: Gods and Kings." In *A New Hollywood Moses: On the Spectacle and Reception of Exodus: Gods and Kings*, edited by David Tollerton, 9–39. London: Bloomsbury T&T Clark, 2017.

Corlett, J. Angelo. *The Errors of Atheism*. New York: Continuum, 2010.

Davis, David Brion. *The Problem of Slavery in the Age of Emancipation*. New York: Alfred A. Knopf, 2014.

Dawkins, Richard. *The God Delusion*. New York: Mariner, 2006.

Dennett, Daniel C. *Breaking the Spell: Religion as a Natural Phenomenon*. New York: Penguin, 2006.

Dever, William G. *Who Were the Early Israelites and Where Did They Come From?* Grand Rapids: Eerdmans, 2003.

Dix, Andrew. *Beginning Film Studies*. New York: Manchester University Press, 2008.

Donald, Stephanie Hemelryk. *There's No Place Like Home: The Migrant Child in World Cinema*. London: IB Tauris, 2018.

Donald, Stephanie Hemelryk, et al., eds. *Childhood and Nation in Contemporary World Cinema: Borders and Encounters*. London: Bloomsbury Academic, 2017.

Dozeman, Thomas P. *Exodus*. Grand Rapids; Cambridge: Eerdmans, 2009.

Edwards, Katie. "Exodus: The Tantastic Gods and Kings Epic is Suspect But Well Worth a Watch." *Conversation*, December 24, 2014. Online. https://theconversation.com/exodus-the-tantastic-gods-and-kings-epic-is-suspect-but-well-worth-a-watch-35795.

Eisen, Robert. *The Peace and Violence of Judaism: From the Bible to Modern Zionism*. New York: Oxford University Press, 2011.

Eslinger, Lyle. "Freedom or Knowledge? Perspective and Purpose in the Exodus Narrative (Exodus 1–15)." *Journal for the Study of the Old Testament* 52 (1991) 43–60.

*Exodus: Gods and Kings*. Directed by Ridley Scott. DVD. Beverly Hills, CA: Twentieth Century Fox Home Entertainment, 2015.

Faulkner, Joanne. *The Importance of Being Innocent: Why We Worry About Children*. New York: Cambridge University Press, 2011.

Ford, William A. *God, Pharaoh, and Moses: Explaining the Lord's Actions in the Exodus Plagues Narrative*. Waynesboro: Paternoster, 2006.

Foundas, Scott. "'Exodus: Gods and Kings': Director Ridley Scott on Creating His Vision of Moses." *Variety*, November 25, 2014. Online. http://variety.com/2014/film/news/ridley-scott-exodus-gods-and-kings-christian-bale-1201363668.

French, Peter A., and Howard K. Wettstein, eds. *The New Atheism and Its Critics*. Boston: Wiley Periodicals, 2013.

Fry, Karin. *Beyond Religious Right and Secular Left Rhetoric: The Road to Compromise*. New York: Palgrave Macmillan, 2014.

Gluck, Andrew L. *Religion, Fundamentalism, and Violence: An Interdisciplinary Dialogue*. Scranton, PA: University of Scranton Press, 2010.

Golding, William. *The Hot Gates and Other Occasional Pieces*. New York: Harcourt, Brace & World, 1966.

———. *Lord of the Flies*. London; Boston: Faber and Faber, 1954.

———. "Lord of the Flies as Fable." In *Readings on Lord of the Flies*, edited by Clarice Swisher, 40–46. San Diego: Greenhaven, 1997.

Göle, Nilüfer. "Manifestations of the Religious-Secular Divide: Self, State, and the Public Sphere." In *Comparative Secularisms in a Global Age*, edited by Linell E. Cady and Elizabeth Shakman Hurd, 41–55. New York: Palgrave Macmillan, 2010.

Gopin, Marc. *Between Eden and Armageddon: The Future of World Religions, Violence, and Peacemaking*. New York: Oxford University Press, 2000.

Grad, Héctor, and Luisa Martín Rojo. "Identities in Discourse: An Integrative View." In *Analysing Identities in Discourse*, edited by Rosana Dolón and Júlia Todolí, 3–29. Philadelphia: John Benjamins, 2008.

Greifenhagen, F. V. *Egypt on the Pentateuch's Ideological Map: Constructing Biblical Israel's Identity*. New York: Sheffield Academic, 2002.

Haslam, Nick. "What *Is* Dehumanization?" In *Humanness and Dehumanization*, edited by Paul G. Bain, et al., 34–48. New York: Routledge, 2014.

Harris, Sam. *The End of Faith: Religion, Terror, and the Future of Reason*. New York: Norton, 2004.

Heberer, Patricia. *Children During the Holocaust*. Plymouth, MA: AltaMira, 2011.

Hitchens, Christopher. *God Is Not Great: How Religion Poisons Everything*. Toronto: McClelland & Stewart, 2007.

Hogan, Erin K. *The Two Cines Con Niño: Genre and the Child Protagonist in over Fifty Years of Spanish Film (1955–2010)*. Edinburgh: Edinburgh University Press, 2018.

Hubert, Jane. "Introduction: The Complexity of Boundedness and Exclusion." In *Madness, Disability, and Social Exclusion: The Archaeology and Anthropology of "Difference,"* edited by Jane Hubert, 1–8. New York: Routledge, 2000.

*The Island on Bird Street*. Directed by Søren Kragh-Jacobsen. DVD. Los Angeles, CA: First Look Home Entertainment, 2008.

Jackson, Kathy Merlock. *Images of Children in American Film: A Sociocultural Analysis*. Metuchen, NJ: Scarecrow, 1986.

James, Allison, and Adrian James. *Key Concepts in Childhood Studies*. 2nd ed. Thousand Oaks, CA: Sage, 2012.

Jenks, Chris. *Childhood*. 2nd ed. New York: Routledge, 2005.

Johnston, Mark. *Saving God: Religion after Idolatry*. Princeton: Princeton University Press, 2009.

Jones, Phil. *Rethinking Childhood: Attitudes in Contemporary Society*. New York: Continuum, 2009.

Juergensmeyer, Mark. *Global Rebellion: Religious Challenges to the Secular State, from Christian Militias to al Qaeda*. Berkeley, CA: University of California Press, 2008.

———. *Terror in the Mind of God: The Global Rise of Religious Violence*. 4th ed. Berkeley, CA: University of California Press, 2017.

Juergensmeyer, Mark, et al., eds. *The Oxford Handbook of Religion and Violence*. New York: Oxford University Press, 2013.

Kapur, Jyotsna. *Coining for Capital: Movies, Marketing, and the Transformation of Childhood*. London: Rutgers University Press, 2005.

Kearney, Richard. *Strangers, Gods, and Monsters: Interpreting Otherness*. London and New York: Routledge, 2003.
Kenny, Anthony. "Agnosticism and Atheism." In *Philosophers and God: At the Frontiers of Faith and Reason*, edited by John Cornwell and Michael McGhee, 117–24. New York: Continuum, 2009.
King, Philip J., and Lawrence E. Stager. *Life in Biblical Israel*. Louisville, KY: Westminster John Knox, 2001.
Kord, T. S. *Little Horrors: How Cinema's Evil Children Play on Our Guilt*. Jefferson, NC: McFarland, 2016.
Lacey, Liam. "Exodus: Gods and Kings—A Clumsy Retreat into Biblical History." *Globe and Mail*, December 12, 2014. Online. http://www.theglobeandmail.com/arts/film/film-reviews/exodus-gods-and-kings—-a-clumsy-retreat-into-biblical-history/article22047863.
Laird, Jay. "Dice." In *Encyclopedia of Play in Today's Society*, edited by Rodney P. Carlisle, 171–73. Thousand Oaks, CA: Sage, 2009.
Lancy, David F. *The Anthropology of Childhood: Cherubs, Chattel, Changelings*. 2nd ed. Cambridge: Cambridge University Press, 2015.
Le Poidevin, Robin. *Agnosticism: A Very Short Introduction*. New York: Oxford University Press, 2010.
Lebeau, Vicky. *Childhood and Cinema*. London: Reaktion, 2008.
LeDrew, Stephen. *The Evolution of Atheism: The Politics of a Modern Movement*. New York: Oxford University Press, 2016.
Lee, Nick. *Childhood and Society: Growing Up in an Age of Uncertainty*. Philadelphia: Open University Press, 2001.
Lee-Koo, Katrina. "Children and Peace Building: Propagating Peace." In *Children and Global Conflict*, by Kim Huynh, et al., 185–210. Cambridge: Cambridge University Press, 2015.
Leirvik, Oddbjørn. *Interreligious Studies: A Relational Approach to Religious Activism and the Study of Religion*. New York: Bloomsbury, 2014.
Lemire, Christy. "Exodus: Gods and Kings." *RogerEbert.com*, December 11, 2014. Online. http://www.rogerebert.com/reviews/exodus-gods-and-kings-2014.
Lemmelijn, Bénédicte. *A Plague of Texts? A Text-Critical Study of the So-Called "Plagues Narrative" in Exodus 7:14–11:10*. Boston: Brill, 2009.
Lennard, Dominic. *Bad Seeds and Holy Terrors: The Child Villains of Horror Film*. Albany: State University of New York Press, 2014.
Low, Brian J. *NFB Kids: Portrayals of Children by the National Film Board of Canada, 1939–89*. Waterloo: Wilfred Laurier University Press, 2002.
Lury, Karen. *The Child in Film: Tears, Fears, and Fairytales*. New Brunswick, NJ: Rutgers University Press, 2010.
Macnicol, John. *Age Discrimination: An Historical and Contemporary Analysis*. Cambridge: Cambridge University Press, 2006.
Magee, James. "Cinematic Childhood(s) and Imag(in)ing the Boy Jesus: Adaptations of Luke 2:41–52 in Late Twentieth-Century Film." MA thesis, Trinity Western University, 2019. Online. https://twu.arcabc.ca/islandora/object/twu%3A523.
Markham, Ian S. *Against Atheism: Why Dawkins, Hitchens, and Harris Are Fundamentally Wrong*. Oxford: Wiley-Blackwell, 2010.
Martin, Deborah. *The Child in Contemporary Latin American Cinema*. New York: Palgrave Macmillan, 2019.

Masters, Kim. "'Exodus': How Ridley Scott Chose His 11-Year-Old Voice of God." *The Hollywood Reporter*, November 12, 2014. Online. http://www.hollywoodreporter.com/news/exodus-how-ridley-scott-chose-748373.

Mayall, Berry. *A History of the Sociology of Childhood*. London: Institute of Education Press, 2013.

McCallum, Robyn. *Screen Adaptations and the Politics of Childhood: Transforming Children's Literature into Film*. London: Palgrave Macmillan, 2018.

Merry, Stephanie. "'Exodus: Gods and Kings' Movie Review: Source Material One of Many Sore Spots for Ridley Scott." *Washington Post*, December 11, 2014. Online. https://www.washingtonpost.com/goingoutguide/movies/exodus-gods-and-kings-movie-review-source-material-one-of-many-sore-spots-for-ridley-scott/2014/12/11/f933084e-7ca6-11e4-9a27-6fdbc612bff8_story.html.

Meyers, Carol. *Exodus*. New York: Cambridge University Press, 2005.

Miles, Margaret R., and S. Brent Plate. "Hospitable Vision: Some Notes on the Ethics of Seeing Film." *Cross Currents* 54 (2004) 22–31.

Mohan, Marc. "'Exodus: Gods and Kings' Review: Ridley Scott's Wannabe Bible Epic is a Miscast Mess with Christian Bale as a Macho Moses." *Oregonian*, December 11, 2014. Online. http://www.oregonlive.com/movies/index.ssf/2014/12/exodus_gods_and_kings_review_r.html#incart_river.

Montgomery, Heather. *An Introduction to Childhood: Anthropological Perspectives on Children's Lives*. Oxford: Wiley-Blackwell, 2009.

Moore, Roger. "Movie Review: Exodus: Gods and Kings." *Movie Nation*, December 9, 2014. Online. http://rogersmovienation.com/2014/12/09/movie-review-exodus-gods-and-kings.

Murphy, Andrew R., ed. *The Blackwell Companion to Religion and Violence*. Oxford: Wiley-Blackwell, 2011.

Musgrave, Andrew. *Children in Films*. Lightship Guides, 2013.

Ng, Andrew Hock-Soon. *Dimensions of Monstrosity in Contemporary Narratives: Theory, Psychoanalysis, Postmodernism*. New York: Palgrave Macmillan, 2004.

Olson, Debbie C. *Black Children in Hollywood Cinema: Cast in Shadow*. Cham: Palgrave Macmillan, 2017.

———, ed. *The Child in Post-Apocalyptic Cinema*. Lanham, MD: Lexington, 2015.

———, ed. *The Child in World Cinema*. Lanham, MD: Lexington, 2018.

———, ed. *Children in the Films of Alfred Hitchcock*. New York: Palgrave Macmillan, 2014.

Olson, Debbie C., and Andrew Scahill, eds. *Lost and Othered Children in Contemporary Cinema*. Plymouth, MA: Lexington, 2014.

Peck, William H. *The Material World of Ancient Egypt*. New York: Cambridge University Press, 2013.

Phillips, Patrick. "Spectator, Audience, and Response." In *Introduction to Film Studies*, edited by Jill Nelmes, 91–128. 5th ed. New York: Routledge, 2012.

Phillips, William H. *Film: An Introduction*. 4th ed. New York: Bedford; St. Martin's, 2009.

Phipps, Keith. "Exodus: Gods and Kings." *Dissolve*, December 11, 2014. Online. http://thedissolve.com/reviews/1268-exodus-gods-and-kings.

Pinch, Geraldine. *Egyptian Mythology: A Guide to the Gods, Goddesses, and Traditions of Ancient Egypt*. New York: Oxford University Press, 2002.

Plate, S. Brent. "Introduction: Images and Imaginings." In *Imag(in)ing Otherness: Filmic Visions of Living Together*, edited by S. Brent Plate, 3–15. Atlanta: Scholars, 1999.

Pomerance, Murray, and Frances Gateward, eds. *Where the Boys Are: Cinemas of Masculinity and Youth*. Detroit: Wayne State University Press, 2005.

Pramaggiore, Maria, and Tom Wallis. *Film: A Critical Introduction*. 3rd ed. London: Laurence King, 2011.

Propp, William H. C. *Exodus 1–18: A New Translation with Introduction and Commentary*. New York: Doubleday, 1999.

Prout, Alan. *The Future of Childhood: Towards the Interdisciplinary Study of Children*. New York: RoutledgeFalmer, 2005.

Randall, Rachel. *Children on the Threshold in Contemporary Latin American Cinema: Nature, Gender, and Agency*. Lanham, MD: Lexington, 2017.

Rea, Steven. "'Exodus: Gods and Kings': God as a Bratty Kid." *Philadelphia Inquirer*, December 13, 2014. Online. http://articles.philly.com/2014-12-13/entertainment/56993712_1_gods-and-kings-ridley-scott-ramses.

Reinhartz, Adele. *Bible and Cinema: An Introduction*. New York: Routledge, 2013.

Reitan, Eric. *Is God a Delusion? A Reply to Religion's Cultured Despisers*. Oxford: Wiley-Blackwell, 2009.

Renner, Karen J. *Evil Children in the Popular Imagination*. New York: Palgrave Macmillan, 2016.

Richardson, Michael. *Otherness in Hollywood Cinema*. New York: Continuum, 2010.

Rocha, Carolina, and Georgia Seminet, eds. *Screening Minors in Latin American Cinema*. Lanham, MD: Lexington, 2014.

Rosen, David M. *Child Soldiers in the Western Imagination: From Patriots to Victims*. New Brunswick, NJ: Rutgers University Press, 2015.

Scahill, Andrew. *The Revolting Child in Horror Cinema: Youth Rebellion and Queer Spectatorship*. New York: Palgrave Macmillan, 2015.

Schober, Adrian. *Possessed Child Narratives in Literature and Film: Contrary States*. New York: Palgrave Macmillan, 2004.

Schober, Adrian, and Debbie Olson, eds. *Children in the Films of Steven Spielberg*. Lanham, MD: Lexington, 2016.

Schwartz, Regina M. *The Curse of Cain: The Violent Legacy of Monotheism*. Chicago: University of Chicago Press, 1997.

Scott, A. O. "'Exodus: Gods and Kings': Ridley Scott's Biblical Drama." *New York Times*, December 11, 2014. Online. http://www.nytimes.com/2014/12/12/movies/exodus-gods-and-kings-ridley-scotts-biblical-drama.html.

Scott, Ridley, and Jeffrey Caine. "Audio Commentary." *Exodus: Gods and Kings*. DVD. Beverly Hills, CA: Twentieth Century Fox Home Entertainment, 2015.

Selengut, Charles. *Sacred Fury: Understanding Religious Violence*. 2nd ed. Lanham, MD: Rowman & Littlefield, 2008.

Sikov, Ed. *Film Studies: An Introduction*. New York: Columbia University Press, 2010.

Sinyard, Neil. *Children in the Movies*. New York: St. Martin's, 1992.

Smith, Jonathan Z. "Differential Equations: On Constructing the Other." In *Relating Religion: Essays in the Study of Religion*, by Jonathan Z. Smith, 230–50. Chicago: University of Chicago Press, 2004.

Smith, Mark S. *The Early History of God: Yahweh and the Other Deities in Ancient Israel*. 2nd ed. Grand Rapids: Eerdmans, 2002.

Speidel, Suzanne. "Film Form and Narrative." In *Introduction to Film Studies*, edited by Jill Nelmes, 79–112. 5th ed. New York: Routledge, 2012.

Stainton Rogers, Rex, and Wendy Stainton Rogers. *Stories of Childhood: Shifting Agendas of Child Concern*. London: Harvester Wheatsheaf, 1992.

Stainton Rogers, Wendy. "What is a Child?" In *Understanding Childhood: An Interdisciplinary Approach*, edited by Martin Woodhead and Heather Montgomery, 37–53. Chichester: John Wiley & Sons, 2003.

Steffen, Lloyd. *Holy War, Just War: Exploring the Moral Meaning of Religious Violence*. Plymouth, UK: Rowman & Littlefield, 2007.

Szpakowska, Kasia. *Daily Life in Ancient Egypt: Recreating Lahun*. Oxford: Blackwell, 2008.

Teehan, John. *In the Name of God: The Evolutionary Origins of Religious Ethics and Violence*. Oxford: Wiley-Blackwell, 2010.

*The Unborn*. Directed by David S. Goyer. DVD. Universal City, CA: Universal Studios Home Entertainment, 2009.

Utzschneider, Helmut, and Wolfgang Oswald. *Exodus 1–15*. Translated by Philip Sumpter. Stuttgart: Verlag W. Kohlhammer, 2015.

Verstraten, Peter. *Film Narratology*. Translated by Stefan van der Lecq. Toronto: University of Toronto Press, 2009.

Vishnevetsky, Ignatiy. "Christian Bale Leads a Slog Through the Old Testament in Ridley Scott's *Exodus*." *A. V. Club*, December 11, 2014. Online. www.avclub.com/review/christian-bale-leads-slog-through-old-testament-ri-212694.

Walsh, Richard. "'What Child Is This?': Reflections on the Child Deity and Generic Lineage of *Exodus: Gods and Kings*." In *T&T Clark Companion to the Bible and Film*, edited by Richard Walsh, 311–21. London: T&T Clark, 2018.

Ward, Keith. *Is Religion Dangerous?* Cambridge: Eerdmans, 2006.

Watson, Paul. "Cinematic Authorship and the Film Auteur." In *Introduction to Film Studies*, edited by Jill Nelmes, 142–65. 5th ed. New York: Routledge, 2012.

*Whisper*. Directed by Stewart Hendler. DVD. Universal City, CA: Universal Studios Home Entertainment, 2007.

Willis, Lawrence M. *Not God's People: Insiders and Outsiders in the Biblical World*. Plymouth, UK: Rowman & Littlefield, 2008.

Wilson, Emma. *Cinema's Missing Children*. New York: Wallflower, 2003.

Wojcik-Andrews, Ian. *Children's Films: History, Ideology, Pedagogy, Theory*. New York: Garland, 2000.

Woodhead, Martin. "Child Development and the Development of Childhood." In *The Palgrave Handbook of Childhood Studies*, edited by Jens Qvortrup, et al., 46–61. Basingstoke: Palgrave Macmillan, 2009.

Wright, Alexa. *Monstrosity: The Human Monster in Visual Culture*. New York: IB Tauris, 2013.

Wright, Sarah. *The Child in Spanish Cinema*. New York: Manchester University Press, 2013.

Wyness, Michael. *Childhood and Society*. 2nd ed. Basingstoke: Palgrave Macmillan, 2012.

Yeo, Colin. "Doesn't Everyone Want their Parents Dead? Monstrous Children in the Films of Ridley Scott." In *Monstrous Children and Childish Monsters: Essays on Cinema's Holy Terrors*, edited by Markus P. J. Bohlmann and Sean Moreland, 96–106. Jefferson, NC: McFarland, 2015.

# *II.*

# THEOLOGY AND PRACTICE OF ENCOUNTER

# 9

# Encountering the Other
## Positive Lessons from Contemporary Science

### Marc Gopin

SEEKING THE STRANGER—THE OTHER in this world—and coming to know the other, entails a confrontation with our most fundamental understanding of what we know and how we know it. I have been fascinated all my life with the struggle between evidence for empiricism and positive science, versus the evidence for a world that is entirely of our own making, of our own conjuring.

Positive science and empiricism present us with persuasive evidence of an objective universe in which we explore and discover "truths" together. But as we experience relationships and then struggle to communicate about them, it seems that people often live in different universes of their own conjuring. We seem to construct reality with as much difference as conceivable. How is it that Spinoza, Nietzsche, Dostoevsky, Tolstoy, Gandhi, and the Dalai Lama live in and describe the same universe, when what they *see* in human nature and human potential is so diametrically opposed? Read their writings in detail, get into what they see, and then tell me they live in the same universe! Their approach to the "other" is as different as galaxies separated by millions of light years. How can this be? What does it say about reality, and the capacity to know the "other"?

The truth is somewhere in between empiricism and postmodern/idealist constructs of reality. Our sense of objective reality is sufficiently reliable that millions of people build planes and skyscrapers together, and they do not all come crashing down. At the same time, our massive differences on moral values and moral conclusions, and our very limited ability to even describe the same events under ethical or political debate, suggests that we do create much of what we see. We each build social reality to some important degree, and conflicting groups always build completely opposed visions of reality.

This paradoxical reality about the nature of knowing has had a challenging impact on the history of human ethical debates, and specifically the history of debates regarding human violence, conflict, and peacemaking. Let me relate this to my most recent research and writing project. I have immersed myself in social psychological, sociobiological, and neuroscientific analysis of what constitutes the ethical state of mind and the ethical gesture. I did this in order to better comprehend nineteenth-century attempts to understand moral feelings. Specifically, I wrote my most recent book, *Compassionate Judaism* on Samuel David Luzzatto (1800–1865, Italy).[1] In it, I traced Luzzatto's effort to understand ethics and moral sense theory, and to articulate and defend a Judaism of compassion. One aspect of his search for the truth of Judaism, and the truth of Divinely created nature itself, was to take very seriously his own autobiography, his own human nature. So much so that he wrote three autobiographies. This was not uncommon in the modern era of philosophical quests for understanding humanity. Following Rousseau, Luzzatto took his own psyche as a key place to begin to ask fundamental questions about what we as humans see; what we feel; and how, when and why we act ethically.

For Luzzatto, the inner life became a clue into and a window onto the world, because in the end we often only have what is going on inside of us to understand the nature of reality, especially ethical reality. Ultimately a religious thinker like Luzzatto joined those autobiographical insights with a very pious commitment to and particular interpretation of sacred texts of Judaism. The basic question for so many of these thinkers was, "Who am I in relationship to the other? In my encounter with the other?" "In discovering myself in relation to others, I will discover myself," they thought, "and in discovering myself and the other, I will also discover the right and the true."

Let's return to the contemporary period, and to scientific investigation of reality for a moment. Although the inner life and the encounter with the other is a vital window onto the nature of ethics, we cannot forget positive

1. Gopin, *Compassionate Judaism*.

science and its indispensable lessons. Much of what I rely on for the positive science of the human encounter, and the cutting edge of psychological research into violence, peace, and the core of human ethics, comes from a large volume of data gathered by Steven Pinker.[2] There are extensive empiricist investigations of the history of violence and nonviolence. Specifically, there has been an unprecedented historic drop in the number and frequency of wars in the last fifty years, despite the fact that the technology of mass murder and the immediacy of instant news make us feel otherwise. There has been a dramatic drop in wars and domestic murder rates, and in fact this is a trend for five hundred years but especially the last hundred years, certainly in Western Europe. And this is in spite of the mass deaths of the world wars. There has been a complete plummeting of state-based torture as punishment for minor or major crimes that used to be commonplace. There were lynchings just a few decades ago in the United States for looking at a woman in a way that a white observer or mob did not like. Torturous death for stealing a piece of bread was commonplace in various parts of Europe, and not many centuries ago being either Protestant or Catholic was a literal death sentence, in much the same way that we see in parts of the Muslim world today regarding Sunni and Shia divisions. There is nothing that ISIS has done that did not used to be commonplace in the United States toward Native Americans or African Americans. Much more recently, New York City used to be a far more dangerous and deadly place when I went to school in the 1970s, and yet the voters today are willing to allow the police far more abuses because they *think* it is more dangerous than ever. The facts are actually the opposite. The fear of increasing violence skews many of our moral decisions.

That less violence is a profound change is a given historical fact. But it is also a fact that we do not *feel* this to be the case, because our view of the world is through a constructed lens. It is the same with many crimes. For example, many crimes against women that used to be commonplace and acceptable to men were then outlawed in the last hundred years. But then the perceptual and emotive shock and dismay comes when it is clear that vast numbers of men continue to commit these crimes in private, when they can get away with it. History is moving in a definite direction toward fewer crimes against women, but it often feels to us as if those crimes are worse than they used to be. In reality, it is our perception of thinking a crime is gone because we made a law; followed by shock that it is not; and then terror at its persistent reality. It is good news that we are vigilant and outraged about persistent ethical and legal crimes. However,

---

2. Pinker, *Better Angels of Our Nature*.

a lack of balance in understanding where things are going often makes for bad strategic decisions.

History moves far slower toward nonviolence than our sense of fear and need for safety demand, but it does move. Infanticide of girls used to be a commonplace of India, widespread to the point that millions seem missing from the census.[3] The paradox of modernity is that prenatal care designed to protect and empower women has led to an abuse of the technology to abort the girls. But the trend toward exposure of these barbaric choices is clear. There are mass demonstrations now when a woman is brutally killed, demonstrations that are comprised of many men and women. This suggests that there is a conscious shift and trend in Indian society toward the suppression of violence against women both legally and socially, and this seems like a permanent trend.[4]

It is not just instant bad news or manipulated Facebook pages by hostile regimes that make us fear each other today. It is millions of years of programming of the mind to look for what to be afraid of, to be in a heightened state of alert, in other words, to do the opposite of research and rational planning. The amygdala portion of the brain has been designed for fight and flight for millions of years.

This is our challenge when it comes to how to engage the other in loving ways when our minds suffer from so many distortions of viewpoint, from fear and dread that seem hard-wired. My own field of conflict analysis and resolution has made tremendous advances on shifting people in violence and conflict away from adversarial positions and attacks, and instead toward mental and interactive concentration on common problems to be solved, for example. We have also done a good job of teaching how to lessen violence as we point out the system's foundation of conflict and violence, and how structures of violence and injustice cut across lines of analysis, from individuals and families to nations. We have explored many contributors to violence, such as relative deprivation and structural injustice.

Here is the challenge from my own critical point of view, however. Much of the field was formulated by a generation of scholars and social critics reeling from the after-effects of two world wars and the constant shadow of nuclear war—the technical capacity of omnicide. This reality foisted many men into depression, and into a somewhat desperate search for what is wrong with us humans as a species, perhaps epitomized by the books of Arthur Koestler, and the reflections on this of Martin Seligman.

---

3. "Where Are India's Millions of Missing Girls?"
4. Biswas, "Protests in India."

The problem is that Seligman pointed out that the lens of depression, of looking for problems, of fixating on those problems, is actually a skewed view of reality.[5] The dark challenges are a part of reality but nowhere near all of reality, so that this has distorted our analysis, distorted therefore our vision of what is real and what is possible.

We are understanding on many scientific levels that we create and distort reality. The empirical reality of uncertainty in quantum physics at the subatomic level of particles and waves, even though 99 percent of us do not understand it very well, has created a new dynamism to looking at reality from multiple perspectives. Pioneering researchers and philosophers of the human condition, from E. O. Wilson, Martin Seligman and Steven Pinker, to Elise Boulding and the Dalai Lama, are coming to an important consensus which is essentially this: we must begin to look anew at *what is right about us humans, not always what is wrong with us*; less on a dark past, more on a promising future; less on the negative, and more on the positive. Whole new schools of positive psychology, appreciative inquiry, rooted in cognitive psychology and therapy, have emphasized the centrality of how we ourselves form our minds. They have concluded that it is possible to regularly check our mental lens, and make sure we are not falling back into a primordial habit of searching nervously and exclusively for what we must fear or loathe or rage against.

Light is a wave or particle depending on the way you look at it, and it is both. This is *reality* at the subatomic level. We are internalizing the reality that things change *when* you look at them, and how you look changes everything. Thus, in a very real sense we construct reality in some aspects.

It also turns out that at the neuroscientific level we are plastic, that with every thought we are creating or reinforcing neural pathways and biochemical reactions. We are constructing our minds. With every prayer, meditation, loving intention (but also hateful thought), we create or strengthen new neural pathways that are real and concrete. This is the essence of neuroplasticity and its new discoveries. The more we follow these new neural pathways the more real they become, and thus, we are very plastic in our entire cognition. But here is the thing, we can eventually harden and make ourselves into many alloys of steel, e.g., the steel of racism, the steel of paranoia, or by contrast, the steel of absolute love. It all depends on what we think, what we repeatedly think, and what we regularly do based on those repetitive thoughts.

When I tell a story and it surprises you, delights you, makes you laugh, and makes you cry, it literally lights up all quadrants of your brain,

---

5. Seligman, "New Era of Positive Psychology."

according to the functional Magnetic Resonance Imaging (fMRIs). I change your reality when I surprise your mind. Here is another tough reality: I can addict you to that. God help us and save us from demagogues in power, or aspiring to it, who know this well. But thank God for the saints who know it as well, and give us so much inspiration with their repeated surprising actions and delightful words.

It is what you do that defines you, and perhaps it is repeated thoughts that move you to those deeds. What you think, however, is free and fluid, or more plastic. I have come to believe therefore that the art of wonder that is the human mind is one aspect of Divine Revelation that is miraculous, an ongoing epiphenomenon of the universe thinking upon itself. I keep my ancient behaviors and practices, such as Sabbath, and then I roam with my mind. That roaming has led to creative interactions between ancient texts and sayings, such as on angels, and contemporary brilliant rules of the universe, such as $E=mc^2$, that energy and mass are interchangeable—the same really. What looks like energy is mass in another guise, and vice versa. This science seems to me, coming out of my religious tradition, like an exploration of an angelic universe dancing before our human mind, a mind that reflects in its essence all that is before us across the universe, and all the poetry and majesty of a fluid universe of mass and energy as angels of the Divine Universe.

That our minds have so much power to create also creates great moral responsibility. What we say and what we emphasize makes a difference. When we focus on and talk about sickness and evil, we get sickness and evil. But if we dream great dreams, we create the skills and the collaboration necessary to revolutionize history. As Martin Seligman noted in his TED talk, there is so much good that has been accomplished by decades of research on depression that it is now considered a curable disease. But there is a need now to focus our collective minds less on depression and more on optimism, resilience, hope, and the science of creating cognitive structures that help us not only heal but even flourish.

This perspective is still missing in peacemaking and conflict resolution. Most people in the field are responding negatively to the outrages of injustice, war crimes, and violations of human rights and dignity. But the key moving forward is building mental constructs that make us meet the other, in love. If we wish to conquer the terrible crimes of war, we need to overwhelm many situations with new habits of thought and deed practiced at every moment, habits that strengthen the power of love, compassion, and eagerness to meet and care for the strange or estranged other.

We need to work on how our minds can make us fall in love with the world—every hour of every day that we practice peace. We must go from an exclusive focus on danger and violence to the kind of mentality that seeks what is the reality of *nonviolence* every day. Of course, we must remain vigilant to danger from criminals in and out of government. That is natural and necessary, but we must shift ourselves back to a fuller picture of reality if we truly want to eliminate war. Where is the breaking news globally, the news flash of nonviolence? Where is the big news of breakthroughs in love and care? Today, for example, "News flash! At this moment, an overwhelming majority of the billions of parents globally continued today, as every day, to sacrifice for the children they love." But instead we read about the tiniest fraction of the tiniest fraction of parents who tortured a child—with pictures. Which is the delusion, the nonviolence story, or the torture story? Which is true when we try to see with Divine-like eyes all of reality?

Problem solving in our field has also been too past-focused. What's wrong out there, what has been wrong in my history or your history, what were the outrages? This fixation on the past pushes the brilliant neocortex to get locked up, because the neocortex can only investigate what our will tells it to investigate, what our minds tell it to actually see.

Real change in ourselves and in the world is not past-oriented, it is future oriented. The neocortex, our higher reasoning, loves it when we wonder, when we ask future questions, "what is to be done?" questions. Then it goes to work on building new realities, on the future as long as we focus the brain on the future. But when the neocortex hears endless Facebook laments—"What is wrong with us?"; "How did this happen to us?"; "Why can't we be kind the way we used to be?"—then the neocortex has nothing productive to do in terms of peace, or discovery of the other. It just becomes a slave to research on how many of us have died horrible deaths, for example. It just becomes a slave working for bad feelings, for empathy with victims, for despair, for longing for imaginary pasts, for withdrawal from humanity. In other words, it becomes a slave for the fight/flight habits of the amygdala. But, if we push our thoughts and our habits toward the present and the future, if we push ourselves to think and imagine a better reality, the neocortex can come alive with ingenious discoveries.

When, for example, much of humanity recently has been convinced that fossil fuels are killing life on earth, and that to survive we must replace them, there has been an explosion of inventions, an acceleration of deep and extraordinary genius that is being directed toward life sustainability, because of hope for the future. Tens of thousands of scientists, entrepreneurs and simple do-gooders around the world are inventing new ways to fuel our lives every day, completely unlike the thousands of scientists who banded together with understandable fear to create weapons of mass destruction just a generation ago. Of course, there are many still creating dangerous weapons and toxins everywhere. Essentially, we create our nightmares, but we also create our dreams. The key is to embrace our capacity to do this, as we seek out love and care of the other.

When you are in a refugee camp as I have been in desperate circumstances, you have a choice. You can see only the negative, and there is so much of it. You can lament, you can feel the pain of a thousand people, as I did once, and it can rip your heart to shreds. It still hurts so deeply to my core. But you can also look around that camp, you can fall in love with the humanity of this person, and that person, and that person. And you can say to yourself, tears in your eyes, "This is what I am going to do, for the rest of my life: to care for others who need me, no matter who. This is what I will do, this is what I will teach, this is who I will be." Then your neocortex comes alive, it goes to work, scheming, planning, researching, making connections across all your neurons and synapses, and your heart and soul fire up as if you are an immortal. You are engaged deeply with the other, and they and you are in an unshakeable bond that gives you life and purpose that no death can conquer.

We have been plagued for too long by the results of the Stanley Milgram experiments; we know now very well that we are all capable of following orders to become fascists and killers; and it makes us moderns sick, withdrawn, and in despair.[6] We know what crime an officer can order us to do, and remarkably we will do it. But what if we imagine an experiment in which we discover what happens when a scientific experiment tells us to love a stranger, to hug a stranger, to cry with an unhappy person, to have joy with a joyous person? How will we do? What will the experiment yield? And why do we not even know the answer to this? Why has the opposite of the Stanley Milgram experiment never been tried? Because we are shell-shocked by fear, enslaved to the amygdala, because we have not yet imagined the good we can unleash in the human mind when we truly train ourselves for vision, for the future, for love over hate.

There is also some exciting new research that may revolutionize our lives. New research on compassion training is confirming the critical importance of compassion and the possibility of its being strengthened as a critical foundation of ethics. Compassion and higher reasoning are the core and most promising ingredients of nonviolence and universal ethics that can apply across all cultures as we work on common ethical commitments to the other. It is possible to train in compassion successfully, and we have proof from brain research that it can be effective.[7] We do need to distin-

---

6. Milgram, *Obedience to Authority*.
7. See Klimecki et al., "Functional Neural Plasticity"; Klimecki, "Empathy and

guish, however, between empathy which tends to depress and isolate and discourage (what many of us call burnout) and compassion, which is closer to love and what several religions refer to as lovingkindness (*hen* and *hesed* in Jewish tradition, *metta* in Buddhism).

Compassion is the core practice in reaching out to the other. We are discovering the parts of the mind that this involves, and we are in an exciting moment of synergizing neuroscience, neuroplasticity, and the emergence of universal compassion as a powerful and positive agent of change.

For too long we were tyrannized by the idea that reason is cold. We associated that cold objectivity with the more educated, with Western civilization, with men, and with the wealthy and successful. Now we know, however, that compassion is the *foundation* of reason. Immanuel Kant, whose categorical imperative is the foundation stone of rational universal ethics, was enamored of Jean Jacques Rousseau precisely because he understood, long before neuroscience, that compassion was a critical foundation upon which a "good will" intends to carry out universal obligations. Now we know that compassion and higher reasoning go hand-in-hand with a peaceful mind that engages the other. We embrace a good will; we embrace its compassion; then our rational mind sees the reality of needing universal ethical laws, *because* of our positive emotions, not despite our emotions. Our mind says to us, "I can feel what others feel, their suffering and their joy, and so we must have laws that apply to all equally." Compassion leads to universal law; civilization leads to nonviolence; leading to Kant's pathbreaking vision in *Perpetual Peace*; which in turn led to the beginnings of global international law, humanitarian conventions, and the better elements of the United Nations. Good will leads to rational vision, to conjuring a rational world in which human rights becomes a part of the construct of our reality, and a construct of thousands of international and national laws. This is our mind at its best, at its most healthy. We achieve health for our minds through discovery of the other.

The second half of the twentieth century has also seen the most astonishing rise in human history of women's power and equality. Ninety-nine percent of violent crimes in history have been committed by men. While it is absolutely true that women are capable of great cruelty and have aided and abetted the worst killers of history, it is also the case that when men and women cooperate in an equal way on the construction and defense of society, they tend to come to terms on far less violent structures of law enforcement, defense, education, protection, and crime and punishment. This is very good news for the new encounter of history with the gendered other.

---

Compassion in Society."

We have also recognized that just and equal forms of commerce can change human history for the better by binding strangers across the world in mutual interests as never before. This too has been associated with the decline of violence. But here too, Adam Smith, the grandfather of capitalism, argued that commerce only works for the common good if it is rooted in the moral sense of compassion, a lesson that we must hammer away at for generations of future economists and business leaders.[8]

A key challenge for what I am arguing for here is that the scientists figuring out these trends have little understanding of the fluidity and changeability of religion. They (along with millions of young people) see religion as only a problem to be overcome, an impediment to global integration and meeting of the other. They do not see its incredible power to bind together, with the exception of Alain de Botton, in his *Atheism 2.0*.[9] De Botton, an atheist scion of a famous rabbinic family, sees that religion has much to offer in terms of the foundations of civilizations. Furthermore, liberalism has assumed that a secularized mind always makes liberal choices. But this was not the case in Nazi Germany, and it has not been the case of late in the United States. Less religion can also lead to more fascism, idolization of race, and other sicknesses of the mind.

It will be up to many of us who take religion seriously to integrate the most important legacies of the Enlightenment, of social psychology and brain research, with those moral values, rituals, and mental constructs of spirituality and religion that "hardwire" love of the stranger into the depths of human consciousness, and into the power of spiritual community. This way, secular and religious together can watch each other cautiously, and move us forward. We need to envision and move forward step by step with a drama of global family reconciliation. This is the discovery of the long lost other that is us, a simple tribe that trudged out of Africa so long ago, and that, despite great violence, continues to long to meet each other, to unite, to discover the unity of life and the unity of the cosmos in the eyes of each other.

## BIBLIOGRAPHY

Biswas, Soutik. "Protests in India after Delhi Gang-Rape Victim Dies." *BBC News*, December 29, 2012. Online. http://www.bbc.com/news/world-asia-india-20863707.

De Botton, Alain. *Religion for Atheists: A Non-Believer's Guide to the Uses of Religion.* Toronto: Signal, 2013.

Klimecki, Olga. "Empathy and Compassion in Society." December 14, 2012. Youtube Video, 19:12. Online. https://www.youtube.com/watch?v=GxH-Oiqz-14.

8. Smith, *Theory of Moral Sentiments*.
9. De Botton, *Religion for Atheists*.

Klimecki, Olga, et al. "Functional Neural Plasticity and Associated Changes in Positive Affect After Compassion Training." *Cerebral Cortex* 23 (2013) 1552–61.

Milgram, Stanley. *Obedience to Authority: An Experimental View*. London: Tavistock, 1974.

Pinker, Steven. *The Better Angels of Our Nature: Why Violence Has Declined*. New York: Viking, 2011.

Seligman, Martin. "The New Era of Positive Psychology." February 2004. Ted Talk Video, 23:30. Online. https://www.ted.com/talks/martin_seligman_on_the_state_of_psychology.

Smith, Adam. *Theory of Moral Sentiments*. 2nd ed. Edinburgh: Millar, Kincaid & Bell, 1761.

"Where Are India's Millions of Missing Girls?" *BBC News*, May 23, 2011. Online. http://www.bbc.com/news/world-south-asia-13264301.

# 10

## Vibration of the Other
### A Kabbalistic Ecumenism

LAURA DUHAN-KAPLAN

AS AN INTER-RELIGIOUS EDUCATOR representing Jewish traditions, I seek inclusive theological models. Ideally, these models combine universal and particular elements, welcoming multiple traditions without ignoring any tradition's uniqueness. In that spirit, I offer what I call a "kabbalistic ecumenism." The term "Kabbalah" communicates that I speak the language of a particular tradition, using Judaism's view of Divine infinity and ineffability. "Ecumenism," a term borrowed from Christianity, communicates my intent to leave room for multiple approaches.[1] In this essay, I will introduce kabbalistic theology and then use kabbalistic concepts to speak of a multifaith ecumenism. In particular, I will draw on the work of Hasidic teacher Rabbi Nachman of Breslov, suggesting his work offers one of many possible ecumenical applications of Kabbalah. Noting that these possibilities are influenced by a theologian's time and place, I point to several historical variations, concluding with my own.

---

1. Matthew Fox is well known for adapting this Christian term to multi-faith discourse. See Fox, *One River, Many Wells*.

## KABBALISTIC PHILOSOPHY

Many respected Jewish scholars say that Kabbalah *is* the theology of the Jewish people.[2] Here is where we discuss the big questions that exist at the boundaries of everyday thought, questions about the nature of God, divine revelation, ultimate truth, and creation and what came before it. Here we propose creative metaphors for answering these questions and push those metaphors to their logical limits. It is true that kabbalistic study slipped into the background during the hyper-rational early modern period of history.[3] But it was preserved in the Hasidic movement, and is re-emerging today.

Kabbalah literally means "received tradition." More specifically, it is a mystical tradition handed down from biblical times; a tradition that re-appears over and over again in the language and cultural style of different places and different eras. The kabbalistic tradition focuses on direct knowledge of the divine—through theological modeling of God's inner nature; metaphorical interpretations of biblical words and phrases; use of traditional prayers as reflective tools; cultivation of psycho-spiritual qualities; sound, music and chanting; visions; imaginative astral travel; silent meditation; and eating with special intention. It is quite diverse.[4]

Within this diversity, we can find something like a unified theology. The kabbalistic tradition takes the idea of monotheism, one god, very seriously. So seriously that it turns monotheism into monism—the view that the entire universe is a single substance.[5] Here is the reasoning: God is *Eyn Sof,* infinite; thus God has no limits or boundaries. If anything besides God existed, that would imply a boundary or a limit to God. So, nothing else can exist.[6] Of course, it *looks like* other things exist. But those other things are just costumes, appearances, or garments of God. If you perceive things correctly, you will recognize they are emanations of divine energy. Human beings do have the potential to develop this kind of spiritual perception. We already experience multiple worlds of consciousness in our daily life, operating on pragmatic, emotional, rational, and spiritual levels. We know how to shift our attention between them. Through both study and grace, we can increase our focus on spiritual consciousness, becoming more aware of the divinity that underlies the surface of everyday life.[7]

2. Steinsaltz, *Thirteen Petalled Rose*, xi.
3. Scholem, *Major Trends in Jewish Mysticism*, 22.
4. Dan, *Kabbalah*, 5–7.
5. Idel, *Kabbalah*, 117.
6. Tishby, *Wisdom of the Zohar*, 263.
7. Green, *Ehyeh*, 19–28; Jacobson, *Hasidic Thought*, 69–84; Schneersohn, *True Existence*, 26–27. See also Elior, *Mystical Origins of Hasidism*.

If everything is an emanation of God, so is each of us. So is our good behavior; so is our bad behavior; so is our pleasure; so is our suffering. We are part of the divine field and everything we do shifts that field in a tiny way.[8] Every ritual action that reminds us of God's presence strengthens the God field. Every ethical action that, to our human understanding, raises up someone improves the God field. When the God-field is fully perfected, through a combination of human and divine action, we will have achieved a messianic time.[9]

## HASIDIC PHILOSOPHY OF REB NACHMAN OF BRESLOV

In Eastern Europe of the late eighteenth and nineteenth centuries, Kabbalah took a popular form in the Hasidic movement. The word "hasidic" means "pious," though its innovators were often criticized as impious. Hasidic philosophy focused on seeing Divinity in everyday life. Hasidic practice cultivated spiritual perception through music, personal prayer, and inner development. Hasidic teaching was quite eclectic. Each teacher taught about their own inner journey, and each practitioner followed a particular spiritual teacher or rebbe.[10]

Rabbi Nachman of Breslov (1772–1810) was a Ukrainian Hasidic spiritual teacher or Rebbe. Reb Nachman was an introverted and intense teen. Because he was raised in a well-known Hasidic family, he learned to give his existential struggles a spiritual interpretation. Over his short career as a teacher, he offered teachings based on the themes of his own inner work to a close circle of disciples. He struggled with depression, so he offered many teachings about finding inner joy. He loved music, especially the Hasidic *niggun*, a wordless melody that attunes a singer's heart to a particular spiritual key, so he often used vibration, sound, and melody as spiritual metaphors. He quarreled intensely with rival teachers, so he taught about how to navigate controversy by finding the good points in everyone. When he was depressed or under professional attack, he wondered what was the point of his life as a spiritual teacher. Sometimes he concluded he was to play a special role in bringing messianic time.[11]

In a particularly self-reflective moment, documented in sermon 64 of *Likutey Moharan* (Collected Works of Our Teacher Rabbi Nachman), he

---

8. Prager, *Path of Blessing*, 13–15.
9. Scholem, *Messianic Idea in Judaism*, 37–48.
10. Holtz and Green, *Your Word Is Fire*, 2–18.
11. Green, *Tormented Master*; Gabel, *Kitzur Likutey Moharan*.

criticized his own tendencies toward conflict. Hasidic teachers, he said, should not be in conflict. We all agree that only one infinite God exists, that every religious tradition is an emanation of the Divine, and that humans recognize and reach for divinity with whatever tools chance and culture provide. When we Hasidim focus on our religious disputes, we waste our time, and give religion a bad reputation. As religious people, we should stop our contentious talk and learn to listen to one another.

## A HOMILETIC EXPLORATION

In sermon 64, Reb Nachman wraps his teaching around the biblical motif of the Exodus. He uses the idea of slavery and the figures of Pharaoh, God, and Moses as metaphors to explore inter-religious conflict resolution. God is the infinite vibration of reality, present to all willing to listen. Slavery is the addiction to proving oneself right on theological matters. Pharaoh, the atheist, has observed this addiction in religious people and thus rejected spirituality. Moses, who knows God, uses his listening skills to show Pharaoh a respectful, unifying spirituality. This social drama, hints Reb Nachman, is also a psychological drama. Each of us has inner voices turning us away from God, as well as an inner Moses who can bring us back. Below is my summary and contemporary rendering of Reb Nachman's Hebrew.

Each wisdom tradition vibrates at a unique frequency. Each tradition is a unique slice of the infinite eternal vibration of *Eyn Sof*, divine infinity. Were our ears spiritually attuned, we would hear a cosmic symphony of paths to God.

If only our ears were so attuned! Most of us get so used to our own melody that others just seem wrong. So we disagree, we argue, we split, we compete, we fight. And to people not attached to the religious life, our disputes look ridiculous. Look how contentious religion is, they say! Look at the tiny differences that rip apart communities into teams of enemies! I want nothing to do with it.

Imagine religious debates as a flowing river. Opposing opinions about religion are like silt piled up on the banks, leaving a void in the middle where atheism can take root—not simply an atheism that rejects a particular metaphor for God, but an atheism that completely denies the spiritual life.

Pharaoh, the slave-owning, God-denying king featured in the Bible, is the biblical archetype of that atheist. Who has the power to confront Pharaoh? Why, the Hebrews—the *Ivrim*, literally "those who cross" the river—do! Not the historical people, but the ones who know how to bypass disputes and differences.

Who leads these Hebrews? A Moses, one who calls himself a speaker of few words. One who knows she cannot win over a Pharaoh with words or arguments, but only with silence. Only by meeting a Pharaoh where they are, moving with their vibration, and quietly demonstrating a living faith in God, a living, non-divisive faith.

"*Bo el Par'oh*—Approach Pharaoh," says God to Moses (Exod 7:26). These words were not addressed just to one historical Moses, but speak to the Moses in all of us.[12]

## EVOLVING APPLICATIONS

Reb Nachman's beautiful teaching draws on open-minded views of God's infinity central to Jewish theology. However, universality is not always highlighted in Jewish teaching. Theology responds to social context, politics, and cultural dynamics. As the *Zohar*, a classic thirteenth-century work of Kabbalah, says: God appears to each generation in a guise that speaks to their time and place.[13] For over a thousand years, European Jews have been a religious minority—a "marginalized group." When social change happens, and chunks on the social map shift, the people in the margins get squeezed—they might get pushed up, they might get squashed down. And they use their theology—its language and its images—to understand their situation.

For example, Jewish poet Solomon ibn Gabirol lived in Andalusia (Islamic Spain) in the early eleventh century—a time of open intellectual exchange between Islamic, Jewish and Christian thinkers, including writers of religious philosophy and spiritual poetry. In this time, Ibn Gabirol could simply say: every creature seeks to get close to the one God.[14]

Kabbalistic writer Yosef Gikatilla also lived in Spain—but about one hundred years later, as Christians warred with Muslims to retake the region. It's true, Gikatilla wrote, there is only one God whose energy infuses everything. But God sends representatives in the form of political leaders to "judge and adjudicate" within each nation. Although they have no power in themselves, God chooses to give them power to determine the fate of the world.[15]

Kabbalistic teacher Isaac Luria lived in the Holy Land three hundred years later, in the sixteenth century, shortly after Jews were expelled from Christian Spain and Portugal. Yes, Luria said, all reality emanates from God,

---

12. Duhan-Kaplan, "Come to Pharaoh," 2016. Based on Rabbi Nachman of Breslov, *Likutey Moharan* 64.

13. Tishby, *Wisdom of the Zohar*, 262–63.

14. Ibn Gabirol, "Keter Malchut," 82–123.

15. Gikatilla, *Gates of Light*, quoted in Brill, *Judaism and Other Religions*.

and all creatures affect the God field. But history shows us that the task of perfecting the God field has been left to the Jewish people alone.[16]

Philosopher Baruch Spinoza (1632–77) lived only one hundred years later in the Netherlands, in a Jewish community built by refugees expelled from Portugal. Spinoza found hope in the very beginnings of secular democracy. If you believe, he wrote, as philosophers do, that God is infinite, without boundaries or limits, then you must agree that God is everything. God is the sum total of nature, following the laws of nature, incapable of acting against its nature, immune to our influence.[17] We humans should learn to work out problems ourselves, through inner ethical reflection and democratic process.[18]

Rabbi Zalman Schachter-Shalomi, a refugee from Nazi Germany, lived in the United States in the twentieth century—when the US saw itself as a "melting pot" of cultures that would blend into something new and uniquely American. Reb Zalman felt all of planet earth as a single spiritual organism, and each religious tradition as a vital organ. Together, we would learn from our spiritual teachers how to care for each organ and the planetary body as a whole.[19]

## TWENTY-FIRST-CENTURY CANADIAN KABBALAH

Kabbalistic concepts shape interfaith visions against particular cultural backdrops. This remains true in early twenty-first-century Canada. Our immigrant-rich country imagines itself a new kind of "secular" society. The new secularism avoids establishing a dominant religious tradition. Instead, it creates public space for multiple traditions.[20] When tensions arise between traditions, we try to identify and address specific causes.[21] For example, disputes around workplace religious practice may be eased with guidelines and training.[22] Conflicts in schools may be prevented with multicultural education.[23] With the help of clear concepts, we hope to create a shared public

---

16. Scholem, *Major Trends in Jewish Mysticism*, 244–86.
17. Spinoza, *Ethics*.
18. Spinoza, *Theological Political Treatise*.
19. Schachter-Shalomi, "Deep Ecumenism."
20. Taylor, *Secular Age*.
21. Carwana, "Big Sort."
22. Bromberg, "Next Frontier."
23. Hiren Mistry, "But—Are They Religions, Sir?"

space in which each of us can recognize all of us. My own mystical vision echoes the contemporary Canadian hope.

A few years ago, I took my seat on an airplane flying from New York to Vancouver, Canada. As soon as I sat down, the man next to me put on large headphones. He had his reasons for wanting to be alone and they had nothing to do with me. Still, his actions, and the thoughts and feelings behind them, affected me. Despite the walls he put up, we were not actually separate. For the next five hours, I saw that clearly. I understood:

> *His psyche is inside him, and also outside of him.*
> 
> *Consciousness is both inside and outside each of us.*
> 
> *To imagine my consciousness centered in my body, as I usually do, is an illusion.*
> 
> *The source of experience lies beyond my body, brain, or mind.*
> 
> *What I am, what we are, is not bounded by our bodies.*
> 
> *Of course there is life after death, because the source of life does not die.*
> 
> *My old view of an "I" centered within me and generated by my brain is a false product of unclear thinking.*
> 
> *Just as gossip makes it hard to see people truly, so the conventions of language and dogmas of science make it hard to see myself truly.*
> 
> *To see clearly, I have to lift veils of opinion over and over again.*

During this time, I was not at all "out of it." I sat in my seat, typed a report on my laptop, entertained someone's bored baby, walked through the airport, and endured the chaotic crush at baggage claim. I just did it all with a beatific smile on my face. Many people smiled back, delighted to be lifted for a moment out of their traveler's stress.[24]

The words I use to describe my vision, i.e., my way of seeing, are influenced by kabbalistic writers, such as Hasidic teacher Rabbi Schneur Zalman of Liadi (1745–1812). In his *Likutei Amarim Tanya* (Collected Teachings), Rabbi Schneur Zalman speaks of human perceptions of God's essential reality. No one, he says, can perceive God fully as God is in itself. Using a metaphor of God as light, he says we receive the light through successive filters.[25] Many of the filters, such as our selective sense organs, cannot be removed. But we can learn more about how the filters work, and gain a fuller image of the Divine light.

For me, Schneur Zalman's metaphors of "divine light" and "filters" speak into our Canadian context. Our multicultural approach to religion acknowledges that humans know God through particular cultural filters.

---

24. Adapted from Duhan-Kaplan, "Mysticism in Midlife."
25. Schneur Zalman, *Likutey Amarim Tanya*, chapters 35–36.

Each tradition has its own languages, music, origin stories, rituals, and more. As an educator, my goal is to learn and teach more about those traditions. Because each tradition's set of filters projects a different image of God, I hope to learn more about both humanity and divinity. And, following the teaching of Reb Nachman, I hope to call on my inner Moses: listening carefully, meeting people where they are, and quietly demonstrating a non-divisive faith in God.

## BIBLIOGRAPHY

Brill, Alan. *Judaism and Other Religions: Models of Understanding.* New York: Palgrave Macmillan, 2010.

Bromberg, Anita. "The Next Frontier: Managing Situations Arising out of Religious Practices and Cultural Values." Workshop at Metropolis Conference, Vancouver, Canada, March 26, 2015.

Carwana, Brian. "The Big Sort: Religion, Secularism & Misunderstandings in Canada's Public Sphere." Lecture at Ontario Multifaith Council Educational Conference, Toronto, October 27, 2014.

Dan, Joseph. *Kabbalah: A Very Short Introduction.* Oxford: Oxford University Press, 2007.

Duhan-Kaplan, Laura. "Come to Pharaoh." Sermon presented at OHALAH: Association of Rabbis for Jewish Renewal, Boulder, CO, January 11, 2016.

———. "Mysticism in Midlife." In *Spiritual Voices,* edited by Eleanor Clitheroe and S. Brooke Anderson, 48–55. Vancouver, BC: Clitheroe and Anderson, 2018.

Elior, Rachel. *The Mystical Origins of Hasidism.* Translated by Shalom Carmy. Portland, OR: Littman Library of Jewish Civilization, 2006.

Fox, Matthew. *One River, Many Wells: Wisdom Springing from Global Faiths.* New York: TarcherPerigee, 2004.

Gabel, Yakov. *Kitzur Likutey Moharan [Abridged Teachings of Our Teacher Rabbi Nachman].* Jerusalem: Breslov Research Institute, 2009.

Gikitilla, Yosef. *Gates of Light.* Translated by Avi Weinstein. San Francisco: HarperCollins, 1994.

Green, Arthur. *Ehyeh: A Kabbalah for Tomorrow.* Woodstock, VT: Jewish Lights, 2002.

———. *Tormented Master: The Life and Spiritual Quest of Rabbi Nahman of Bratslav.* Woodstock, VT: Jewish Lights, 1992.

Holtz, Barry W., and Arthur Green. *Your Word Is Fire.* Mahwah, NJ: Paulist, 1977.

Ibn Gabirol, Solomon. "Keter Malchut [Crown of Divine Sovereignty]." In *Selected Religious Poems of Solomon ibn Gabirol,* edited by Israel Zangwill. Translated by Israel Zangwill. New York: Jewish Publication Society, 1922, 82–133.

Idel, Moshe. *Kabbalah: New Perspectives.* New Haven: Yale University Press, 1990.

Jacobson, Yoram. *Hasidic Thought.* Tel Aviv: MOD, 1998.

Mistry, Hiren. "But—Are They Religions, Sir?" Lecture at Ontario Multifaith Council Educational Conference, Toronto, Canada, October 27, 2014.

Nachman of Breslov. *Likutey Moharan.* Jerusalem: Breslov Research Institute, 1995.

Prager, Marcia. *The Path of Blessing.* Woodstock, VT: Jewish Lights, 1998.

Schachter-Shalomi, Zalman. "Deep Ecumenism." Lecture at Elat Chayyim Retreat Center, Accord, New York, July 1988.

Schneersohn, Shmuel. *True Existence.* Translated by Yosef Marcus. Brooklyn: Kehot, 1992.

Schneur Zalman of Liadi. *Likutey Amarim Tanya.* Bilingual ed. New York: Kehot Publication Society, 1998.

Scholem, Gershom. *Major Trends in Jewish Mysticism.* New York: Schocken, 1995.

———. *The Messianic Idea in Judaism.* New York: Schocken, 1971

———. *Origins of the Kabbalah.* Translated by Allan Arkush. Philadelphia: Jewish Publication Society, 1987.

Spinoza, Baruch. *Ethics.* Indianapolis: Hackett, 1991.

———. *Theological Political Treatise.* Cambridge: Cambridge University Press, 2007.

Steinsaltz, Adin. *The Thirteen Petalled Rose: A Discourse on the Essence of Jewish Ethics and Belief.* New York: Basic, 2006.

Taylor, Charles. *A Secular Age.* Cambridge, MA: Harvard University Press, 2007.

Tishby, Isaiah. *Wisdom of the Zohar.* Translated by D. Goldstein. Washington, DC: Littman Library of Jewish Civilization, 1989.

## 11

# "Unitive Being" in the Face of Atrocity

## North American Contemplative Christian Responses to Terrorism

### Paula Pryce

> We cannot keep saying it is "those terrorists" who have done this, but must look deeply into the violence we live out ourselves . . . by turning more fully towards it, accepting it as our very selves.

UNITIVE BEING, *UNIO MYSTICA*, phenomenological intersubjectivity. By whatever name, the central endeavor of contemplative Christianity is a classic form of eros: to make whole what is separate or broken. For the most committed and knowledgeable of these practitioners, the cultivation of unitive being with the divine, people, and creation is not a fair-weather venture reserved for times when contemplation is a kind of pleasant entertainment. Rather, among those with whom I have done years of ethnographic research, North American contemplative Christians saw their efforts as a chosen intention to "build energy" and to facilitate the flow of that energy from person to person through their porous boundaries into the world. Ideally, they felt that the attempt to foster unity should be enacted in every moment and in every situation. A product of both action and contemplation, such unitive being is a phenomenological sense of fusion between self and other that practitioners believe manifests as a creative power which is simultaneously integrative and "spacious." Religious philosopher Raimón Panikkar[1] described it as a way of being that is distinct to a particular kind of Christian spirituality: not the discrete categories of "creature" and "creator" prominent in many transcendence-oriented Christianities, nor the oceanic monism of Vedanta Hinduism in which self and other fully merge, but instead a state of being in which self and other mingle and yet retain their identities—what Cynthia Bourgeault, one of the spiritual teachers in my ethnographic research, described as "not one, not two, but both one and two." Ideally their task was not focused on individual enlightenment, but on service. Cultivated through service to others, surrender to the divine, and the disciplined practice of formal rites and intentional ways of living (which often included political and social activism), contemplative Christians said that this form of union between self and other has a capacity to heal and to reconcile. My ethnographic research as a cultural anthropologist who has worked since 2009 in North American Christian monasteries and among a global network of Centering Prayer practitioners reveals how this variety of Christianity views contemplation as the necessary labor of responsible citizens who wish to ameliorate breaches between self and other as a way to bring peace into the world.

Terrorists, believed many of these practitioners of contemplative Christianity, are part of the unified whole regardless of their horrific actions. Some North American contemplative Christians' responses to the terrorist activities at the end of 2015 in Paris, Beirut, San Bernardino, California, and other locations show how seriously these practitioners take the endeavor to foster unitive being as an alternative to more common oppositional sociopolitical rhetoric and behaviors. Their responses both to the attacks and to the reactionary positions of some public figures in the United States and Canada show their sense of responsibility to act in ways which they believed would help establish peace. They called for what one teacher in the movement described as "effective action on behalf of all humanity." This paper describes how these contemplative practitioners attempted to take effective action through the roles of prophetic teacher, social activist, and contemplative. Their actions and statements reveal their metaphysical understanding of how self and other are causally interconnected and ontologically linked in a way that informed a belief that prayer, contemplation, and "unitive being" are effective, cultivatable forces for peacemaking.[2]

1. Panikkar, *Christophany*.
2. For the purposes of this paper, I draw my evidence from social media postings

Let me briefly describe the people whom I call "contemplative Christians," a vast category which could include innumerable streams. I have done extensive ethnographic research with cross-denominational (and often interreligious) North American practitioners of Centering Prayer, a form of Christian meditation that American Trappist Cistercian monks modelled in the 1970s from Christian monastic theologies and practices and Vedanta Hindu and Buddhist meditation techniques. Inspired by the interreligious diplomacy and Asiatic explorations of their novice master Thomas Merton, the Trappist monks Thomas Keating, William Meninger, and Basil Pennington's motivation to teach Christian forms of contemplation initially came from a desire to serve non-monastic Catholics whose spiritual passions drove them to other religions.[3] Today many thousands of people practice Centering Prayer around the world.[4] My research focused on particularly devoted and learned North American practitioners, both monastic and non-monastic.

There are several characteristics which the North American Centering Prayer practitioners in my research tended to share. They often had personal histories which included a critique of and subsequent distancing from institutional churches. During periods of searching outside the confines of Christianity, many studied and practiced other religious streams, then reconsidered the potential of Christianity when they discovered its historical and contemporary mystical expressions. Key traits of this community include an openness to religious and social others, an emphasis on divine immanence rather than transcendence, the formalized practice of contemplative rites (including meditation), an appreciation for complex epistemological theories which highlight ambiguity, and a commitment to social reform and service. Important to note, the people with whom I have worked were not only pie-in-the-sky dreamers: while I know of no one in the network who has been directly impacted by terrorist activities, many people did active work on the frontlines of social problems like domestic violence, substance abuse, racial inequality, and poverty.

---

which refer to the cluster of violent actions in late 2015, particularly the terrorist attacks in Paris and San Bernardino. My sources include social media groups of contemplative Christians, as well as their blogs, articles, lectures, and sermons. I also conducted several online interviews with teachers and members of those communities. I use first-name pseudonyms for those who posted on social media sites, but I cite the real names of authors of published sermons and lectures.

3. These men have been prolific writers. See, for, example Merton, *Chuang-Tzu*; *Zen and Birds*; *Contemplative Prayer*; Keating, *Intimacy*; "Introduction"; Meninger, *Loving Search*; Pennington, *Place Apart*; *Listening*.

4. See, for example, the website of Contemplative Outreach, the main organization of Centering Prayer practitioners.

To some degree this form of contemplative Christianity is a product of a pluralistic outlook. Having grappled with the ambiguity and doubt that accompanies stepping out of one's well-known religious confines, many Centering Prayer practitioners have a deep appreciation for other religious ways of approaching the divine. They fit well into what Richard Kearney has described as "anatheistic" Christianity.[5] Kearney's "anatheism," or "god after god," recognizes the need to adjust one's view of the divine in a world of immeasurable diversity and interconnection. The term describes the lived theology of people, like those in my research, who have abandoned the triumphalism of a Christian-centered universe in favor of an hermeneutical posture which replaces defensive certitude with humility. Where the hostility of Crusade-oriented Christianities rose out of an us-against-them mentality, anatheistic Christianities have emerged out of the ambiguity which comes from greeting the stranger in a pluralistic, globalized world. Truly welcoming the other has required people to be open enough to make doctrinal tenets secondary and to try to perceive the universe without preconception, which creates a world of increasing ambiguity. Anatheists, then, are those who recognize the poverty of their own conceptualizations. Yet rather than rejecting God in so uncertain and expansive a universe, they emphasize the need to welcome God in the stranger, thus taking on hospitality and openness as the central rubric in their stance of unknowing and creating a potential for intimacy.[6]

This combination of openness and desire for intimacy informs how the North American contemplative Christians in my research have responded both to terrorist activity and to their own societies' sometimes aggressive reactions. They are pacifists who act with the intention of making significant changes in a world in which people suffer. The difference lies in how they envision the best way to effect change.

How then did this community respond to the cluster of violent events at the end of 2015? Their initial responses expressed shock and horror, followed immediately by convictions about the unity of humanity and all creation. Many of their postings on social media featured memes of evocative earthrise photographs with comments like "One world, one love" and "I am not a 'me.' There is only 'we.'" Julie, a teacher in the contemplative Christian network, wrote on her students' group Facebook page in response to the events at Paris, "This is an attack on all humanity, on all that civilization has stood for and brought to pass. . . . My real prayers are for how I, as part of

---

5. See Kearney, *Anatheism*.

6. See also Seligman and Weller, *Rethinking Pluralism,* for insightful analysis regarding creative religious responses to pluralism and ambiguity.

humanity, can (and must) help." Her student Alexandra then posted a piece showing the idea that one must recognize and foster unity between self and other, even under detestable circumstances. She wrote,

> If my own recent experiences of suffering have taught me anything, it is to allow the outrage to rise into the alchemy of love. Are we not even now being unified by this horror? [That which] is most repellent, detestable and hideous . . . if we have the courage to bear it (and not by running from it, but by turning more fully towards it, accepting it as our very selves) . . . does it not bind us even more deeply to each other and to the Source of Life itself? We cannot keep saying it is "those terrorists" who have done this, but must look deeply into the violence we live out within [ourselves] (in the name of religion. The many ways we split ourselves . . . into "true" and "false" selves. Creating more and more polarizing dualities) . . . [Peace and reconciliation] must begin within.

## PROPHETIC TRUTH TELLING

In this network of Christian contemplatives, the work of peacemaking began with calls for prophetic truth telling. Jeremy was a scholar of Islam from the American South who wrote a blog in December 2015 which proclaimed that the contemplative Christian community must voice alternatives to animosity and violence. He wrote, "Ordinary individuals must boldly speak the wisdom they know. They must raise their voices to call alternative communities into formation. . . . They must speak a new and powerful narrative that redefines the ways we see ourselves and the world around us," a way which he called "interbeing." Elizabeth, another member of the network, used Facebook to share a short article by Clarissa Pinkola Estes which proffered a similar prophetic call to action.[7] The piece acknowledged people's "righteous rage over the latest degradations of what matters most to civilized, visionary people," but proclaimed that "we were made for these times." It encouraged contemplative practitioners by saying that their years of training and practice have prepared them "to display the lantern of soul in shadowy times like these—to be fierce and to show mercy towards others; both are acts of immense bravery and great necessity."

Contemplative Christian prophetic truth-telling included educating non-Muslims. People in my research wrote blogs and articles which distinguished between extremism and majority expressions of Islamic cultures and theologies, described the sociocultural foundations of terrorism, and

---

7. Estes, "We Were Made for These Times."

noted the history of Christian violence. The website of the Worldwide Community of Christian Meditation, for example, posted an article entitled "Love and Compassion in Islam."[8] Colin, a priest living in western Canada, similarly wrote educational blogs with titles like "Is Islam Inherently Violent?," "The Violent Bible," and "Responding to Terrorism."

Furthermore, people in the network upheld modern historical political and religious activists as exemplary models of the kind of pacifism that could be rallied in response to terrorist activity. They uploaded photos and blogs about famous individuals like Mahatma Gandhi, Nelson Mandela, and Martin Luther King Jr., whose actions had significant political effects, as well as lesser known, ordinary citizens who were equally dedicated to serving the community in situations of organized violence. A five-part blog told the story of French Trappist monks who were murdered in Algeria when they collectively decided to remain among and support their Muslim neighbors as Islamic extremists became more active in their region. Several other people posted comments about Etty Hillesum, a young Jewish woman born in the Netherlands and killed at Auschwitz, who kept a wartime journal in which she wrote, "Each of us moves things in the direction of war every time we fail to love" and "Ultimately we have just one moral duty: to reclaim large areas of peace in ourselves, more and more peace, and to reflect it towards others."[9]

## SOCIAL ACTIVISM

Members of the contemplative Christian network saw social activism and political critique of their own society as crucial to their prophetic response to terrorism and a primary site of their responsibility. The people in my study emphasized the link between Islamic extremism and the 2015 Syrian refugee crisis because of people's fear that immigrant communities might harbor terrorists. American xenophobia was exacerbated with the shootings at San Bernardino, California on December 2, 2015, which were purported to have been planned by a radicalized Muslim couple of Pakistani descent.[10] Donald J. Trump, then a frontrunner in the 2015–16 campaign for the Republican presidential candidacy, vowed to ban Muslim immigration, sparking a media furor which polarized debates about American refugee/immigration policies and gun laws that make firearms easily accessible.[11] Notably, the *New York*

---

8. Hidden, "Love and Compassion in Islam."
9. Salenson, *Christian de Chergé*; Woodhouse, *Etty Hillesum*.
10. Nagourney et al., "San Bernadino Shooting."
11. Johnson, "Trump Calls for Total Shutdown."

*Daily News* published a front page critique, "God Isn't Fixing This," which ridiculed politicians who did nothing but offer "thoughts and prayers" to the victims and families of the San Bernardino massacre. The paper denounced them as "cowards who could truly end the gun scourge [but instead] continue to hide behind meaningless platitudes."[12]

How did contemplative Christians in the network respond to this sociopolitical divisiveness? A few days after the San Bernardino incident, Br. James Koester, a monk at the Society of Saint John the Evangelist in Cambridge, MA, gave a sermon which acknowledged the despair that people can feel when faced with the brutal realities of "the shootings in California, the bombing in Paris, ISIS in the Middle East, the very real and justified anger behind Black Lives Matter, climate change around the world, not to mention the daily ups and downs of our own lives." Yet Br. James Koester advocated action and called on people to make demands of people with power, especially those who have the capacity to change public policy. He gave an example of courageous social activism in the rare occurrence of a front-page editorial in the *New York Times* which decried politicians' refusal to amend gun laws as "a moral outrage and a national disgrace." Br. James Koester concluded by saying that this kind of truth telling, whether people choose to hear it or not, has the reconciling effect of bringing the divine into our "present reality."[13] In other words, he understood prophetic truth telling itself as a kind of prayer which had the capacity to invoke transformative energy.

George, a priest with a Midwestern American parish, posted on Facebook a December 2015 sermon that advocated social activism in response to the American backlash against immigrants and refugees after the terrorist attacks. He said, "Displacement is the hidden by-product of terrorism and terrorism reinforces the evil of displacement as people around the world react in fear and close their borders." George appealed to the government to open its doors to refugees, criticizing especially the "governors of 31 states [who have called for] an immediate ban of all Syrian refugees to the United States." Making strategic reference to the common foundation of Abrahamic religions, George likened the refugee crisis to Exodus stories in which Jews escaped the oppression of Egypt to wander in the "true no-man's-land" of the desert before arriving at Canaan. He then called on his listeners to take pragmatic, but contemplatively inspired social action, like Moses did when he commanded water to flow from a rock for the thirsty travellers. "We are designed to bring water from rocks" said

---

12. Schapiro, "God Isn't Fixing This."
13. Koester, "Lord Jesus, Come Soon"; "End the Gun Epidemic."

George, "to bring justice to the needy," then added, "All of this 'otherness' on display in our political culture today that says we are fundamentally separate from one another is the great lie of our times."

In Canada, where a newly elected federal government had committed to taking large numbers of Syrian refugees within a short period of time, contemplative Christians' call for justice had a warmer tone. For example, Colin, the blogger-priest, wrote about his parish's January 2016 public forums on Syrian culture that helped raise funds for refugee sponsorship. He was heartened: "I cannot call to mind anything that has ever enabled our congregation to raise $100,000 within three months." Colin saw the refugee crisis not only as a way to serve those displaced by war, but also as a unifying force in his local community. He said, "There is a depth of compassion and responsiveness in the community beyond the church that deserves our full respect." One can see the boundary-crossing impulses of the contemplative Christian network in Colin's comment, "We do ourselves and the world around us a great disservice when we fail to honour the light and beauty present in the lives of many people who have absolutely no interest in the church." He emphasized the need "to continue listening carefully to people" outside the church environment, saying "the only way forward is with deep openness to the wisdom and goodness of people for whom the church is profoundly foreign territory." Through his blog and his role as rector of a parish which took social activism seriously, Colin attempted to ameliorate the distance between disparate peoples, both locally and globally. His endeavors to reconcile unjust circumstances and to foster intimacy was illustrative of Kearney's theory about the relationship between pluralism, hospitality, and "anatheistic" Christianity.

## CONTEMPLATIVE PRAYER

Contemplative prayer is the foundational work of this kind of peacemaking, believe the people in my study. Those well versed in this variety of Christianity did not consider practices like meditation to be qualitatively different from teaching, speaking out, or political activism. Rather, they saw serious contemplative practices as interactive, productive, and indeed the necessary grounding of any kind of "effective action." Their perspective on the causal relationship between prayer and social change belies a concept of the human being as a porous entity which had the capacity to send inner gestures, thoughts, and demeanors beyond the boundaries of the physical body and to receive the energy of others. This movement of energy manifests as a phenomenological connection with the divine, all people, and all creation. In this community's view, generating and sharing energy through contemplation is a way to heal the rift between inner self and outer other, to change perception, and to hone awareness of the integral unity of all things. Thus, while the contemplatives in my research would not contest the *New York Daily News*'s insistence on a political solution by way of gun reforms, they had quite a different view from the paper's editors who mocked prayer as an impotent, careless response to violence. To the contrary, they understood prayer as potentially transformative at the levels of person and society, even cosmos, particularly when enacted with disciplined focus.

Jeremy's blog is instructive; it saw a profound difference between ineffectual prayer and serious, mature prayer. Cautioning people to distinguish between "religious entertainment that garbs itself as contemporary spirituality" and responsible spiritual action, Jeremy said that contemplative Christianity, like Islamic Sufism, possesses "an immense treasury of spiritual wisdom," but that "this treasury can only be wielded by those who are awake and have power enough to take effective action on behalf of all humanity." He added that practicing and teaching intensive varieties of contemplation could help repair "the deficit of meaning" in the materialistically oriented societies of North America and Europe and thereby help staunch the flow of disillusioned youth toward religious extremism.

After the terrorist attacks, the contemplative Christians in my research organized virtual and real-space communal prayer activities as a way to foster peace and reconciliation in the hope of offering "effective action on behalf of all humanity." Alexandra asked members of her contemplative Christian social media group to practice a form of Buddhist intercessory prayer called *tonglen* together, in which practitioners envision breathing in the suffering of the world and breathing out peace. She said, "Let's join our hearts and intentions in prayer for the world. . . . I encourage us to be mindful of the energy we send out to our world every time we sign on to [social media]. . . . Let us practice tonglen and cultivate compassion and love, while encouraging hope in the midst of our world's turmoil."

Cynthia Bourgeault, a teacher of significance to contemplatives in my research, led an Advent retreat on the Spirituality and Practice website just after the Paris attacks. During the retreat, Cynthia Bourgeault encouraged the 1000 international participants to "pool our energy to reclaim the world" by meditating together with the intention of generating and sharing unitive being and peace. She also performed a "Mass for the World" (inspired by the Jesuit priest, Pierre Teilhard de Chardin) at a lecture in Aspen, Colorado, in which she used evocative language and chant in the company of "a gathering of human beings who are seriously concerned and [hold] in our hearts our planet at this dangerous and potentially fruitful time." Together, she said, "we are lifting up our hearts to the collective vision of humanity." The Mass ended with a benediction, "Believer and unbeliever alike, Lord, make us one."[14]

Br. Geoffrey Tristam of the Society of Saint John the Evangelist, who was in Paris just two weeks before the November 2015 attacks, also upheld prayer as an effective force. In his sermon, Br. Geoffrey Tristam described the refugee camps in Calais, France: "I was aware of the terrible human suffering all around me in Europe—people lost, homeless, exiled. Two weeks ago, lighting a candle in Notre Dame, and praying for those exiled families, I could not have imagined the awful killings and bloodshed which have taken place this weekend." He went on to say that prayer "actually *does* something. The prayer of intercession is powerful and can change lives," he said, then went on to explain that the word intercession comes from the Greek *entynchanein*, meaning "to meet or be with someone, on behalf of another." Br. Geoffrey Tristam said that this kind of prayer is about being "intimately close" with the divine and carrying others "into the heart of God.... True intercession ... is not just a detached impassioned shopping list of the needs of the world.... Rather, it is a profound, loving, and costly holding up of others who are on our hearts before God." He said that we have "the incredible privilege of being able to draw very close to the heart of God, and bringing with us ... those whom we long to be healed and restored." Thus, Br. Geoffrey Tristam described prayer as a form of intersubjectivity between the self, the divine, and other people, which can act as a reconciling force.[15]

## UNITIVE BEING

How can we understand these people's convictions about the causal force of prayer? What are they doing when they describe their practices as "effective action on behalf of all humanity"? Drawing from years of fieldwork with Centering Prayer practitioners, I crafted a model which attempts to show how contemplative Christians intentionally followed ritual practices and the ritualization of everyday activities in an effort to facilitate an on-going process of transformation which they said generates unitive being, even in situations which horrify them. My model highlights how contemplatives worked to change perception through a combination of "intention" (agency), a learned capacity to "keep attention" (focus), and "surrender" or "unknowing" (creative ambiguity)—that is, a simultaneous practice of action and contemplation, or doing and not-doing, which one teacher described as having "alchemical" properties that can prompt "awakening to the divine." With

---

14. Bourgeault, "Lectures."
15. Tristam, "Holding Those on Our Hearts."

dedication and perseverance, their practices could potentially shift perception, they believed, so that one could better sense the divine and see the world and other people in new ways, especially with love and compassion. They said that, in partnership with divine will, this was a way that they could encourage a manifestation of unitive being in any situation.

My model uses the analogy of a convection current's flow of heating and cooling water to depict the lengthy process of transforming *habitus* (unconscious cultural and historical ways of being and knowing) and *doxa* (critical awareness).[16] Using the metaphors of "upward" for greater doxa and "downward" for habitus, the movement towards contemplative maturity ideally flows in continuous circuits of critical thought and contemplative ways of being. Practitioners believed that the doxa which results from reflexivity could be redirected and subsumed towards a renewed habitus of being and thinking by way of contemplative practices like meditation. The idea is that, with committed practice over time, chosen ideals and intentions could become the undercurrent of the "new normal" out of which first impulses rise.

This transformative "convection current" takes its "heat source" from a combination of personal agency, intentional openness to the unknown, and what they call divine will or grace. They saw the second factor, honoring and cultivating ambiguity instead of dogmatic belief, as key to finding ways beyond the confines of human philosophical, social, and phenomenological capacity. As we saw in Kearney's theory of anatheism, ambiguity was an important motivating factor that rises from social engagement with others in pluralistic society. Such ambiguity acted as a catalyst for wonder which loosened the intellectual, social, and ontological constraints that erected boundaries between people.

Individuals clearly had a crucial role in their own transformation. Even so, their personal agency was an ambiguous factor. Engaging intentional practices and critical thought were seen as primary responsibilities of the contemplative: by rigorously training themselves in practices that combined the strange bedfellows of focus and ambiguity, and by pursuing intellectual study and self-examination, contemplatives worked to shift their thought habits and behaviors towards chosen ideals, including facilitating social change. Despite the critical importance of personal action, however, they asserted humility as a key tenet. That is, in their view, personal capability and responsibility coexisted with human frailty and ineffectuality, and above all, they emphasized the divine as the fundamental source of any transformation. Indeed, their contemplative way was a paradox of action

16. Bourdieu, *Outline of a Theory of Practice*.

and contemplation, of responsibility and surrender to the divine. Morphing habitus and consciousness came degree by degree through a combination of doing and not-doing, they believed, effecting subtle or substantial changes with each cycle of ascent and descent.

Even so, among learned practitioners this transformative process was not primarily about individual enlightenment but about serving and transforming the community. We have seen that contemplative Christians understood humans as porous entities and that with training and focus, the "energy" of their prayer practices could flow to affect others at any distance. We also saw in Jeremy's comments about effective prayer that they saw people as having varying abilities to cultivate and direct that energy. In my book, *The Monk's Cell*,[17] I develop a second model which describes the intentional contemplative process which results in variable degrees of phenomenological experiences of *collective* unitive being. Depending on degrees of experience, understanding, and capacity for "keeping attention," contemplatives bring together intentional unknowing, cultural capital, and varieties of intellectual, rhetorical, and ontological knowledge to become greater or lesser facilitators of collective unitive being. Though they may or may not have a formal position in the institutional churches, from their perspective people who are adept at cultivating unitive being and manifesting "divine flow" have a role as community servants who help bring peace into the world. Whether that flow manifests between fellow contemplative practitioners or between practitioners and those for whom they pray, the people with whom I did research did not see geographic distance as a barrier to the pragmatic cultivation of unitive being. They saw seriousness of purpose, training, and "consent to the divine" as the factors that together constituted a way of generating energy and love in the world in varying intensities.

When people in the network of this variety of contemplative Christianity talk about the goodness of human diversity and pluralism, they do not mean the rather low-bar community vision that is expressed on bumper stickers which proclaim "Tolerance" and "Co-existence." Those statements seem to be less about love than a kind of ceasefire. The contemplatives in my research mean something altogether more fully engaged: they mean diversity that manifests as deep love and visceral union. We saw one description of their vision from the teachings of Cynthia Bourgeault: "not one, not two, but both one and two." Another image they used was Paul's "Body of Christ" in which each part has its distinct role, but together they make a unified, living, breathing being. Such a vision demands that neither terrorists nor political reactionaries may be excluded. People in this contemplative

---

17. Pryce, *Monk's Cell*.

network believed that their high-agency efforts at teaching, social activism, and honing attention to the divine through disciplined contemplative practices could help establish peace and reconciliation in a raucous, suffering world, even among those whose actions they found abhorrent. They saw their work as essential, to be enacted regardless of positive or negative feelings. Still, most did not find these efforts easy and often had their share of doubts. Written not long after the Paris attacks, Rachel's social media posting conveys the weighty sense of responsibility, as well as some uncertainty of her personal capacity to follow through. Her mixture of necessity and hesitancy, the desire to make a substantial difference, and the awareness of human frailty stand as a final image of the complexity of these people's ways of knowing and being in the face of atrocity:

> This year I'm going to end war.
> It won't be easy but I think I can do it one
> thought at a time.
> . . .
> . . .
> . . . . . .
> . . .
> Maybe tomorrow.

## BIBLIOGRAPHY

Bourdieu, Pierre. *Outline of a Theory of Practice*. Cambridge: Cambridge University Press, 1977.

Bourgeault, Cynthia. "Lectures." Aspen Chapel, Aspen, CO, December 17–18, 2015.

Contemplative Outreach. "Silence Solitude Solidarity Service." 2019. Online. www.contemplativeoutreach.org.

"End the Gun Epidemic in America." *New York Times*, December 4, 2015. Online. https://www.nytimes.com/2015/12/05/opinion/end-the-gun-epidemic-in-america.html.

Estes, Clarissa Pinkola. "We Were Made for These Times." 2001. Online. http://www.grahameb.com/pinkola_estes.htm.

Hidden, Sheelah Treflé. "Love and Compassion in Islam." *World Community for Christian Meditation* (blog), 2018. Online. http://wccm.org/content/love-and-compassion-islam.

Johnson, Jenna. "Trump Calls for 'Total and Complete Shutdown of Muslims Entering the United States.'" *Washington Post*, December 7, 2015. Online. https://www.washingtonpost.com/news/post-politics/wp/2015/12/07/donald-trump-calls-for-total-and-complete-shutdown-of-muslims-entering-the-united-states.

Kearney, Richard. *Anatheism: Returning to God after God*. New York: Columbia University Press, 2010.

Keating, Thomas. *Intimacy with God: An Introduction to Centering Prayer*. New York: Crossroad, 2002.

———. "Introduction: The Points of Agreement." In *The Common Heart: an Experience of Interreligious Dialogue*, edited by Netanel Miles-Yepez, xvii–xix. New York: Lantern, 2006.

Koester, James. "Lord Jesus, Come Soon." *Society of Saint John the Evangelist* (sermon), December 6, 2015. Online. https://www.ssje.org/2015/12/06/lord-jesus-come-soon-br-james-koester.

Meninger, William. *The Loving Search for God: Contemplative Prayer and the Cloud of Unknowing*. New York: Continuum, 1997.

Merton, Thomas. *Contemplative Prayer*. New York: Doubleday, 1968.

———. *The Way of Chuang-Tzu*. New York: New Directions, 1965.

———. *Zen and the Birds of Appetite*. New York: New Directions, 1968.

Nagourney, Adam, Ian Lovett, and Richard Pérez-Peña. "San Bernadino Shooting Kills at Least 14; Two Suspects Are Dead." *New York Times*, December 2, 2015. Online. https://www.nytimes.com/2015/12/03/us/san-bernardino-shooting.html.

Panikkar, Ramón. *Christophany: The Fullness of Man*. Maryknoll, NY: Orbis, 2004.

Pennington, Basil. *Listening: God's Word for Today*. New York: Continuum, 2000.

———. *A Place Apart: Monastic Prayer and Practice for Everyone*. Garden City, NY: Doubleday, 1983.

Pryce, Paula. *The Monk's Cell: Ritual and Knowledge in American Contemplative Christianity*. New York: Oxford University Press, 2018.

Salenson, Christian. *Christian De Chergé: A Theology of Hope*. Trappist, KY: Cistercian. 2012.

Schapiro, Rich. "God Isn't Fixing This." *New York Daily News*, December 3, 2015. Online. https://www.nydailynews.com/news/politics/gop-candidates-call-prayers-calf-massacre-article-1.2453261.

Seligman, Adam B., and Robert P. Weller. *Rethinking Pluralism: Ritual, Experience, and Ambiguity*. Oxford: Oxford University Press, 2012.

Tristam, Geoffrey. "Holding Those on Our Hearts Before God." *Society of Saint John the Evangelist* (sermon), November 15, 2015. Online. https://www.ssje.org/2015/11/15/holding-those-on-our-hearts-before-god-br-geoffrey-tristram.

Woodhouse, Patrick. *Etty Hillesum: A Life Transformed*. New York: Continuum, 2009.

# 12

# Searching for the Sacred Other in the Palestinian/Israeli Conflict

### Lynn E. Mills

THE SCOPE OF THE cosmic war[1] being enacted in the lands of Palestine and Israel today leaves little hope for a peaceful solution. There are, however, numerous peace activists and conflict resolution organizations which refuse to give up. Their approaches differ widely with varying degree of success. This paper will focus on Martin Buber's concept of "I and Thou" and how it has permeated nonviolent approaches to peace efforts. The key to unlocking a genuine "I-Thou" encounter with a perceived enemy is a willingness on our part to be open and vulnerable, and a gift of grace on God's part in achieving such openness. Compassionate Listening is a method or process which beautifully facilitates this and empowers citizen diplomacy to effect fundamental change at a grassroots level.

---

1. Juergensmeyer, *Terror in the Mind of God*, 148–68, defines cosmic war as a religious war which is beyond human armies, nations or identities. It is an inevitable war of epic significance between the forces of good and evil and therefore no compromise is possible, no peace sought, only victory to be won.

## "I AND THOU"

Martin Buber, a German Jew, wrote his little book, *Ich und Du*, in 1923; it was first translated into English as *I and Thou* in 1937. The German word *du* carries a meaning which is not translated into the English "thou," or more modern "you." German has two words for the English equivalent of "you," the informal *du* and the formal *sie*. For Martin Buber, use of *du* signals not just the familiar, but the beloved. This is not simply a casual "you," it is the beloved "you." His use of this term suggests layers of meaning in his concept before he starts to unpack it. We know that we are starting from a position of respect, honor, and love of the Other. The importance of this understanding of the Other is indicated by the use of the capital "O."

Buber proposes that humans are defined by two primary word pairs, "I-It" and "I-Thou."[2] The first denotes a connection to the world of pragmatic experience while the second denotes a connection of pure relation. The first experiences the Other in terms of use, how it affects or impacts the I. The second relates to the Other as a sacred being, entering into the being of the Other with no analysis, but simply love, acceptance and compassion. This is not an easy concept to understand and even more difficult to achieve, while impossible to sustain. Our human nature does not allow us to stay in a state of pure love in this broken world. We can however, pursue it passionately. Maurice Freidman in his excellent and comprehensive collection and commentary on Buber's life work, *Martin Buber: The Life of Dialogue*, says, "The two I's are not the same: 'The primary word I-Thou can only be spoken with the whole being. The primary word I-It can never be spoken with the whole being.'"[3]

To passionately pursue this paradigm of connecting with the Other requires an act of will. One must be willing to put aside one's preconceptions, fear, and ego to genuinely step into this paradigm. Once there, it is God's grace which encounters the "I" and lovingly assists the death of the small ego in order to be fully open to the reality of the Other in all its pain and joy. As Friedman asserts, "The Thou, on the other hand, cannot be sought, for it meets one through grace. Yet the man who knows Thou must go out to meet the Thou and step into direct relation with it, and the Thou responds to the meeting."[4]

---

2. Buber, *I and Thou*, 3.
3. Friedman, *Life of Dialogue*, 65.
4. Friedman, *Life of Dialogue*, 67.

## THE PALESTINIAN/ISRAELI CONTEXT

The scope of this paper does not allow for any in-depth summary of the Palestinian-Israeli conflict. Suffice to say that it is an incredibly long standing and complex conflict which has caused massive harm to all sides: bodily, emotional, mental and cultural. This paper is not concerned with taking sides, but with the efforts of healing and preventing further harm. Sami Awad, peace activist, nonviolence educator, and founder of the Holy Land Trust, sums up the current emotional reality in Israel and Palestine:

> One of the greatest barriers to peace is fear; fear prevents mutual trust and respect between the different groups to be established. The behavior of communities living in the Holy Land is frequently driven by fear. For example, the Jewish community lives a fear of eradication and the Palestinian community lives a fear of ethnic cleansing or marginalization. The violence and trauma of current conflicts and historic experiences of past conflicts have resulted in people developing fear of "the other," fear that past events will be repeated, fear that current patterns of behavior will continue, and fear that a step forward will expose them to great danger. All this ultimately perpetuates victimization, blame, hatred, and even racism.[5]

The current state of occupation of the Palestinian territories causes harm both to the occupiers and the occupied. As Munib Younan, Bishop of the Evangelical Lutheran Church of Jordan and the Holy Land states: "For us, occupation is a sin against God and humanity. It deprives people of their human rights and dignity. It demoralizes first the occupier and then the occupied. . . . I want to liberate both Israelis and Palestinians alike from the evils of occupation."[6]

Daphna Golan-Agnon teaches human rights at the Hebrew University of Jerusalem. She was a co-founder and research director of *B'Tselem* and the founding director of *Bat Shalom*.[7] She is currently a research fellow at the Harry S. Truman Institute for the Advancement of Peace in Jerusalem. Golan-Agnon is a Jewish Israeli mother who watches her daughter board the bus to school with no little amount of fear for her safety, and then leaves to stands in front of a bulldozer to protest the demolition of Palestinian homes. In a conversation in September 2007, Golan-Agnon described the occupation as destroying the soul of Israelis. One must at the very least

---

5. Holy Land Trust, "Barriers & Core Challenges."

6. Younan, "Visions of Peace," 19.

7. For an inside look at Israeli peace activism, see Golan-Agnon, *Next Year in Jerusalem*.

make the Other less than you, at worst demonize them, in order to occupy their land and dominate their existence. This is not good for the soul of the occupier nor the occupied. Current violence and trauma recall past experiences which expediently escalates the fear. Fear prevents a move toward peace which could make one vulnerable and open to further attack. This all creates a spiral of fear, accusations, bitterness, and racism.

One way out of this abyss is to actively seek the sacred in the Other. As Bishop Younan says, "I call Israelis to see God in the face of the Palestinian, and I call Palestinians to see God in the face of the Israeli. I call on each of us to accept the other's humanity."[8] This one to one grassroots approach is painfully slow, but perhaps the only real "roadmap to peace." Awad, who has been actively working for peace the past few decades and follows in the footsteps of his uncle, Mubarak Awad,[9] states:

> Real calmness in the Holy Land can only manifest itself if a real peace emerges between the communities of the land, not the politicians. It is a peace that is founded on the principles of mutual trust and respect and a desire to truly bring a sense of justice, equality and equity to all those who live in the Holy Land. It is a peace that addresses the existential fears of the past on both sides and does not allow that fear to be manipulated by the political establishments.[10]

## "I-THOU" IN PRACTICE

Martin Buber wove his concept of "I-Thou" and the sacred Other into all his life's work; long before he articulated this concept in book form, he proposed a bi-national state for Jews and Palestinians to the twelve Zionist Congress in September of 1921.[11] He recognized that accords and agreements with third parties, i.e., Great Britain, would not lead to a workable solution with the Palestinians as he stated in *Notes from the Congress Concerning Zionist Policy* in October 1921: "The Land [of Israel] already contains a non-Jewish population without whose expressed or tacit agreement all of our accords with a third party are likely to encounter severe difficulties. We are therefore obliged immediately to begin direct negotiations with this population on social and economic issues."[12] Buber

---

8. Younan, "Visions of Peace," 20.

9. Mubarak Awad established the Palestinian Center for the Study of Nonviolence in 1983 and Nonviolence International in 1989.

10. Awad, "Illusion of Calmness."

11. Buber, "Proposed Resolution," 60–61.

12. Buber, "Notes from the Congress," 66.

continued his peace efforts in Israel in founding *Brit Shalom* in 1925 and his co-founding of the *Ihud* party in 1942 which were both committed to a bi-national state. In a speech delivered at the Sixteenth Zionist Congress in August of 1929 Buber stated that "Another thing we need is the ability to put ourselves in the place of the other individual, the stranger, and to make his soul ours."[13] He never shrank from or glossed over how difficult this encounter with the Other would be. Maurice S. Friedman in *Martin Buber: The Life of Dialogue* acknowledges this when he writes:

> Perhaps no other phrase so aptly characterizes the quality and significance of Martin Buber's life and thought as this one of the "narrow ridge." It expresses not only the "holy insecurity" of his existentialist philosophy but also the "I-Thou," or dialogical, philosophy which he has formulated as a genuine third alternative to the insistent either-ors of our age. Buber's "narrow ridge" is no "happy middle" which ignores the reality of paradox and contradiction to escape from the suffering they produce.[14]

Haim Gordon, Professor Emeritus in Philosophy of Education at Ben-Gurion University of the Negev, instituted a project in 1979 called Buberian Learning Groups. The aim was to heal the relationships between Arabs and Jews, to create mutual understanding and cooperation, and to promote peace between them. This project ran for three years with the involvement of approximately two hundred participants. Gordon himself was disappointed in the results, hoping for more concrete outcomes in peacemaking.[15] However, evaluators Riffat Hassan and Leonard M. Grob both praise the project for what it achieved and even take Gordon to task for his own negative appraisal. Hassan states:

> Dr. Gordon deserves recognition and commendation for his ability to translate a number of Martin Buber's ideas about dialogue into a philosophy of education and to test this philosophy in a real-life encounter between Jews and Arabs. To me the Education for Peace project is exciting and challenging both as concept and as actuality. The fact that it has shortcomings does not diminish either its uniqueness or its significance. . . . I believe that the project taught them how to decrease the "existential mistrust" between Jews and Arabs and led in some cases (I observed at least two instances personally) to the

---

13. Buber, "Proposed Resolution," 79.
14. Friedman, *Life of Dialogue*, 3.
15. For Gordon's own appraisal of this project, see Gordon, "Buberian Learning Groups," 628–29.

establishing of an authentic one-to-one relationship between a Jew and an Arab.[16]

Grob proposes that Gordon is using an incorrect measuring stick for success when he says, "dialogue is not on the other side of the practice of peacemaking, but is rather its very ground."[17] As painful as it is not to see immediate hard qualitative results, Grob points out that "For Buber the world of dialogue, the world of so-called I-Thou relationships, is fundamentally atemporal and aspatial. To meet my partner in dialogue is to step out of the clock time and ordinary space."[18] "I-Thou" happens in *kairos* time, not *chronos* time. Chronos is quantitative, one minute after another, while Kairos is qualitative. Time is suspended. It is pregnant with possibility and meaning. It is time out of chronological time. While political diplomacy rarely happens outside of *chronos* time, citizen diplomacy must happen in *kairos* time to be truly open to God's grace to transcend fear and pain.

Inspired by the success of *Neve Shalom ~ Wahat as-Salam* (Oasis of Peace), a village where Jewish and Palestinian Israeli families live and learn together in Israel, the Traubman Foundation started the Jewish-Palestinian Living Room Dialogue in 1992 in the San Francisco area. Through a facilitated process in an environment of compassionate listening, Jews and Palestinians share their stories with each other. Buber's concept of entering into relationship with the Other with no analysis or judgement is at the heart of the process the Foundation has developed.[19] In the past twenty-four years, the program has been used to great success in person and via the internet across the US, in the Middle East, and in other conflict zones.[20]

In 2016, the Jewish-Palestinian Living Room Dialogue facilitated a concert audience dialogue for Heartbeat, a group of Israeli and Palestinian youth musicians on their North America tour. Heartbeat boldly states its purpose to "build awareness, respect and trust across a critical mass of 25 percent of the population; thereby making respect and trust unstoppable."[21] Heartbeat was started by Washington, DC, native Aaron Shneyer in 2007. Shneyer has been living in Jerusalem since 2006 and has worked as a dialogue facilitator with various grassroots peace organizations which

---

16. Hassan, "Response to 'Buberian Learning Groups,'" 226.
17. Grob, "Buberian Critique," 432.
18. Grob, "Buberian Critique," 425.
19. Traubman, "Engaging the Other."
20. Traubman and Traubman, "Jewish-Palestinian Living Room Dialogue."
21. Heartbeat, "About."

practice Buber's theory of I-Thou dialogue such as Seeds of Peace[22] and the Sulha Peace Project.[23]

The Compassionate Listening Project (CLP),[24] founded in 1997 by Leah Green, works with Israelis and Palestinians in Citizen Diplomacy. The CLP website states their application of Buberian dialogue in this way:

> The intelligence of the heart is confirmed in research in the field of Neurocardiology. In Compassionate Listening, our emphasis is on strengthening the influence of the heart through cultivating compassion for ourselves and others, and learning to listen and speak from the heart—even in the heat of conflict. The practice of Compassionate Listening teaches us how to reach through layers of defensiveness and reactivity to our essential core. From there, we can shift communication and relationships into heart-to-heart interaction.[25]

CLP has facilitated hundreds of compassionate listening sessions and has trained many facilitators in the process. Tal Shai, a participant states, "This format and compassionate listening allows us to move through our stories, our shadows, our wounds . . . to connect with our own humanity, and with the humanity of the Other, and to see this happening with Israelis and with Palestinians is extremely, extremely, extremely transformational."[26]

The Holy Land Trust teaches nonviolence and provides opportunities to continue a Buberian Dialogue in its peacemaking efforts. Awad proposes that this peacemaking process must: "start locally, and at the most basic local level, which goes to the individual themselves. It is creating this awareness and this possibility for transformation to take place within individuals."[27] When a Buberian dialogue happens among Jews, Christians and Muslims, they are reminded that they are all children of Abraham; there is more that is common between them than what is different. The acceptance of this first commonality can lead to the discovery of others. When one is in a state of openness and compassion rather than analysis and judgment, experiencing the Other's pain is inevitable. This leads to a desire to heal that pain. Awad daringly asserts, "The transformation for Israeli society and community, and to engage in healing with them, in my opinion, has to be the responsibility of Palestinians, and it starts with Palestinians. Any act of resistance

22. See Seeds of Peace, "Home."
23. See Sulha Peace Project, "What is Sulha?"
24. See Compassionate Listening Project, "Home."
25. Compassionate Listening Project, "Home."
26. Tal Shai in Green, "Compassionate Listening."
27. Awad, "Sami Awad."

and defiance to the occupation has to be linked in parallel to an act in healing as much as it is an act of resistance."[28]

Marc Gopin brings up an excellent point in his book *Between Eden and Armageddon: The Future of World Religions, Violence, and Peacemaking* when he asserts that there are times when dialogue is not possible; ritual is required to break through preconceived ideas and birth a new beginning. There are some things which humanity cannot express in words. They are instead, deeply expressed in ritual, transcending mere words to touch the soul of the Other.[29]

Integration of the concept of "I-Thou" in peacemaking processes is revealed in the concept of "honoring the highest ideals of each community. . . . The free gift of honor is an ancient method of discovery of the Other in Jewish life, and it has dramatic effects on conflict and interpersonal injury."[30] Gopin provides a useful caveat that the smaller the encounters are, "the more authentic and effective they are likely to be. The more national and political, the more endangered they are in terms of the perception of politicization and hypocrisy."[31] However, he also states that real change on a societal level requires large-scale endeavors. To solve this dilemma, he suggests nationwide events which provide the opportunity for one on one encounters. He emphasizes the power of personal stories, "because people believe personal narratives in a way that they believe nothing else from an adversary."[32]

## CHALLENGES

There are of course, many challenges in using a Buberian approach to dialogue and peacemaking. A significant factor is our failure to achieve the "I-Thou" connection and to maintain it. There are a few issues which Hassan and Grob addressed in the Buberian Learning Groups which illustrate this. They both highlighted the inequality between the Jews and the Arabs in the project which was exposed in numerous ways such as: there were very few Arabs in leadership positions, and the lack of Islamic sources in the reading material.[33] This inequality suggests paternalism, which is both endemic in a society of

---

28. Awad, "Sami Awad."

29. Gopin describes a ritual in a predominately Christian American setting where the participants engaged in a re-enactment of history which had a profound effect on the participants. See Gopin, *Between Eden and Armageddon*, 47.

30. Gopin, *Between Eden and Armageddon*, 19.

31. Gopin, *Between Eden and Armageddon*, 129.

32. Gopin, *Between Eden and Armageddon*, 130.

33. For the full evaluations of the Buberian Learning Group, see Hassan, "Response to Buberian Learning Groups"; Grob, "Buberian Critique."

dominant and dominated peoples and extremely difficult to overcome. This very state makes the putting aside of oneself to encounter only the Other even more challenging. Our will to do so is not enough. We need God's grace in the encounter to create a safe place to let go of our ego.

There was a sense from some of the Arabs that this project was contrived in some sense with the goal of pacifying them in the guise of peacemaking. Grob speaks very strongly against this as he states:

> Do I respond to the other as merely a means to the realization of my ends, as merely an instrument, (in Buber's terms) an "It"? Am I open to the encounter with the other as an absolute, as (again in Buber's terms) a "Thou" who is my partner in ongoing living events? . . . Peace education must aim for ontological or structural change in which one calls into question the nature of that (merely) self-interested seeing which has from the very outset led to bias and prejudgment at the core of conflict. Only thus can existential mistrust be overcome.[34]

Hassan made another very important point regarding dialogue and confrontation in the Buberian Group, "They [the participants] had learned about confrontation but not about compassion and thought that they could carry on a dialogue with the other with the detachment of a surgeon performing an operation under clinical conditions."[35] Hassan goes on to say, "Jesus' golden words 'Love thy neighbor as thyself' are, in fact, the foundational principle of authentic dialogue, for if I could love the other as myself then I would be willing not only to confront the other with the "painful truth" but also to share in the pain."[36]

The success of the Jewish-Palestinian Living Room Dialogue, the Compassionate Listening Project, Heartbeat, Seeds of Peace, the Sulha Peace Project, and The Holy Land Trust suggests they have achieved some progress in overcoming the challenges experienced by the Buberian Learning Groups through the practice of compassionate listening, where the ego is set aside to be fully present and open to the Other.

## CONCLUSION

Despite the enormity of the challenge, there is hope for a peaceful solution to the Palestinian/Israeli conflict. Awad states that even with forty trainers, the Holy Land Trust cannot keep up with the demand from both Palestinians and

---

34. Grob, "Buberian Critique," 424, 427.
35. Hassan, "Response to 'Buberian Learning Groups,'" 229.
36. Hassan, "Response to 'Buberian Learning Groups,'" 229.

Israelis for training in nonviolence. This is a massive shift in their society as just a few years ago they were shunned as traitors and collaborators and now they are respected and sought after as citizens working for peace.[37]

Marc Gopin shares the encouraging stories of Arab and Jewish peacemakers in his moving book *Bridges Across an Impossible Divide*. Sufi Sheikh Abdul Aziz Bukhari speaks of the futility of war and violence: "We have been fighting for the past sixty years, show me where violence can achieve peace? Only dialogue, only understanding, only respect, only seeing the other with your own eyes as a human being, that's where we'll achieve peace, that will solve the problem, that will stop the rockets, not war, not bombing, not killing will stop the rockets from coming to Israel."[38]

Gopin states in *Between Eden and Armageddon* that "the most important goal of conflict resolution and peacemaking should be the humanization of the Other . . . the treatment of the Other with absolute dignity, even love."[39] As stated earlier, this is a very difficult thing to achieve, particularly when the Other is perceived as a dangerous enemy. It demands an act of will, to willingly put aside one's own ego. However, as Richard Rohr cautions, "If we try to change our ego with the help of our ego, we only have a better-disguised ego."[40] The answer is grace. The important piece on our part is the willingness to put ourselves in a vulnerable position of encountering the perceived enemy, the rest is up to God. Riffat Hassan beautifully asserts: "I believe that the ability to touch the deepest levels of the other's self requires a kind of "gift from heaven.""[41]

Towards the end of his life, Martin Buber wrote these words to Professor Giorgio La Pira:

> Modern history claims to teach us that peace is not possible unless governments first achieve an understanding: that the masses are behind them. We think otherwise. . . . What is now needed is that human beings of good will should speak to each other as only they know how. . . . Let human beings help each other to behold and to desire truly to speak to each other, truly to understand each other, and the masses will follow, and the governments will follow the masses. This is the time.[42]

---

37. Awad, "Sami Awad."
38. Gopin, *Bridges Across an Impossible Divide*, 91–92.
39. Gopin, *Between Eden and Armageddon*, 133.
40. Rohr, "Power of Powerlessness."
41. Hassan, "Response to 'Buberian Learning Groups,'" 230.
42. Mendes-Flohr, "Buber's Legacy," 322.

I propose with Martin Buber, that it is only when we cease to view the Other as an enemy and instead see them as a sacred Other that a true and lasting peace can be achieved. When enough are willing to encounter the Other, to discover and experience the things we share in common, the joy *and* the pain, the world can experience a paradigm shift towards peace.

## BIBLIOGRAPHY

Awad, Sami. "The Illusion of Calmness." *Huffington Post*, October 15, 2015. Online. https://www.huffpost.com/entry/the-illusion-of-calmness_b_8306162.

———. "Sami Awad: Complete Interview." Global Oneness Project Video, 34:06. Online. https://www.globalonenessproject.org/library/interviews/sami-awad-complete-interview.

Buber, Martin. *I and Thou: A New Translation with a Prologue "I and You" and Notes by Walter Kaufmann*. Reprint, Mansfield Center, CT: Martino, 2010.

———. *A Land of Two Peoples: Martin Buber on Jews and Arabs*. Edited by Paul R. Mendes-Flohr. Chicago: University of Chicago Press, 2005.

Compassionate Listening Project. "Home." Online. http://www.compassionatelistening.org.

Friedman, Maurice S. *Martin Buber: The Life of Dialogue*. New York: Routledge, 2002.

Golan-Agnon, Daphna. *Next Year in Jerusalem: Everyday Life in a Divided Land*. Translated by Janine Woolfson. New York: New Press, 2005.

Gopin, Marc. *Between Eden and Armageddon: The Future of World Religions, Violence, and Peacemaking*. Oxford: Oxford University Press, 2002.

———. *Bridges Across an Impossible Divide: The Inner Lives of Arab and Jewish Peacemakers*. Oxford: Oxford University Press, 2012.

Gordon, Haim. "Buberian Learning Groups: Education for Peace in Israel." *Journal of Ecumenical Studies* 21 (1984) 628–29.

Green, Leah. "Compassionate Listening for Israeli and Palestinian Peace Leaders." December 12, 2015. Youtube Video, 11:50. Online. https://www.youtube.com/watch?v=WMiKXUCaH38.

Grob, Leonard M. "Buberian Peace Education in the Mideast: A Buberian Critique." *Educational Theory* 35 (1985) 423–32.

Hassan, Riffat. "Response to 'Buberian Learning Groups: The Quest for Responsibility in Education for Peace' by Haim Gordon and Jan Demarest." *Teachers College Record* 84 (1982) 226–31.

Heartbeat New Sound Foundation. "Home." Online. http://heartbeat.fm.

Holy Land Trust. "Barriers & Core Challenges." Online. http://www.holylandtrust.org.

Juergensmeyer, Mark. *Terror in the Mind of God: The Global Rise of Religious Violence*. 3rd ed. Berkeley: University of California Press, 2003.

Mendes-Flohr, Paul. "Buber's Legacy: 1993." In *A Land of Two Peoples: Martin Buber on Jews and Arabs*, edited by Paul R. Mendes-Flohr, 321–22. Chicago: University of Chicago Press, 2005.

Rohr, Richard. "The Power of Powerlessness." *Center for Action and Contemplation*, November 16, 2015. Online. https://cac.org/the-power-of-powerlessness-2015-11-16.

Rosenberg, Marshall B. *Nonviolent Communication: A Language of Life*. Encinitas, CA: PuddleDancer, 2003.
Seeds of Peace. "Home." Online. https://www.seedsofpeace.org.
Sulha Peace Project. "What is Sulha?" Online. https://www.sulhapeaceproject.com.
Traubman, Leonard. "Engaging the Other." 2009. Online. http://traubman.igc.org/engagingtheother.pdf.
Traubman, Leonard, and Linny Traubman. "Jewish-Palestinian Living Room Dialogue Group." *Len & Libby Traubman*. Online. http://traubman.igc.org/dg-prog.htm.
Younan, Munib. "Visions of Peace in Israel and Palestine: A Palestinian Christian View." *Church & Society* 96 (2006) 17–20.

# 13

# For the Love of Strangers
## A Theology of Hospitality in Colonial Canada

ANITA FAST

## INTRODUCTION

FOR EURO-CHRISTIANS WHO BENEFIT from the spoils of imperialism and empire, theologies of hospitality have often failed to lead to practices which sufficiently confront or dismantle oppressive systems of colonialism and racism, particularly as they are manifest in Christian settler relationships with Indigenous peoples and their lands. The aspects of a Euro-Western worldview which bolster the twin evils of superiority and entitlement have become so entangled with Christian teachings and practice for so many centuries that it becomes a deep and complex work to relax their grip on cultural prejudices and practices.[1]

The query driving this paper is to ask what a theology of hospitality looks like if it is to have teeth sharp enough to cut through the hardened sinews and ossified walls built up by centuries of racism and imperialism in Canada, and move settler Christians into a new relationship with the land and the Indigenous peoples from whom it was stolen. To explore this question, I will pursue three main avenues of inquiry:

---

1. Said, *Orientalism*; Mackey, "Apologizer's Apology"; Heinrichs, *Buffalo Shout, Salmon Cry.*

First, our setting can quite fairly be named as one that is largely ignorant of and indifferent to Indigenous worldviews and ways of knowing. Because I believe that the means we use have significant impacts on the ends we get, developing a theology of hospitality accountable to Indigenous people in Canada must, itself, be hospitable to Indigenous voices, world views, and theologies. This means not only imagining hospitable relationships with Indigenous peoples, but imagining hospitality itself only while holding Indigenous world views and perspectives as central.

Second, although the term "hospitality" generally conjures up positive images of friendship and generosity, we must not assume that a theology of hospitality is free from re-enacting, underwriting or bolstering colonialism, imperialism, and racism. This is particularly true as hospitality is imagined and practiced by those benefitting most from the systems of power and privilege. Therefore, this paper will examine how theologies of hospitality may aid in reinforcing oppressive systems rather than undermining them. Is viewing hospitality as primarily rooted in "welcome" enough to challenge such oppressive systems? Is a focus on diversity and multiculturalism sufficient? In what ways does the Bible situate hospitality such that paternalism and racism in our Canadian churches is confronted and challenged?

Third, a theology of hospitality in the context of a racist and colonial Canada asks what Christian hospitality means for congregations which are largely made up of uninvited guests on stolen and exploited Indigenous land. It will explore concrete actions Christian communities might take in order better to live out God's vision of hospitable relations among all peoples.

## HOSPITABLE THEOLOGY OF HOSPITALITY: RECIPROCITY AND THE GIFT

Although the training of my ear towards Indigenous voices and the opening of my heart and mind to Indigenous perspectives are in their infant stages, this paper seeks to orient hospitality around some key aspects I have learned about Indigenous epistemology and worldviews. These include the centrality of relationship; respect; responsibility; and reciprocity with and within all of creation, with a clear emphasis not only on people but also on the lands we inhabit.[2] As hospitality is often imagined firstly as a gift from God, I suggest that we begin by intentionally situating our theology of hospitality within what Ruana Kuokkanen calls the "logic of the gift." Within Indigenous communities where the logic of the gift is operative, gifts are

---

2. Kuokkanen, "What Is Hospitality in the Academy?"; Ross, *Returning to the Teachings*; Deloria, *Spirit and Reason*; Tinker, *American Indian Liberation*.

given "to actively acknowledge the relationships and coexistence with the world without which survival would not be possible."[3]

The logic of the gift is an alternative economy to the economy of exchange, an economy more typical of Euro-Western capitalist thinking. In an economy of exchange, where balance is maintained through a perceived equal exchange of goods and services, a gift either upsets the balance, or becomes entangled with a sense of indebtedness to the giver. In the logic of an exchange economy, if a gift is given, whether by God or by one another, the notion of reciprocity becomes suspect, as reciprocity appears to lean towards indebtedness. In an economy of exchange, a gift is only considered truly a gift if there are no strings attached.

In addition, within the economy of exchange, being able to offer the gift of hospitality is often associated with having enough power (and property/possessions) to be able to host/give. As such, Jacques Derrida questions whether a "free gift" is even possible. Within this economy of exchange, as Jacques Derrida has so aptly noted, hospitality always, already, contains the seeds, if not the fruit, of violence.[4]

Alternatively, the logic of the gift assumes and acknowledges those strings as the web of all relations. Rather than understanding the importance of hospitality as a form of gift-giving which expects nothing in return, hospitality becomes a gift offered in recognition that we all, God included, bear responsibility for relationships of love and justice. Furthermore, an Indigenous logic of the gift keeps our relations to the land and living well in the land central to our considerations. It orients itself to respectful, responsible, and reciprocal relationships with others, whether human or other-than-human.

## MOVING BEYOND PATERNALISM AND RACISM: IS "WELCOME" ENOUGH?

Keeping in mind, then, a hospitality rooted in the logic of the gift, let us consider the next important question—how a theology of hospitality might help recognize and challenge, rather than reinforce, paternalism and racism in Canada.

Though there are diverse Christian theological and practical approaches to the question of hospitality, by and large theologies of hospitality have been given traction in biblical and theological themes of welcome such as that articulated in Romans 15:7, "Welcome one another, therefore, just as

---

3. Kuokkanen, "What Is Hospitality in the Academy?," 66.
4. Derrida, "Hospitality"; *Of Hospitality*.

Christ has welcomed you, for the glory of God." Christine Pohl, author of *Making Room: Recovering Hospitality as a Christian Tradition*, notes that as early as the fourth century, a definition arose of Christian hospitality that clearly distinguished it from the surrounding Greco-Roman world, which also emphasized the importance of hospitality. For Jerome, Lactantius and Chrysostom, Christian hospitality "was defined as welcoming the 'least' with no concerns for advantage or ambition."[5]

Pohl then notes that this definition arose at the same time that the church was gaining in power and prestige in the Roman Empire. She wonders at the "ironic" timing but does not explore whether any connection might be made between this "uniquely Christian definition" and the social and political reality of gaining power. However, I wonder whether the timing is not so ironic after all. Could it be that as an institution or community becomes more powerful and stable in its place within society, welcoming outsiders actually becomes less risky, particularly outsiders who are "the least"? This would be true because those with less worldly power are easier to control, to assimilate into the status quo, to define on their behalf what is in their own good.

This dynamic of "welcome" or "generosity" serving to solidify rather than undermine power and privilege is not lost on many thinkers critical of imperialism and oppression. As Paulo Freire points out in his *Pedagogy of the Oppressed*, "The generosity of the oppressors is nourished by an unjust order, which must be maintained in order to justify that generosity."[6] Notions of "welcome" can conjure up pleasantries, gratitude, and even cooperation while leaving real power imbalances unaddressed.

Like talk of reconciliation, emphasis on welcome within a theology of hospitality might duplicate a danger of the Truth and Reconciliation Commission: the production "of an illusory sense of resolution that conveniently brackets ongoing colonial injustices."[7] Indigenous theologian George E. "Tink" Tinker adds that "the nature of colonization is such that it entices the strong to take advantage of the weak in all aspects of life: social, political, economic, and religious."[8] As Cobus van Wyngaard notes throughout his work with racism in South Africa, even listening carries the danger of repeating paternalistic behavior if it doesn't require conversion.[9]

---

5. Pohl, *Making Room*, 47.
6. Freire, *Pedagogy of the Oppressed*, 60.
7. McCall, "My Story Is a Gift," 111.
8. Tinker, *American Indian Liberation*, 103.
9. Van Wyngaard, "Whiteness and Public Theology," 486.

Instead, we need a theology of hospitality that moves our communities beyond welcome and into a posture of humility, taking our own social situation and that of others very seriously, learning to recognize signs and effects of our privilege and power.[10] Welcome may still be one motif within this call, yet under the present circumstances I believe other trajectories of a biblical vision of hospitality ought to predominate.

## BIBLICAL FOUNDATIONS OF A THEOLOGY OF HOSPITALITY: LIBERATION, ENTANGLEMENT, AND COVENANT SOLIDARITY

So where, if not only or primarily in welcome, does the Bible root its teachings about hospitality? The Greek word in the New Testament text that is translated as "hospitality" is *philoxenia*, literally "loving as a brother one who is a stranger." This is the opposite of *xenophobia*, a term still operative in contemporary usage to indicate a fear of others who are different from us, most often in a context where violence and/or injustice arise out of that fear. Whereas in the ancient world, hospitality, or *philoxenia*, was seen as a civilizing concept and commended as a virtue,[11] the biblical witness situates this duty differently in its own memory and story. Both Deuteronomy and Leviticus root Israel's responsibility to the stranger in their remembrance of being brought out of Egypt by God (Deut 10:18–19; Lev 19:33–34). As such, significantly, the call to love the foreigner and the stranger is bound not primarily to welcome but to the act of liberation and the execution of justice. Israel is not told merely to "welcome" the alien, but to *not oppress* the alien (Lev 19:34).

Secondly, both the Hebrew Bible and the New Testament reflect the ancient world's understanding of the close intermingling among the divine and the earthly. Long before Jesus walked the earth, God strolls through the garden with Adam and Eve (Gen 3:8), visits Abraham and Sarah with two friends (Gen 18), and promises to "walk among" the people of Israel (Lev 26:12). Indeed, one of the New Testament teachings about loving strangers, Hebrews 13:2, refers directly back to Genesis 18: "Do not neglect to show hospitality to strangers, for by doing that some have entertained angels without knowing it." This ancient insight into a divinely entangled world in which our actions towards others are quite possibly being offered to Godself sits comfortably within the Indigenous logic of the gift, which "does not separate the self from

---

10. Russell, *Just Hospitality*; Peters, "Decolonizing Our Minds."
11. Sutherland, *I Was a Stranger*, xv.

the world to an extent that it would be possible to view human beings as independent from the rest of the socio-cosmic order."[12]

As within a gift-logic, the biblical texts ground hospitality not in having much to give within this entangled web, but in remembering one's own dependence on others, human and non-human. Hospitality does not reinforce possession, but dispossession. As opposed to Derrida, who claims that hospitality reinforces hierarchy and power because "it is only possible on the basis of having power to host and exert control over the people hosted,"[13] the Bible again and again emphasizes that it is predominantly those who are poor who, in offering hospitality, have an encounter with the holy (Gen 18; 1 Kgs 17:7–16; Luke 6:20). Self-sufficiency is not required. In fact, it likely puts us at a distinct disadvantage (Luke 6:24; Matt 19:24).

This challenges commonly held views of hospitality that involve those who "have" giving to those who don't, a view which can reinforce notions of superiority rather than reciprocity and partnership. Alternatively, the purpose of giving to or receiving from a stranger is to establish and build respect and relationship. It acknowledges that one is not able to go it alone, and that solidarity with all creation is critical to our survival. Furthermore, in the end there is not one who benefits more than the other, but both receive the fruits of the relationship. Just as the Latin word "hospitality" comes from the root *hostes*, which means both host and guest, the sort of hospitality that we are after also blurs the lines between "giver" and "receiver," the roles becoming far less predictable.[14]

Finally, another place where New Testament writers see evidence of God's hospitality is in the opening up of the kingdom of God to Gentiles. Both 1 Peter 2:10 and Romans 9:25 refer to the prophetic text of Hosea to express this action of God. Hosea 2:23, the primary text quoted in these passages, reads, "And I will have pity on Not pitied, and I will say to Not my people, 'You are my people'; and he shall say, 'Thou art my God.'"

Again, many reflections on God's hospitality see in these texts evidence that God's love of strangers is primarily rooted in welcome. Yet when we look at Hosea closely, it is questionable whether the main theme is God's welcome. Instead, we read about covenant, alienation, judgment and the longing for a renewed relationship of reciprocity and love.[15] The central emphasis is on love and repentance within a renewed covenantal relationship. God is a lively member of the community who is angered when covenant

---

12. Kuokkanen, "What Is Hospitality in the Academy?," 66.
13. Brander, "Hosts and Guests," 102.
14. Pohl, *Making Room*, 72–84.
15. Brueggemann, "Recovering God of Hosea"; Light, "New Covenant in Hosea."

fidelity is broken because the estrangement that occurs breaks the harmony of all of life. While we must not ignore the violent patriarchal imagery in Hosea, what is remarkable is that God passionately loves the stranger, or in this case the estranged, back into relationship. This new relationship "concerns new vows of fidelity on YHWH's part, new commitment to the well-being of creation through covenant, disarmament, the end of military threat, and the restoration of the fruitfulness of creation."[16]

If we imagine the God of Hosea within Indigenous epistemology and the logic of the gift, God's action towards restoration is part of God's commitment to the life and wellbeing of all. This is not a welcoming of those who were once nobodies[17] but God's actual turning away from the violence levied against Israel for unfaithfulness, and a choice made instead to pursue a renewed covenant.[18] God acts in this way because this is what God must do in order for healing to take place.

Gary W. Light, too, emphasizes the deeply expressed love of God intermingled with harsh threats of violence and destruction. He argues that the move Hosea makes is to re-conceptualize the meaning of covenant on relational terms. Hosea declares that the reason for the failure of the original covenant was the failure to love and know God (4:1). Thus, in order to renew the original intent of the covenant, the loving relationship needs to be emphasized and restored. It is here that we then enter into the poem that is picked up by New Testament writers, Hosea 2:2–23. While only the final verse is quoted in the New Testament, this verse is inextricable from the whole. Light names 2:16 as the central verse. Within this marriage metaphor, God longs to be Israel's "husband," using the more intimate word *ish*, and no longer Israel's "husband," using the more familiar contemporary term for husband, *baʼal*, also meaning lord, owner, ruler. The relationship God most deeply desires is a reciprocal, mutually faithful one, not merely a legal one.[19]

Light also emphasizes Hosea's use of agricultural metaphors. These, too, have significance for our attempts to understand hospitality in the context of colonial Canada and the exploitation of Indigenous people and their lands. Light notes that the same words, *ish* and *baʼal*, can also mean "keeper of tillable ground" or "land owner." Once again, the former connotes intimacy and care, and the latter connotes possession. In 2:21–22, verses just prior to the ones quoted in Romans and alluded to in 1 Peter, the restoration of relationship between God and Israel is reflected in God, the farmer's, living relationship

---

16. Brueggeman, "Recovering God of Hosea," 15.
17. Russell, *Just Hospitality*, 102.
18. Brueggeman, "Recovering God of Hosea," 8–9.
19. Light, "New Covenant in Hosea," 223–28.

with his farm, heard through the intimate conversation between elements of heaven and earth themselves. Later in Hosea, the broken covenant is reflected by a broken relationship with the land (e.g., 4:3; 8:7–8).

As we take the epistemology of Indigenous people seriously, and the racist and paternalistic relationship between settler Canadians and First Nations as the context of our own broken covenant or treaty, the sort of hospitality imagined in Hosea is precisely the sort we must pursue. First, the purpose is not so much "welcome" as it is mutual covenantal relationship built on reciprocal and intimate love. Second, there is a recognition of the violence, betrayal, and alienation that has been characteristic of the relationship, and that any restoration requires repentance and concrete change. And finally, the forest, animals, wind, and grain are all actors in the interconnected web of the covenant such that the brokenness of one impacts the other, and the wellbeing of one leads to the wellbeing of the other.

## THE CHALLENGE OF THE BIBLICAL CALL TO HOSPITALITY

Our exploration of some biblical themes, then, supports a theology of hospitality that insists on keeping God's welcome embedded firmly within God's definitive action towards liberation and God's expectation that we love strangers and do not oppress them. Furthermore, it cannot be disentangled from our own entanglement with all other forms of life—divine, human, and other-than-human—in heaven and on earth.

And so, then, on to some practical considerations. What, concretely, does such a theology of hospitality have in store for the mainline churches in this country, those made up primarily of people of European descent who benefit most significantly from the dispossession and exploitation we have spoken of thus far?

### *Movement #1: From Diversity to Dispossession*

Within the liberal democracies of global capitalism, multiculturalism and pluralism are valued. However, we must be cautious in too quickly celebrating institutionalized multiculturalism, as it easily becomes "a propaganda vehicle of Western capitalism."[20] In a sharp critique of liberal multiculturalist discourse, Meyda Yegenoglou warns that "the racism of multiculturalism does not reside in its being against the values of other cultures. Quite the contrary: it respects and tolerates other cultures, but in respecting and tolerating the different,

---

20. Augustine, "Pentecost and the Hospitality of God," 19.

it maintains a distance which enables it to retain a privileged position."[21] In other words, the disadvantaged "other" is encouraged to speak and express their views, all the while being made "irrelevant to the economic and political mechanisms of global governance."[22] Diversity becomes a smorgasbord of delightful and palatable "difference" on which to feast.

A biblical call to hospitality rooted in liberation, entanglement, and covenant solidarity within all of creation is, rather, an invitation to indigestion at such a multicultural banquet. As Chris Budden says in *Following Jesus in Invaded Space: Doing Theology on Aboriginal Land*, it requires that our communities face our racism and paternalism, and sincerely engage not only the joys of cross-cultural encounter, but real people in their anger and pain. "It is important that people meet and share their lives. It is particularly important that Second peoples hear the stories of First peoples first hand. But this is not enough. People need to be able to name the past for what it was, to own the injustice, and to act to help put it right."[23]

Sophie McCall, reflecting on the Truth and Reconciliation Commission, calls this becoming a witness both to the self, who "acknowledges historical responsibility for their privileges," as well as to the trauma being expressed by the Indigenous person telling their story.[24] Because "as colonizers our very souls are imperiled by our attitudes and actions towards others,"[25] the purpose of meeting and listening is about the same movement of the life of faith—living, dying, and rebirth. Our act as witness is a sort of martyrdom of the privileged self.

Fr. Pierre-Francois speaks of expecting a profound disorientation in our encounters with those we have learned to consider "other."[26] If hospitality primarily induces warm feelings and self-congratulatory gestures, it isn't the biblical hospitality we are talking about. Confronting the legacy of colonialism and the racism of our Christian communities should lead to repentance and, rather than guilt, an acceptance of responsibility for the piece our community can do to bear the burden and move in a new direction. Steve Heinrichs, Director of Indigenous Relations for Mennonite Church Canada calls this the path of learning and unlearning. Among other things, it involves deep exploration of the critical issues, listening to Indigenous voices, discovering the way our own families have engaged host peoples and the land in the past,

---

21. Yegenoglou, "Liberal Multiculturalism" 11.
22. Augustine, "Pentecost and the Hospitality of God," 20.
23. Budden, *Following Jesus in Invaded Space*, 161.
24. McCall, "My Story Is a Gift," 121.
25. Peters, "Decolonizing Our Minds," 96.
26. De Bethune, "Interreligious Dialogue and Sacred Hospitality," 3.

understanding the treaty history in our own area, and deconstructing Indigenous stereotypes in our heart and community.[27]

Croatian theologian Mirslav Volf has written extensively on the complexities of life in a fractured world out of his own experience of the horror of the Balkan warfare. Volf has developed the theological motif of the embrace as a way to think about and engage in the challenging and costly work of confronting injustice and violence, and moving in a different direction. His vision has import, too, for a renewed theology of hospitality. Volf speaks of the first movement of the embrace as the act of opening the arms. First we must signal to the other that we are open and no longer desire to be closed in on ourselves. We want to know something of the other's life, their hopes and their hurts. As gentle and non-threatening as the metaphor of "embrace" may be, Volf notes that "open arms suggest a fissure in the self. They signify an aperture on the boundary of the self through which the other can come in."[28] To offer a true embrace of the other means that we are willing to let go and detach ourselves from whatever we have created the other to be.

### *Movement #2: From Hosting to Being the Guest*

Being hospitable is usually imagined as positioning oneself as the host and welcoming the other as guest into our space. However, it is worthwhile to imagine how we might configure this host/guest relationship so that it leans into the biblical hospitality we are imagining. It seems to me that in a colonial context where one group has a disproportionate amount of unearned power and privilege, only by the dominant group intentionally taking the posture of the guest will there be any hope of enacting a biblically inspired hospitality.

In more and more settings, including places of worship, gatherings begin with an acknowledgment that we are guests on traditional, unceded Indigenous territory. While this may be an important recognition of Indigenous protocol, it is unclear just how this spoken recognition that we are guests of Indigenous nations is actually leading us into the posture of being so. Do our communities accept the invitations offered to them to visit Indigenous communities, attend powwows, and volunteer at Indigenous led organizations? Or are they more likely to invite an Indigenous speaker to one of our Sunday School classes? Do we take classes about Indigenous issues, or in all areas of the curriculum learn from Indigenous instructors alongside other Indigenous students? Are Indigenous ways

---

27. Heinrichs, *Paths for Peacemaking*.
28. Volf, *Exclusion and Embrace*, 141–42.

of teaching, learning, and knowing given central place in our schools, churches, and communities?

Amos Yong, evangelical theologian and professor of theology writes extensively of the importance of being guests of religious others. He notes that discourse about hospitality has only secondarily reflected on what it means to be a guest. Although he does not take up the critical question of being a guest of those whom we have exploited, or towards those whom we hold either a racist or a paternalistic attitude, his insights are important. Yong emphasizes cultivating friendships so that we receive an invitation in the first place. Being a guest entails "an intentionally deferential posture"[29] which cedes "power and initiative . . . to their hosts."[30] And perhaps most powerfully, from his evangelical commitment to "the affective and dispositional center of evangelical life,"[31] Yong insists that being a guest "invites us to risk vulnerability and place ourselves in the hands of others so that they may examine us and forgive our offenses."[32]

This "placing ourselves in the hands of others" entails not only vulnerability but a willingness to move slowly and wait. Unlike hosts who might even compel people to enter and partake of what they have provided (like the banquet host in Luke 14:21–23), the posture of guest entails a waiting to be received. This waiting reflects "act two" of Miroslav Volf's movement of the embrace. An embrace is not an embrace if it is grasped at or forced, and therefore, it may take a long time. There is no guarantee, having made the difficult and crucial transition into a willingness to open to the other and be their guest, that the other will respond and welcome us in. Here we must have patience. Here is the test of whether our willingness to embrace and be embraced is an authentic action of hospitality or not. For if it isn't—if it is really only a self-serving attempt to manipulate the other by empty expressions of love and acceptance, then our arms will tire and we will once again close off. Only if we have truly let go of our control of the relationship can we successfully engage in the patient act of waiting.[33]

## *Movement #3: From Support to Solidarity*

The final aspect I will explore is the movement from support to solidarity. Support conjures up images of giving out of our strength, donating money,

---

29. Yong, "Guests of Religious Others," 76.
30. Yong, "Guests of Religious Others," 78.
31. Yong, "Guests of Religious Others," 78.
32. Yong, "Guests of Religious Others," 79.
33. Volf, *Exclusion and Embrace*, 142–43.

signing petitions, attending rallies. All of these things have their important place, yet they are not primarily what hospitality in colonial Canada must be about. While they may not necessarily prevent repentance and reciprocal relationship, neither do they necessarily imply them. It is possible, in other words, to be "supportive" of Indigenous people without ever having that support bring us through repentance and into relationships of reciprocity, respect, and love.

Solidarity names something much deeper. Anti-racism trainer Anne Bishop highlights in her work and trainings that a root of all oppressions is a relationship of "power-over" such that the powerful group benefits at the expense of the less powerful.[34] Thus it becomes critical to deconstruct and reconstruct the basis of relationship between Indigenous and non-Indigenous people to one of reciprocity and respect, or "power-with." This, of course, echoes the central posture of dispossession and vulnerability named earlier. Yet from there it names something else critical to the new covenantal relationship, something central to an Indigenous worldview. It entails responsibility on the part of each party, a deep recognition and confession that not only are our histories entwined, but so are our futures.[35] Part of healing is to realize that we can't fix ourselves by ourselves. This is the opposite of triumphalism and superiority in that it both names our own lack and need as Euro-Christians, as well as recognizing that any healing depends upon mutual and equal relationships with Indigenous people.

This final movement from support to solidarity is like the final two acts of Miroslav Volf's embrace. In acts of solidarity, we realize the embrace itself. The embrace is a free and mutual giving and receiving. The other is not consumed into oneself, nor is the self consumed into the other, but the two encounter one another as a question—curious as to who the other is, what their perspective might be, and offering the vulnerability of one's own perspective. If the first two movements have been authentic, this is the act that fully transforms the relationship from one of possession, fear, and otherness, into one of freedom, love, and unity.

However, the embrace does not create unity by dissolving and making one body in the place of two. If the embrace is not to cancel itself out and finally result in the violence of assimilation, the arms must open again. The other must be let go so that the movement can continue on with the arms newly opened. The end of the embrace is already the possible

---

34. Bishop, *Becoming an Ally.*
35. McCall, "My Story Is a Gift," 121.

beginning of another embrace, for "the movement of the self to the other and back has no end."[36]

## CONCLUSION

My search for a post-colonial theology of hospitality has merely touched the surface of the implications for the Euro-Christian church in Canada, let alone its implications for Christian theologies, ecclesiologies, and missiologies. However, from its biblical roots in the memory of liberation and our call not to oppress, to its call to repentance and a renewed covenant with God, others, and the land, such an expanded view of what Christian hospitality entails is needed if we are to be faithful to our calling as a people of God.

For hospitality involves so much more than welcome, both on the part of God and on the part of human beings. It cannot be divorced from an awareness of, and the dismantling of, oppressive and violent relationships and social structures. It requires that all—whether divine, two-legged, winged, or four-legged—do their part in keeping covenant and treaty. And in the patient, careful journeying through it all, it means a willingness to be stretched into a different mode of perceiving and living in the world. Repentance. Reciprocity. Respect. Responsibility. Renewal. These become the defining features of the call to love the stranger. If Arthur Sutherland is right, and "hospitality is the practice by which the church stands or falls,"[37] may we have the courage to enter into its beckoning and its promise.

## BIBLIOGRAPHY

Allard, Silas Webster. "In the Shade of the Oaks of Mamre: Hospitality as a Framework for Political Engagement between Christians and Muslims." *Political Theology* 13 (2012) 414–24.

Augustine, Daniela C. "Pentecost and the Hospitality of God as Justice for Others." *Brethren Life and Thought* (2002) 17–26.

Bishop, Anne. *Becoming an Ally: Breaking the Cycle of Oppression in People*. 3rd ed. Halifax: Fernwood, 2015.

Brander, Tobias. "Hosts and Guests: Hospitality as an Emerging Paradigm in Mission." *International Review of Mission* 102 (2013) 94–102.

Brett, Mark G. *Decolonizing God: The Bible in the Tides of Empire*. Sheffield: Sheffield Phoenix, 2008.

Brueggemann, Walter. "The Recovering God of Hosea." *Horizons in Biblical Theology* 30 (2008) 5–20.

Budden, Chris. *Following Jesus in Invaded Space: Doing Theology on Aboriginal Land*. Eugene, OR: Pickwick, 2009.

---

36. Volf, *Exclusion and Embrace*, 143–45.
37. Sutherland, *I Was a Stranger*, 83.

Byrne, Brendan. *The Hospitality of God: A Reading of Luke's Gospel*. Collegeville, MN: Liturgical, 2000.

de Bethune, Pierre-Francois. "Interreligious Dialogue and Sacred Hospitality." *Religion East & West* 7 (2007) 1–22.

Deloria, Vine. *Spirit & Reason: The Vine Deloria Jr. Reader*. Edited by Barbara Deloria, et al. Golden, CO: Fulcrum, 1999.

Derrida, Jacques. "Hospitality." In *Acts of Religion*, edited by G. Anidjar, 358–420. New York: Routledge, 2002.

———. *Of Hospitality: Anne Dufourmantelle Invites Jacques Derrida to Respond*. Stanford: Stanford University Press, 2000.

Freire, Paulo. *Pedagogy of the Oppressed*. 30th anniversary ed. New York: Bloomsbury Academic, 2012.

Heinrichs, Steve. *Buffalo Shout, Salmon Cry: Conversations on Creation, Land Justice, and Life Together*. Waterloo, ON: Herald, 2013.

———. *Paths for Peacemaking with Host Peoples*. Winnipeg: Mennonite Church Canada, 2014.

Kuokkanen, Rauna. "What Is Hospitality in the Academy? Epistemic Ignorance and the (Im)Possible Gift." *Review of Education, Pedagogy, and Cultural Studies* 30 (2008) 60–82.

Light, Gary W. "The New Covenant in the Book of Hosea." *Review and Expositor* 90 (1993) 219–38.

Mackey, Eve. "The Apologizer's Apology." In *Reconciling Canada: Critical Perspectives on the Culture of Redress*, edited by Jennifer Henderson and Pauline Wakeham, 47–62. Toronto: University of Toronto Press, 2013.

McCall, Sophie. "'My Story Is a Gift': The Royal Commission on Aboriginal Peoples and the Politics of Reconciliation." In *First Person Plural: Aboriginal Storytelling and the Ethics of Collaborative Authorship*, 109–136. Vancouver: University of British Columbia Press, 2011.

Newman, Elizabeth. *Untamed Hospitality: Welcoming God and Other Strangers*. Grand Rapids: Brazos, 2007.

Peters, Rebecca Todd. "Decolonizing our Minds: Postcolonial Perspectives on the Church." In *Women's Voices and Visions of the Church: Reflections from North America*, edited by Aruna Gnanadson, et al., 93–110. Geneva: World Council of Churches, 2005.

Pohl, Christine D. *Making Room: Recovering Hospitality as a Christian Tradition*. Grand Rapids: Eerdmans, 1999.

Rosello, Mireille. *Postcolonial Hospitality: The Immigrant as Guest*. Stanford, CA: Stanford University Press, 2001.

Ross, Rupert. *Returning to the Teachings: Exploring Aboriginal Justice*. Toronto: Penguin, 1996.

Russell, Letty M. *Just Hospitality: God's Welcome in a World of Difference*. Louisville: Westminster John Knox, 2009.

Said, Edward. *Orientalism*. New York: Vintage, 1999.

Sutherland, Arthur. *I Was a Stranger: A Christian Theology of Hospitality*. Nashville: Abingdon, 2006.

Tinker, George E. *American Indian Liberation: A Theology of Sovereignty*. Maryknoll, NY: Orbis, 2008.

van Wyngaard, Cobus. "Whiteness and Public Theology: An Exploration of Listening." *Missionalia: South African Journal of Missiology* 43 (2015) 478–92.

Volf, Miroslav. *Exclusion & Embrace: A Theological Exploration of Identity, Otherness, and Reconciliation*. Nashville: Abingdon, 1996.

Yegenoglou, Meyda. "Liberal Multiculturalism and the Ethics of Hospitality in the Age of Globalization." *Postmodern Culture* 13 (2003). Online. http://muse.jhu.edu/journals/postmodern_culture/vo13/13.2yegenoglu.html.

Yong, Amos. "Guests of Religious Others: Theological Education in the Pluralistic World." *Theological Education* 47 (2012) 75–83.

# 14

# Hindu Traditions
## A Positive Approach to the Other

ACHARYA SHRINATH PRASAD DWIVEDI

THIS ESSAY PRESENTS THOSE cosmic values of Hindu *Dharma* (religion) that help in formulating positive consciousness. Positive consciousness is a healthy environment of support, cooperation, and compassion. It includes a minimizing of negative thoughts of hatred, violence, prejudice, and injustice. Positive consciousness is the cultivation of a desire for the well-being of all humanity. Please note that the essay does not offer a comprehensive review of all psychological or religious theories. Instead, it focuses on various basic concepts that I, in my work as an inter-religious activist, have found most are relevant in stimulating positive awareness.

## DIVERSITY OF HINDU RELIGION

What we call Hindu religion may be understood as a collection of many religions. There is neither a single scripture nor a single founder of the Hindu religion. Hindu traditions are part of the ancient Sindhu (Indus) Valley civilization. These traditions survived the blows of time and invasion while other old civilizations such as Babylonian, Egyptian, Mesopotamian, and Mayan disappeared, living on primarily in books or museums. Over time,

Hindu traditions have evolved. With the passage of time, more scriptures were added to suit changing cultural and intellectual needs.[1]

Hindu traditions include multiple theistic philosophies: *Nyaya* (realism), *Vaisesika* (atomism), *Samkhya* (dualism), *Yoga* (union), *Mimamsa* (textual reflection) and Vedanta (philosophical study of the Upanishad texts). Vedanta itself is composed of different metaphysical schools of thought. These include *dvaita* (Dualism), *Advaita* (Non-dualism), *Vishishta Dvaita* (Specified-Dualism). Hindu traditions include the various Yogic paths of *Moksha* (Liberation): *Karma Yoga* (Action Yoga), *Bhakti Yoga* (Devotional Yoga), and *Jnana Yoga* (Knowledge Yoga).[2] About this, the *Santi Parva*, twelfth book of the ancient epic *Mahabharata* says, "Outwardly, it sounds quite complex to a common person but deep study and understanding may clear all the confusion."[3]

## UNIVERSAL ASPECTS OF HINDU RELIGION

The *Mahabharata* explicitly defines the purpose of religion as "the general betterment of all-beings" (Mahabharata, Santi Parva, 101.10). Across its differing philosophical traditions, Hindu religion endorses the idea that entire cosmos is permeated by the same spiritual power. "Divinity pervades everything," says the *Bhagavad Gita* (18.61), also part of the *Mahabharata*. Thus, there is no difference between energy and matter. Divine light is present in everything. This includes all human beings regardless of race, religion, creed or nationality. The spark of divinity dwells inside us in form of *atman*, spirit or soul. This spark of divinity moves human beings to diverse forms of spiritual expression. As Swami Vivekananda (1862–1902) said, "Religion is the manifestation of divinity that is already in man."[4] From this, it can be argued that inwardly all humans are inter-connected, making all humans part of an extended global family. Just as we take care of our close family members, we are also supposed to take care of the members of our global family. As other authors have said, *dharma* (religion) is the welfare of good men.[5]

Two well-known sayings imply the unity and equality of all religious traditions and belief systems. "Truth alone triumphs" was adopted as the national motto of India in 1950. It is part of a mantra from ancient Sanskrit text, the *Mundaka Upanishads* (3.1.6). This concept reminds us that we do not

1. Flood, *Introduction to Hinduism.*
2. Klostermaier, *Survey of Hinduism.*
3. For a well-known translation, see Subramanian.
4. Swami Vivekananda, *Complete Works of Swami Vivekananda.*
5. Radhakrishnan, "Hindu Dharma."

need to have any confrontation, hatred, or suspicion for each other. Truth, not anger, triumphs. "Truth is one, but scholars interpret it differently," says the *Rig Veda* (1.164.46). This concept can motivate people to think more carefully about the oneness of all, and gradually minimize differences and hostility. Together, the two concepts can work as a unifying force.

The Hindu concept of nonviolence brings these philosophical concepts into action. "Non-violence is the supreme religion," says the *Santi Parva* book of the *Mahabharata*. This refers to avoiding violence in actions, words, and even thoughts. It is meant to be directed at all living beings, and lead to reverence for all of nature. The practice of nonviolence can have a profound impact in cultivating a culture of peace, compassion, and harmony. In our time, philosophers and psychologists influenced by quantum mechanics have taught that the very process of our observation changes the things we observe.[6] What we see depends on how we look. What we do depends on what we see. What we see depends on what we think. "Life is regulated, coordinated, and unified according to the objective one chooses as their life's goal and their whole existence is an expression of that objective."[7]

As explained above, it is a prominent Hindu tradition to look upon human beings as part of nature. Vedic wisdom reflects an encompassing global view of all beings as being pervaded by same spiritual power. Reverence for life is connected with an awareness that the majestic forces of nature are all bound to each other. Thus, the Hindu view of nature is expressed in the call for people not to exploit natural resources to satisfy their greed. Today, global patterns of increasing population, urbanization and accelerated economic expansion have created significant environmental challenges. Hindu teachings about reverence for all forms of life need to be nurtured and emphasized. These teachings can change our thought and our action. Thus, they can help us learn how to support a sustainable environment.[8] The *Vedas* say, "We venerate Mother Earth, the sustainer and preserver of forests, vegetation. She is the source of stable environment" (*Prithvi Sukta, Atharveda*, verse 27). "O Mother Earth! you care for the people who belong to different races, practice various religions and spiritual beliefs, and speak different languages. Like the wish fulfilling cow, may you bless us all in thousand fold-manner" (*Prithvi sukta*, verse 45).

---

6. Weizmann Institute, "Quantum Theory Demonstrated."
7. Little, *Introduction to Sociology*.
8. Pankaj Jain, *Ten Hindu Environmental Teachings*.

## POSITIVE THINKING AND HINDU RELIGIOUS TEACHING

Positive psychology is a contemporary field of research that uses scientific understanding to focus on personal growth rather than on pathology.[9] Religion has been shown to have a positive effect on personal growth. This effect is reinforced when a religious tradition teaches positive thinking. According to National Institutes of Health research, people who are religious show better emotional well-being and lower rates of delinquency, alcoholism, drug abuse and other social problems.[10] According to R. A. Emmons, six religious factors have a positive effect on well-being. Religion provides social support, coping strategies, and a sense of meaning and purpose. It promotes generosity and altruism, personality integration, and a healthy life style.[11]

As seen above in the discussion of nonviolence, the conceptual foundation of Hindu traditions is broadly based on a positive approach to life. The premise is that positive thinking lead to positive emotions and positive behavior. Positive emotions include happiness, joy, excitement, satisfaction, pride, and awe. The health benefits of positive thinking include increased life span, lower rates of depression, lower levels of stress, better psychological and physical well-being, and better coping skills during hardships. Negative thoughts and emotions such as fear, anger, and stress, on the other hand, drain energy and keep us from being in the present moment. They interrupt the clarity of our thought and close off some of our options.[12] Positive thinking does not mean that person should separate himself or herself from less pleasant situations. Rather, they should deal with challenging situations in a more positive and creative way. In every situation, people can ask themselves the age-old question: is your glass half empty or half full? The answer can lead to a person reacting with positive or negative thoughts and emotions. As shown above, thinking and feeling affect what we see, and what we do, and our impact on the world around us.

Religiosity has been recognized as leading to pro-social behavior. Positive relationships are important in feeding positive emotions. In their focus on the oneness of all, Hindu teachings actively emphasize positive relationships. Enmity, hatred and violence based on religion or race are discouraged. Active cooperation and collaboration aimed at building the welfare of all are encouraged. These actions, too, shape thought. The mind

---

9. Seligman and Csikszentmihalyi, "Positive Psychology."
10. Koenig, "Religion, Spirituality, and Health."
11. Emmons, *Psychology of Ultimate Concerns*.
12. Khazan, "Best Headspace for Making Decisions."

is a spiritual facet of the material universe.[13] Behavior affects the mind and the mind's social, emotional, and religious beliefs are formed.[14] Many people work for the happiness and prosperity of their own family. Religious communities often expand that work, creating projects that contribute to the greater good of humanity. Specifically, Hindu principles such as, "for the happiness of all and the welfare of many" and "may all enjoy happiness" inspire people to work and sacrifice for others without any prejudice, bias or narrow considerations.

The inspiration, in turn, must lead to action. Swami Vivekananda used to say that it is a sin to preach religion to one who is hungry or naked.[15] First, religious people must help take care of the basic needs of other people. Only then should they teach about the religion and spirituality that motivated them to reach out. If practiced sincerely, this caring approach will help alleviate poverty, suffering, and hopelessness. I pray that Hindu positive thinking can keep alive our hope in building relationships of trust and cooperation that will assure the peace and well-being of people on earth.

## BIBLIOGRAPHY

Azar, Beth. "A Reason to Believe." *APA Monitor on Psychology* 41 (2010) 52. Online. https://www.apa.org/monitor/2010/12/believe.

Emmons, R. A. *The Psychology of Ultimate Concerns: Motivation and Spirituality in Personality.* New York: Guilford, 1999.

Flood, Gavin. *An Introduction to Hinduism.* Cambridge: Cambridge University Press, 1996.

Jain, Pankaj. "Ten Hindu Environmental Teachings." *Huffington Post*, April 10, 2011. Online. https://www.huffpost.com/entry/10-hindu-environmental-te_b_846245.

Khazan, Olga. "The Best Headspace for Making Decisions." *Atlantic*, September 19, 2016. Online. https://www.theatlantic.com/science/archive/2016/09/the-best-headspace-for-making-decisions/500423.

Klostermaier, Klaus K. *A Survey of Hinduism.* Albany, NY: State University of New York Press, 2007.

Koenig, Harold G. "Religion, Spirituality, and Health: The Research and Clinical Implications." *ISRN Psychiatry*, December 16, 2012. Online. https://www.ncbi.nlm.nih.gov/pmc/articles/PMC3671693.

Kumaris, Brahma. *Journey into Inner Space: Find Your True Self.* Haryana, India: Imprint, 2019.

Little, William. *Introduction to Sociology.* 2nd ed. Vancouver: BC Open Textbook Collection, 2016. Online. https://opentextbc.ca/introductiontosociology2ndedition.

Radhakrishnan, S. "The Hindu Dharma." *International Journal of Ethics* 33 (1922) 1–22.

13. Kumaris, *Journey into Inner Space.*
14. Azar, "Reason to Believe."
15. Vivekananda, *Complete Works.*

Seligman, Martin, and Mihaly Csikszentmihalyi. "Positive Psychology: An Introduction." *American Psychologist* 55 (2000) 5–14.
Subramanian, Kamala, trans. *Mahabharata*. Mumbai: Siddhi, 2014.
Vivekananda, Swami. *The Complete Works of Swami Vivekananda*. Belur, India: Advaita Ashrama, 2014.
Weizmann Institute of Science. "Quantum Theory Demonstrated: Observation Affects Reality." *Science Daily*, February 27, 1998. Online. https://www.sciencedaily.com/releases/1998/02/980227055013.htm.

# III.

## RESPONSIBILITY TO THE OTHER IN CHRISTIAN MISSION

# 15

# Indigenous People as the Other
## Bartolomé de las Casas in Conversation with Tzvetan Todorov

RAY ALDRED

## INTRODUCTION

THIS PAPER PLACES BARTOLOMÉ de las Casas (1484–1566) and Tzvetan Todorov (1939–2017) in dialogue in order to explore the "other," modernity, and the role of Christianity. Both Las Casas and Todorov wrote about the conquest of the Americas. They agreed that the coming of the Europeans to the New World fundamentally altered the European conception of what it means to be a human being. Las Casas believed that the discovery of America by Columbus was God's providential work. It set before Spain the opportunity to spread the kingdom of God over all the earth through evangelism. But Las Casas, moved by his experience and his Christianity, also sought to defend the Indians from Spanish brutality. Todorov, however, criticized Las Casas's mixed motives, claiming that Las Casas did not completely acknowledge the Indigenous people as equal human beings to the Spanish Christians.[1] Todorov offered another vision of "salvation" or vision of progress. Human enlightenment, he wrote, points to humanism and democracy as modes of respecting the "other." Todorov was

---

1. Todorov, *Conquest of America*, 163.

correct that Las Casas's Christianity was polluted with his own nationalism. Nevertheless, the progression of Las Casas's own thought envisioned a way forward that respects Indigenous identity. Todorov's enlightened humanism, however, presumed the inadequacy of Christianity, making a judgment on behalf of Indigenous people about Christian faith.

## BARTOLOMÉ DE LAS CASAS: DEFENDER OF THE INDIANS

### Shaping Forces

Bartolomé de las Casas was born in Seville, Spain, in 1484.[2] During his lifetime, Spain experienced events that advanced the profile of the Catholic Nation. On January 2, 1492, the Spanish monarchs Ferdinand and Isabella took possession of Granada after successfully defeating the Muslims who had taken it from them.[3] That same year, Columbus set out on his initial voyage in search of a direct route to the wealth of the Indies by circumnavigating the globe from the West and arriving in the East.[4] Spain had spent a significant amount of its wealth in advancing the Catholic State, and no doubt the need for wealth was a significant motivator for the Spanish monarchy to finance his voyage. At the same time, they had succeeded in returning a Catholic King as the rightful sovereign to Granada. It was only right, they believed, that the kingdom of the Catholic King continue to advance. The advancement of the Kingdom of God by the Nation of Spain by means of war would continue to be a part of the thinking of the Spanish,[5] but so would the advancement of the Catholic faith. These two forces, war and mission, would shape Las Casas as he encountered Indigenous people of the New World who were brutalized by Spanish fortune hunters and soldiers. As he came to see it, these Indigenous people were in need of both eternal salvation and protection from the Spanish in the present world.

Las Casas's first encounter with the "other" was in his birthplace, Seville. His father was a merchant who sailed with Christopher Columbus. When Columbus returned from his first voyage in 1493, he came to Seville. Las Casas, at the age of eight, "saw them in Seville, where they stayed."[6] He saw the seven "Indians" who had survived Columbus's return voyage to Spain. Las Casas, like everyone else, was filled with awe at the

---

2. Las Casas and Griffin, *Destruction of the Indies*, xlii.
3. Las Casas et al., *Only Way*, 9.
4. Las Casas and Collard, *History of the Indies*, 16.
5. Las Casas et al., *Only Way*, 9.
6. Casas and Collard, *History of the Indies*, 37.

sight of the "Indians" and the beautiful parrots and gold that Columbus had brought. After a subsequent voyage to the new world, Las Casas's father returned with "Indian" slaves or servants given to him by Columbus.[7] He gave the young Amerindian Juanico to his son as a companion. No doubt, Juanico was baptized when he returned with the younger Las Casas to Hispaniola. There, in 1502, Las Casas became an *encomendero* (land and labor grant holder) of an estate. He was administrator of his father's holdings, courtesy of Columbus himself.

Spain was still a feudal state after the pattern of the Middle Ages. Thus, hierarchy of society was a given. But the Spanish approach to servitude shifted with its contact with the New World.[8] Instead of outright slavery, something no doubt many Spanish would have preferred, the system of *encomendero* was established. "Indians" were assigned to *encomenderos* as serfs or servants, not slaves. In exchange for working and paying a tribute to the Spanish overlords, the Spanish overlord was to provide teaching on the Catholic faith. In this way the desire of the State and faith could be balanced.[9] During Las Casas's time as an *encomendero*, the Spanish killed an Indian chieftain whom Las Casas had befriended. This led to an Indian uprising because of Spanish treachery. Despite his horror, young Las Casas and his father helped to finance a campaign to capture the remaining rebellious chiefs.[10] Still, Las Casas began to shift his focus from the expansion of Spain's wealth to his desire for justice for the Indigenous people, flowing out of his own developing Christian faith.

In 1506 Las Casas returned to Seville to seek the priesthood. When he returned as a priest to the New World and helped with the conquest, he did so in a peaceful way. In the conquest of Cuba, he went ahead of the Spanish troops as the "white Shaman." He combined being a priest and healer.[11] He went into Indian villages, preached the gospel, baptized converts and then instructed the natives to leave half of the village houses empty with plenty of food for the arriving Spanish force. He promised the Indigenous people that this would prevent violence against them. However, even this peaceful approach at times could not prevent violence against the Indigenous people. In one Cuban village, Las Casas was unable to stop the slaughter of Indigenous people. This continued to make him question the actions of the Spanish in the New World. But, he did not question the Church or the Christian faith.

---

7. Las Casas et al., *Only Way*, 12–13.
8. Hanke and Casas, *All Mankind Is One*.
9. Hanke and Casas, *All Mankind Is One*, 4–5.
10. Las Casas et al., *Only Way*, 14.
11. Las Casas et al., *Only Way*, 17.

His conversion leading to renouncing his use of "Indian" slaves or serfs began in earnest when he heard the preaching of the Dominicans condemning the practice of enslaving the Indians.[12] The Dominicans' argument was to the effect that "Indians" were rational human beings. They had the right to lands and to the gospel. Anyone who enslaved them was guilty of breaking the second commandment to love your neighbour as yourself. As human beings, Indians had the right to be loved and the Spanish had the obligation to love them. "The preaching of Antón Montesino against the Spanish began to turn Las Casas, 'you are living in deadly sin for the atrocities you tyrannically impose on the innocent people. Tell me, what right have you to enslave them?'"[13] The Dominicans went even further, denying the right to confession and absolution to any owner of "Indian" slaves, including the young priest, Las Casas.[14] He wondered why, as he had been a fair and just overlord. Yet the denial of absolution began a three-year process of reasoning that would culminate in a conversion of attitude and consciousness.

By his own recollection, Las Casas was contemplating a passage from Ecclesiasticus 34 in preparation for a coming sermon he needed to preach around the time of Pentecost, 1514.[15]

> If one sacrifices ill-gotten goods, the offering is blemished; the gifts of the lawless are not acceptable. The Most High is not pleased with the offerings of the ungodly, nor for a multitude of sacrifices does he forgive sins. Like one who kills a son before his father's eyes is the person who offers a sacrifice from the property of the poor. The bread of the needy is the life of the poor; whoever deprives them of it is a murderer. To take away a neighbor's living is to commit murder; to deprive an employee of wages is to shed blood. (Sir 34:21–25, NASB)

Reflecting on that passage, on the preaching of the Dominican Friar three years prior, and on the teaching of the Church, his eyes were opened to his own complicity in the enslavement of the Indians. Thus, around the age of forty, he decided that he would renounce his ownership of "Indians."[16] He did not do this lightly, for he understood that they would in all likelihood end up with a master who treated them with far less respect. However, he was convinced that if he preached against oppression while continuing to own "Indians," people would accuse him of being a hypocrite.

12. Las Casas and Griffin, *Destruction of the Indies*, xx.
13. Las Casas and Collard, *History of the Indies*, 184.
14. Las Casas and Collard, *History of the Indies*, 208.
15. Las Casas et al., *Only Way*, 19.
16. Las Casas and Collard, *History of the Indies*, 209.

## Sin of the Spanish "Conquistadors" and the Need for Restitution

Las Casas's encounters with the Indians had led him to conclude that the Indians were not irrational savages or under-developed human beings. Rather, they were a peaceful, rational people with their own unique characteristics and talents. They lived in freedom, with their own laws, cities, and commerce. In many ways, their form of government was superior to European countries. They did not deserve to be slaves. Instead, they had the right to receive the gospel and to freely come to faith.[17] The church fathers, said Las Casas, never presented the gospel by way of the sword.[18] Missionaries concerned with the "Indians'" free opportunity for salvation would pursue a peaceful method. Only those intent on making money or taking advantage would use violence.[19]

The Spanish, said Las Casas, had been given the privilege of bringing the gospel to the New World. This mission was the primary reason for their presence in the New World.[20] Unless the Spanish project kept to its intended mission, it was sinful. Thus, the Spanish conquistadors, not the Indians, were the uncivilized ones.[21] They had become like irrational barbarians[22] incapable of governing themselves because of their lust for gold and riches. In *A Short Account of the Destruction of the Indians,* Las Casas criticized the Spanish for tearing the "Indians" to shreds. The Spanish settlers' violence revealed that they were just pretending to be Christians.[23] They had proved themselves unfit for the providential gift that God had given them by allowing them to discover the New World.[24] Their unchristian demonic behavior had cast the gospel and the Catholic faith in a negative light and severely damaged the mission of sharing the gospel with the inhabitants of the New World.[25] Spanish violence against Indigenous people had made the gospel odious to them. Indigenous people were killed before they could respond to the gospel. Thus, anyone left alive could not see how this gospel

---

17. Las Casas et al., *Only Way*, 64; Las Casas and Poole, *In Defense of the Indians,* 41–42; Gutiérrez, *In Search of the Poor,* 67, 80.

18. Gutiérrez, *In Search of the Poor,* 264–65; Las Casas and Poole, *In Defense of the Indians,* 175.

19. Las Casas et al., *Only Way*, 103–9.

20. Gutiérrez, *In Search of the Poor,* 82.

21. Las Casas and Poole, *In Defense of the Indians,* 28–42.

22. Las Casas and Poole, *In Defense of the Indians,* 49, 53.

23. Las Casas and Griffin, *Destruction of the Indies,* 12–13.

24. Las Casas and Griffin, *Destruction of the Indies,* 71–72.

25. Las Casas and Griffin, *Destruction of the Indies,* 82.

was a gospel of love.[26] Due to the violence, the Nation of Spain was in danger of coming under the judgment of God for the sin against the Indigenous people.[27] In his final will, Las Casas wrote, "I believe that because of these impious, criminal and ignominious deeds perpetrated so unjustly, tyrannically and barbarously, God will vent upon Spain His wrath and fury, for nearly all of Spain has shared in the bloody wealth usurped at the cost of so much ruin and slaughter."[28]

Thus, Las Casas called on the Spanish crown to make restitution to the Indians. He found support for restitution in the writings of Aquinas on just war.[29] Even if Spain was justified in making war against the Indians, Las Casas argued, the brutality and violence against women, children, and the elderly was unjust and was a mortal sin. The Spanish had systematically destroyed the Indigenous people, using every pretext available to continue to conquer and effectively depopulate some of the Islands. Therefore, since the Spanish soldiers had done injustice, restitution was necessary.[30] Restitution could save the reputation and destiny of Spain, and also see a great harvest of souls amongst the Indigenous people. Las Casas demanded that the Indians receive back their own lands and haciendas near Christian villages and settlements.[31] Ultimately, he envisioned a peaceful coexistence between Spanish and Indigenous people.

By calling for restitution, Las Casas was not attempting to destroy the country of Spain, the monarchy, or the Christian Church. He hoped that Spain would continue to be the sovereign Catholic Nation that advanced the kingdom of God. So that no one would falsely blame the Sovereign of Spain for the violence, he recorded the history of the Indies.[32] He envisioned the Indigenous people willing to embrace the Catholic faith, if it was presented in a peaceful, gentle way, and to live "free" under the Sovereign of Spain.[33]

Las Casas was not a humanist in the modern sense. Rather, his ethics flowed out of his faith in the theology of the Spanish Catholic Church. At one point, he suggested that slaves of other ethnicities could replace

---

26. Las Casas et al., *Only Way*, 158.
27. Las Casas et al., *Only Way*, 170.
28. Todorov, *Conquest of America*, 245.
29. Aquinas, *Summa Theologica*, II–II, Q 59, A 4.
30. Las Casas and Poole, *In Defense of the Indians*, 202–3.
31. Las Casas, "Letter to the Council," 24.
32. Las Casas and Collard, *History of the Indies*, 9.
33. Las Casas et al., *Only Way*, 53; Las Casas and Griffin, *Destruction of the Indies*, 18–19.

the "Indians," who were not well-suited to slavery.[34] Later, he changed his mind, and regretted that perspective. Still, he did not advocate for anything like a democratic nation state. For him, all persons were equal under God, even if they occupied different places within the functional hierarchy of the kingdom. Indigenous people would never occupy the role of the sovereign, but it was not clear where Las Casas thought they would fit in the hierarchy of Church leadership. Nonetheless, as Hanke points out, future modern thinkers did look to Las Casas's Christian values as inspiration for their modern secular values.[35]

## TZVETAN TODOROV

### Shaping Forces

By his own admission, Tzvetan Todorov had a vested interest in seeing democracy defended. He was born in 1939 and grew up under communist rule in Sofia, Bulgaria.[36] Tzvetan grew up knowing what it was like to lack freedom and be controlled by the state. He wrote, "Our whole life was monitored, and the slightest deviation from the party line risked being denounced."[37] He was in danger of being punished, but desired freedom, so he managed to write for a newspaper in which advocated for freedom by alluding to some past heroes who opposed fascism. His desire was to help people remember "freedom must be fought for."[38] Freedom was fundamental to democracy, but freedom was being threatened. Under the guise of democracy, some were seeking to limit freedoms, for the sake of ideologies that seemed to be moving backward toward totalitarian states. Todorov sought to defend people from the intrusion of governments and religions, which, he thought, denigrate human beings.[39] He was therefore a defender of persons like Las Casas. However, Todorov viewed the world through a non-religious lens. He sought to resurrect the humanist values that had initially led to democratic countries that stood for the freedom of human beings. He believed that Las Casas was possibly beginning to develop humanist values but did not go far enough.

---

34. Las Casas, "Letter to the Council," 24; Las Casas and Griffin, *Destruction of the Indies*, 10, 42.

35. Hanke, *Aristotle and the American Indians*, 116.

36. Todorov, *Frail Happiness*, xi.

37. Todorov and Brown, *Inner Enemies of Democracy*, 1.

38. Todorov and Brown, *Inner Enemies of Democracy*, 3.

39. Todorov and Brown, *Inner Enemies of Democracy*, 7.

Todorov examined the literature from the conquest of America, as part of an attempt to understand the enlightenment and the modern era. For Todorov, the founding of the New World marked the beginning of modernity.[40] The encounter with the "other" forced the Old World to face the limitations of its own perception. The Spanish had encountered the other in persons from Africa and the Moors, and even in parts of Asia, but this had been gradual. The Americas represented something sudden and completely new.[41] The Spanish also represented something completely new for the Amerindians. Encountering this "other" forced Europeans to rethink some of their traditional accounts of the world. It pushed the development of humanism. The discovery of people still seen as the "natural" human showed that something had been lost in the development of European people.

Humanism, defined by Todorov, holds the autonomy of the individual to freely choose, with a human morality developed within a social context, i.e., not given by God. This context defines a person's identity, as neither an isolated individual, nor a faceless member of a commune.[42] Todorov identified four phases of encountering the other that progress toward the humanist ideal. When encountering the "other," at first I have only the categories of my own identity, so I put the knowledge of the other into my own categories. Thus, even though I am interested in other cultures, I assimilate them into my prefigured categories. As Todorov wrote, "Knowledge grows quantitatively, not qualitatively. There is only one identity: my own."[43] In the second phase of understanding, I immerse myself in the other culture. I try to become one with the other by giving up my own identity. In the third phase of understanding, I resume my own identity from a new perspective. The difference between the other and me becomes a space for dialogue to occur, not something to be overcome or erased. In the fourth and final phase, I arrive at a reconfigured identity that is neither the other's nor my original identity. Instead it is an identity that is truly inter-subjective.[44]

When the Spanish encountered the Amerindians, they interpreted them through their own "preconfigured" categories. The majority of the Spanish reacted with ethnocentrism. They believed that the Indigenous people were at best like children and at worst guilty of the worst pagan crimes imaginable. These were the only categories that the Spanish possessed. For example, Las Casas's opponent, Juan Gines de Sepulveda,

---

40. Todorov, *Conquest of America*, 5.
41. Todorov, *Morals of History*, 17.
42. Todorov, *Imperfect Garden*, 33.
43. Todorov, *Imperfect Garden*, 14.
44. Todorov, *Imperfect Garden*, 15.

believed that the Indigenous people were pagans and guilty of idolatry, cannibalism and other atrocities.[45] Therefore, they were less than true human beings and could be made slaves or killed by just war. Even Las Casas, who "refused to despise others simply because they were different,"[46] and defended Indigenous people, saw them through familiar Christian categories. Las Casas believed that the Indigenous people had all the markers of civilization.[47] They had government, community, commerce and an economy. However, Las Casas viewed their spirituality as inferior to his. He sought to gently assimilate the Indigenous people into the Spanish Catholic Kingdom. Todorov suggested that Las Casas viewed the Indians as "wild" Christians, who could be assimilated into the Christian Spanish nation.[48] Thus, Las Casas did not evaluate Indigenous people with a universal humanist moral judgement. He was, according to Todorov, guilty of a "prejudice of equality . . . it consists in identifying the other purely and simply with one's own "ego ideal" (or with oneself)."[49] Although he was motivated by love, his religious values constricted his freedom to allow Indigenous people to be who they are. He did not recognize the identity of Indigenous people themselves or their desires to perhaps remain free autonomous people. Thus, while not an ethnocentric advocate of violent conquest, like Sepulveda, he was guilty of a "generous assimilation."[50]

## "Salvation" in Moral Humanism

Todorov defined the enlightenment broadly:

> What we mean by "Enlightenment" was not a rational and coherent doctrine, where the consequences followed from rigorous, universally accepted principles; rather it was a broad discussion, which combined contradictory or complementary proposals, either inherited from the past or newly formulated. It was a debate that took advantage of the widespread and accelerated flow of ideas between individuals and between countries.[51]

It brought about necessary natural evolution towards freedom, best expressed in democracy. Democracy, as defined by Todorov, is a state governed

45. Todorov, *Imperfect Garden*, 34.
46. Todorov, *Conquest of America*, 167.
47. Las Casas and Poole, *In Defense of the Indians*, 42.
48. Todorov, *Conquest of America*, 163–65.
49. Todorov, *Conquest of America*, 165.
50. Todorov, *Morals of History*, 34–35.
51. Todorov and Brown, *Inner Enemies of Democracy*, 25.

by the people, in which equal rights and dignity are extended to all those born or accepted by those born into that particular place.[52] Democracy moves humanity past monarchy and collectivism, past traditional and religious ideals.[53] It moves towards a true freedom, neither individualistic nor totalitarian. It is based in a humanism that accentuates human freedom without eliminating responsibility to society. This humanism can be encapsulated in two main ideas. (1) All human beings have the same rights and dignity by virtue of being of the same "species." (2) An acceptance of the "plurality of cultures."[54] A culture could be judged as better offering freedom and responsibility to its members. But no culture could claim to be superior just because of its being. Humanism, says Todorov, "asserts the universality of the human: all human beings have the same rights and deserve the same respect, whether or not they live in the same way."[55] Christianity was a step towards the humanist ideal, but it relied on God. Some Christians implemented their religious idealism by taking away human freedom.

Enlightenment ideals, according to Todorov, were best expressed in the thought of Montesquieu (1689–1755), who was influenced by Michel de Montaigne (1533–92), and in the thought of Jean-Jacques Rousseau (1712–78). Montaigne was one of the first to put forward a humanist ideal. Generally speaking, he defended the autonomy of the "I," based on our tendency to favor the decisions we have had the freedom to make.[56] When Montaigne read the writings of Las Casas documenting the violence against the Amerindians, he condemned that violence.[57] But Todorov pointed out the limits of Montaigne's humanism. Montaigne had begun to grasp the true humanist ideal of the equality of all human beings and the plurality of cultures. But he did not apply it universally. Instead, for Montaigne, Amerindians represented a "noble savage" or a pristine natural man, an example of an "infant" humanity. Montaigne contrasted that representation with a European culture in decline. He did not take into account the Indians' intrinsic value, nor pay attention to how they perceived the Spanish.[58]

Montesquieu, said Todorov, based his evaluation of Indigenous people in the New World upon more universal humanistic values. In his political writings, Montesquieu recognized that a plurality of societies can exist.

---

52. Todorov and Brown, *Inner Enemies of Democracy*, 8.
53. Todorov, *Deflection of the Enlightenment*, 4.
54. Todorov, *Deflection of the Enlightenment*, 1.
55. Todorov, *Hope and Memory*, 24.
56. Todorov, *Imperfect Garden*, 43.
57. Montaigne, "Of Coaches," 116–17.
58. Todorov, *Morals of History*, 38–39.

He argued for government that respects culture, preserves civil liberty, and upholds he rule of law. Out of his universal sense of justice, he condemned the whole Spanish conquest, and especially the cruelty of the conquerors. He noticed that the Indigenous people who had a less "despotic" ruler or system resisted the Spanish longer.[59] He said he did not know whether the Amerindian society needed to change; to judge, he would need more information. He certainly did not use categories like "childish" or "flowering" to describe it. He did imagine that if Descartes could have come to Mexico before Cortez, and freed the Aztecs from their superstition about the natural world, they would not have been fooled or conquered so easily. (Todorov, however, proposed that the Spanish had a better grasp of the idea of different cultures than the Aztecs. Thus, Cortez was able to defeat them by pretending that he was their "god."[60])

Todorov found the exemplar of moral humanism in the writings of Rousseau. His ideas about what happens when humans come into contact with the "other," Todorov thought, offered a strong foundation for democracy. Rousseau described a balanced tension between the individual and the state, realized in the "moderate human being."[61] The moderate human being does not give up his own freedom but recognizes the importance of the larger society. They evolve from their natural state as primitive individuals, to citizens controlled completely by the state, to people who use their freedom for both their own good and the good of their fellow human beings. At one point, says Todorov, Rousseau had planned to travel to see the Amerindians. For him, they represented the "natural man," the ideal human being in pristine innocence. However, he decided against the trip.[62] Later, he explained that, even if the natural man in his primitive state had existed, that state is gone. It gave way to social man, controlled by the state. But, longing to return to a state of freedom and independence, social man rebels against an all-encompassing state or monarchy, ending up as an isolated individual. A true humanism, however, moves beyond the polarities of the natural man and the citizen of society.

For Todorov, the Enlightenment and the 1492 discovery of peoples no "civilized" person had ever encountered helped move human beings from the constraints of traditions and towards the liberal democratic state. However, humans are still in danger of lapsing back into despotic governments and societies. Hubris can lead to violence and a loss of freedom, a

---

59. Todorov, *Morals of History*, 44–45.
60. Todorov, *Semiotic Conquest of America*.
61. Todorov, *Frail Happiness*, 57.
62. Todorov, *Frail Happiness*, 55–56.

forgetting of the modern humanist ideals of plurality and equality. Pride can lead people to accentuate particular groups over universal humanity.[63] They may idealize past regimes to create collectivist visions, or try to imprison others into an ideology such as religious idealism or scientific determinism. Amartya Sen speaks of this view of a danger when he says that tribalism threatens liberal democracy. Violence can be avoided through the use of responsible choice, arrived at through sound reasoning, to embrace the modern pluralist identity of humanism.[64]

## LAS CASAS AND TODOROV IN DIALOGUE

Todorov was right to say that, in some ways, Las Casas did not take the Amerindian identity seriously. Las Casas believed that the Indigenous people should be taken into the Spanish nation to build up the nation and further the kingdom of God.[65] Even though Las Casas had a positive view of the Amerindians, he still saw them through his own ego as "wild Christians."[66] He was guilty of a "generous assimilationism." And he was overly in his hope that the Sovereign of the Catholic Empire would respond in a positive way toward reports of violence committed against the Amerindians. So, Las Casas may well not have appreciated the identity of the Indigenous people in the way that Todorov saw it might have been recognized during the enlightenment, through a lens of proper humanist values.

Todorov, who grew up in a totalitarian state, was sensitive to failures to embrace a truly human identity. However, he failed to see his own shortcomings with regard to the "other." He did try to take into account the writings of the Aztecs themselves about their encounter with the Spanish.[67] However, he seemed to believe that Indigenous identity, as a collective identity, has nothing to contribute to the ongoing development of a more human existence. He would have liked to introduce humanist thought to Indigenous people so that they could be freed from superstition and conquest. Thus, he presumed to make a decision for Indigenous people about their need to move past Christian faith on the way towards humanism. Todorov's own project was really only a gentler form of assimilation into a humanist perspective.

---

63. Todorov, *Deflection of the Enlightenment*, 12.
64. Sen, *Identity and Violence*, xvii.
65. Las Casas et al., *Only Way*. 53
66. Todorov, *Morals of History*, 34–35.
67. See Todorov, *Morals of History*, 17–33; Durán and Heyden, *History of the Indies*.

Todorov's critique also fails to take into account the positive effect of the Christian faith upon Las Casas. Las Casas viewed the suffering Indigenous people as the suffering Christ. His love for Christ motivated his love for the Indigenous people. It moved him to defend their rights and equality under God.[68] Because of his Christological focus, he believed the Spanish should be in the New World only to spread the gospel,[69] and that their use of violence would bring shame upon the name of Christ.[70] Las Casas was realistic about human beings' propensity to sin, and the need for the grace of God to respond to the violence. His theology enabled him to humble himself. It inspired him to change and correct his own misguided ideals about slavery. His eschatological view of progress opened him up to the ongoing need for repentance, forgiveness, and restitution of wrongs committed. Las Casas's Christian idealism may not have been modern, but it offered a universalism with a built-in humility as well as or better than Todorov's humanism.

In the writings discussed in this essay, the thoughts of Indigenous people themselves were not completely taken into account. Still, Las Casas was with the Indigenous people and continues to have a legacy as one who defended them. That Las Casas was a defender of the "Indian" is put forward by modern Indigenous people themselves. Whether Todorov's defense of the enlightenment as a way to defend all cultures will bear the same fruit as Las Casas's Christian defense of the Amerindians, only time will tell.

## BIBLIOGRAPHY

Aquinas, Thomas. *Summa Theologica*. Translated by the Fathers of the English Dominican Province. 2nd rev. ed. London: Burns, Oates, and Washbourne, 1920.

Casas, Bartolomé de las. "Letter to the Council of the Indies." In *La iglesia y el negro esclavo en Santo Domingo: Una historia de tres siglos*, by José Luis Sáez, 212. Santo Domingo: Editora Amigo del Hogar, 1994.

Casas, Bartolomé de las, and Andrée Collard. *History of the Indies*. New York: Harper & Row, 1971.

Casas, Bartolomé de las, and Nigel Griffin. *A Short Account of the Destruction of the Indies*. New York: Penguin, 1992.

Casas, Bartolomé de las, et al. *The Only Way*. Sources of American Spirituality. New York: Paulist, 1992.

Casas, Bartolomé de las, and Stafford Poole. *In Defense of the Indians: The Defense of the Most Reverend Lord, Don Fray Bartolomé de las Casas, of the Order of Preachers, Late Bishop of Chiapa, Against the Persecutors and Slanderers of the Peoples of the New World Discovered Across the Seas*. DeKalb: Northern Illinois University Press, 1992.

68. Gutiérrez, *In Search of the Poor*, 67.
69. Gutiérrez, *In Search of the Poor*, 67.
70. Las Casas and Poole, *In Defense of the Indians*, 20.

Durán, Diego, and Doris Heyden. *The History of the Indies of New Spain*. Civilization of the American Indian. Norman: University of Oklahoma Press, 1994.

Gutiérrez, Gustavo. *Las Casas: In Search of the Poor of Jesus Christ*. Maryknoll, NY: Orbis, 1993.

Hanke, Lewis. *Aristotle and the American Indians: A Study in Race Prejudice in the Modern World*. A Midland Book. Bloomington: Indiana University Press, 1970.

Hanke, Lewis, and Bartolomé de las Casas. *All Mankind Is One: a Study of the Disputation between Bartolomé de las Casas and Juan Ginés De Sepúlveda in 1550 on the Intellectual and Religious Capacity of the American Indians*. DeKalb: Northern Illinois University Press, 1974.

Martyr, Justin. *The Apostolic Fathers, Justin Martyr, Irenaeus*. Vol. 1 of the *Ante-Nicene Fathers*. Edited by Alexander Roberts and James Donaldson. 1885. Reprint, Grand Rapids: Christian Classics Ethereal Library, 2010. Online. http://www.ccel.org/ccel/schaff/anf01.viii.ii.xlvi.html.

Montaigne, Michel de. "Of Coaches." In *The Essays of Michel De Montaigne*, edited by Jacob Zeitlin, 3. New York: Knopf, 1936.

Sen, Amartya. *Identity and Violence: The Illusion of Destiny*. Issues of Our Time. New York: Norton, 2006.

Todorov, Tzvetan. *The Conquest of America: The Question of the Other*. New York: Harper & Row, 1984.

———. "The Deflection of the Enlightenment." Paper presented at The Novel and the Writer's Life: A Symposium in Honor of Joseph Frank and Ian Watt, Stanford Humanities Center, Stanford, CA, February 3, 1989.

———. *Frail Happiness: An Essay on Rousseau*. University Park: Pennsylvania State University Press, 2001.

———. *Hope and Memory: Lessons from the Twentieth Century*. Princeton: Princeton University Press, 2003.

———. *Imperfect Garde: The Legacy of Humanism*. Princeton: Princeton University Press, 2002.

———. *The Morals of History*. Minneapolis: University of Minnesota Press, 1995.

———. *The Semiotic Conquest of America*. Andrew W. Mellon Lectures. New Orleans: Graduate School of Tulane University, 1982.

Todorov, Tzvetan, and Andrew Brown. *The Inner Enemies of Democracy*. Cambridge: Polity, 2014.

Vickery, Paul S. *Bartolomé de las Casas: Great Prophet of the Americas*. New York: Paulist, 2006.

Wilson, Andrew L. *Black Slaves and Messianic Dreams in Bartolome de las Casas's Plans for an Abundant Indies*. Princeton: Princeton University Press, 2009.

# 16

# The Constructive Iconoclasm of Lamin Sanneh

## Robert S. Paul

Our fractious world is rife with conflicts between groups that view each other with mutual suspicion, enmity, and hostility. Such perceptions may arise for specific reasons, or from simple prejudice—pre-judgments imposed on people we do not know, do not understand, and do not welcome into our company or territory. In either case, we cease to regard other people simply as human beings who happen to be different, and see them instead as "other" in a pejorative sense—as alien, unsafe, inferior, or unworthy.

How this occurs may be illustrated by means of a metaphor. Concrete is made by mixing sand, gravel, water, and cement together, and pouring it into forms. Everything from sidewalks to skyscrapers can be constructed by this method. In the same way, we mentally mix objective observations with our subjective feelings into a kind of slurry of impressions. When this slurry is poured over the mold of certain ideas we regard as important, or moral standards we hold as being normative, it may or may not conform to our ideals. The slurry might fit the mold perfectly, or only partly, or it might spill over as an unruly mess that refuses to fit the mold. In any case, as it hardens a constructed image of another person is formed. It is not the person as they really are, but our idea about them; indeed, our judgment of them. Whether this judgment is positive or negative, once the image is formed in our minds it may become as difficult to deconstruct as actual concrete.

Religion is often criticized for fostering such constructs and, even worse, for doing it in the name of God. To speak of religion, however, is to deal in abstractions. What critics of religion mean concretely is that people who are religious are prejudiced, judgmental, hateful, and even violent on account of their religion. There is no denying that some religious people behave very badly, but it is not only religious people who are guilty of such sins. People who are avowedly *non*-religious are prone to the same problems, as history amply illustrates. Religion is not the only source of trouble in the world.

Indeed, the business of constructing pejorative images of the "other" is an open market, available to all comers. Religious people may go about constructing images using doctrinal or moralistic principles as their criteria of judgment, but non-religious people do the same kind of thing for their own reasons. Broad-brushed criticisms of religion, for example, may involve invidious stereotypes of people who happen to be religious as being ignorant, deluded, backwards, hypocritical, malevolent, and so on. Who gets constructed as "other" by whom varies endlessly, but it is all the same phenomenon in the end. The challenge we must consider is how to reduce the prevalence of such destructive constructions, and the tensions, alienations, and hostilities that result.

To illuminate this subject, Lamin Sanneh is an important resource. He is personally acquainted with the fracture lines that cut across our world, and his prodigious work as a scholar manifests a deep concern to understand and transcend boundaries of alienation and difference. His careful analysis is iconoclastic in its power to deconstruct stereotypes, yet he is not merely a demolitionist. He promotes a methodology that pushes us to look beyond stereotypes, and he models an irenic tone and conciliatory posture in the ways that he interacts with others, including those with whom he may differ in significant ways. As the title of this chapter suggests, Lamin Sanneh is an iconoclast with constructive intent. This brief introduction cannot do justice to the full range of his work, but it may serve to inspire further study and reflection on the life and contributions of a remarkable man.

## LIFE JOURNEY

Growing up in The Gambia, West Africa, where he was born, Lamin Sanneh was rigorously schooled in the Muslim beliefs and practices of his family. At age eighteen, however, he converted to Christianity. He subsequently studied in Africa, the Middle East, Britain, and the United States, and taught at Harvard before becoming the D. Willis James Professor of Missions and World Christianity at Yale Divinity School, and Professor of History at Yale University. Along the way, he became a naturalized citizen of the United States and a Roman Catholic. His life journey, in itself, illustrates the capacity of individuals to transcend religious and cultural categories. As he says,

> Since I personally belong to several cultures at once, I gladly and eagerly support the view that multiple cultural boundaries may coexist harmoniously and fruitfully. . . . Human life in the small individual slice that is mine happens to have subsisted on a great diversity of sources, and I happily and gratefully acknowledge my plural indebtedness.[1]

Sanneh's scholarly work covers a wide range of subjects. His earliest work focused on Muslim and Christian engagement with West African culture.[2] His signature contribution to the study of missions and comparative religion concerns the inherent "translatability" of the gospel from one cultural context to another, a theme he develops by close analysis of the interaction of missionary "transmitters" with Indigenous "receptors" of their message.[3] Entailed in the principle of translatability is the observation that Indigenous receptors of the gospel have been more important in the adoption and assimilation of the faith into new cultural settings than the missionary transmitters who first introduced it. In *Abolitionists Abroad*, Sanneh expands on the theme of Indigenous agency by giving an account of slavery's abolition from the African side, so to speak. He relates the history of Africans enslaved in America who returned to West Africa as free men and women, and of Indigenous Africans who played significant roles in the anti-slavery movement within Africa. Their efforts were crucial to uprooting the transatlantic slave trade in its West African strongholds.

In later works, Sanneh turns his attention to modern Western culture,[4] and to the worldwide Christian movement in its diverse, multicultural, contemporary complexity.[5] Most recently, in a winsome personal memoir, he recounts his childhood experiences growing up in West Africa and his personal journey of faith and conversion to Christianity.[6] The subject that consistently is woven into all of Sanneh's writing is the interaction

---

1. Sanneh, *Encountering the West*, 25.
2. For example, Sanneh, *West African Christianity*; *Jakhanke Muslim Clerics*.
3. See Sanneh, *Translating the Message*.
4. E.g., Sanneh, *Encountering the West*.
5. E.g., Sanneh, *Whose Religion is Christianity?*; *Disciples of All Nations*.
6. Sanneh, *Summoned from the Margin*.

of religion and culture. For the discussion that follows, it is important to consider how he conceptualizes this relationship.

## RELIGION AND CULTURE

Religion and culture are not abstract notions in Sanneh's thinking. He does not locate the essence of a religion primarily in its formal beliefs and doctrines. Beliefs are part of what defines a religion, but when Sanneh speaks of religion he is not referencing a belief system suspended in the realm of abstract concepts. His interest instead is on the character of religion as a lived social reality. Whether Christian, Muslim, or otherwise, he focuses on people who believe, and who express their faith in concrete terms within particular traditions and communities. As he puts it,

> The fact of the matter is that the localization of Christianity is an inevitable and indispensable aspect of the religion qua religion, and that without that concrete, historical grounding Christianity becomes nothing but a fragile, elusive abstraction, salt without its saltness [sic]. That is the problem that dogs all attempts at defining the core of the gospel as a propositional truth without regard to the concrete lives of men and women who call themselves Christian.[7]

Sanneh defines culture in similarly concrete terms, consistent with others who have written on the subject. His discussions are congruent with those of Berger and Luckmann, for example, who describe culture as the cumulative product of the "world building activity of human beings."[8] He is aligned with Richard Niebuhr as well, in the view that culture is not value-neutral since the culture-forming choices that human beings make always imply some intended purpose or good.[9] Indeed, "the value relation is inescapable wherever we encounter culture," as Katherine Tanner puts it.[10] All these insights resist treating culture as an abstraction, and focus instead on human agency as the vital factor in cultural formation. Sanneh's approach is consistent with these insights, but he goes beyond them by ascribing *theological* significance to culture, and to human agency in relation to culture, as well.

Culture, in Sanneh's view, is the historical arena ordained by God where divine revelation occurs and where human beings have the freedom

---

7. Sanneh, *Encountering the West*, 129.
8. Berger and Luckmann, *Social Construction of Reality*, 6.
9. Niebuhr, *Christ and Culture*.
10. Tanner, *Theories of Culture*, 49.

and responsibility to work out the meaning of that revelation in practical and moral terms. In his vocabulary, every culture is both *destigmatized* and *deabsolutized*, meaning that every culture is deemed a worthy venue for divine revelation, but no culture may claim to represent the absolute expression of God's will. All cultures are subject to critique (and ultimately to divine judgment) in relation to the valorizing choices that people make in the ongoing process of constructing, deconstructing, and reconstructing cultural customs, patterns, practices, and structures.

Implicit in Sanneh's view of culture is a high regard for human freedom and agency. People obviously are influenced by various cultural values and religious beliefs, but Sanneh maintains that human behavior is not absolutely determined by such factors. Individuals may or may not conform to cultural customs and religious dictates. They may (and often do) defy cultural norms as an act of rebellion, or sometimes in response to divine revelation. In analyzing interreligious or intercultural encounters, therefore, Sanneh is less interested in generalizations than in the particular choices that particular people make in particular circumstances, especially where those choices diverge from the norm.

To summarize, Sanneh rejects a binary model that would juxtapose religion and culture as abstract entities. Instead, he considers religion and culture in concrete terms, seeing the relationship as intertwined, interactive, and interdependent—a dynamic relationship that is of vital importance to real people involved in both spheres. Religious groups necessarily express their beliefs in cultural forms, such as the Hebrew Scriptures, Christian cathedrals, and the holy shrines of Islam, or in communal practices such as Jewish Sabbath observance as examples. Culture, as it is formed by human actions and valorizing choices, draws upon the moral precepts, symbols, and spiritual nourishment that religion affords, for better or worse. To take a positive example, Christian conscience was a key motivation in the movement to abolish slavery, a cultural shift of profound significance. Negatively, history is rife with instances when a religious group abandoned itself to some pernicious ideology, with horrific results for the wider culture.

When religion and culture interact in a healthy relationship, Sanneh says, they are like marrow to bone, one giving life while the other provides structure, with both the better for it. Critics who attack religion indiscriminately, therefore, are attacking a source of human conviction that lends moral seriousness to the culture-building process. Religionists who regard "culture" as an entity that is always inimical to the interests of faith, and attack it as such, are undercutting the concrete footing that faith requires to make a real difference in the world.

## DIFFERENCE IN THE DETAILS

The way that Sanneh conceptualizes religion and culture, as indicated above, allows him to analyze interreligious and intercultural encounters quite differently than, say, post-colonial criticism as one example. While post-colonial theory illuminates the historical era of European imperialism in many important ways, it is vulnerable to subsuming the particularities of human behavior under *a priori* categories such as foreign, Indigenous, imperialist, native, oppressor, oppressed, etc. Sanneh can stake a claim to being a post-colonial critic himself, but he is also a critic of post-colonial criticism on methodological grounds. This is evident in his response to Edward Said, whose seminal work helped to define post-colonialism as a critical theory. Said's central thesis was that "Orientalism" as an academic discipline was a contrivance of Western scholars who were servile to Western imperialism. Their studies, he averred, though presented under the guise of academic objectivity, actually served to reinforce Western cultural prejudice and power.[11] Sanneh comments:

> I think the issue is over-simplified, but in any case the blame should not be imputed wholly to an incorrigible western bias against the "orient." It has fundamentally more to do with an inherent tendency to allow literary representation to overthrow situational details.[12]

To put it simply, Sanneh sees in Said's critique of Orientalism the same problem that Said saw in Orientalism itself—namely, the tendency to force the complex, living reality of human behavior into a predetermined framework. This problem is especially acute when a strong theoretical point of view is involved: Orientalism is one case in point, and post-colonial criticism, its mirror-opposite, is another. The problem is not limited to those fields, however. Disciplines such as history, anthropology, and theology are also prone to the problem due to the narrative description that is part and parcel of the work done by scholars in such fields. Writing about complex matters is not an easy task, and it is easy to sacrifice details for the sake of generalizations. As he notes, other peoples and cultures may be misrepresented unintentionally, not because of prejudice or malicious intent but simply because we are constrained by our inability to represent reality more fully.

It is precisely for this reason that Sanneh has little regard for postmodernist deconstructionism. A tacit principle of postmodern hermeneutics is that any text should be approached with suspicion, on the presumption that

---

11. Said, *Orientalism*, 66.
12. Sanneh, "Christian Mission in the Pluralist Milieu," 204.

power interests are always involved. Michel Foucault is particularly associated with this line of thinking.

> There is no power relation without the correlative constitution of a field of knowledge, nor any knowledge that does not presuppose and constitute at the same time power relations.[13]

Foucault's assertion is not immune to his own theoretical assumptions, however. The hermeneutic of suspicion he promotes can be deconstructed as a power-interest in itself; a prejudgment the interpreter brings to a text, presumably in service of his or her own power interests. This leads to an infinite regression in which every affirmation is presumed to be suspect and is deconstructed in turn, until nothing remains but a pile of rubble, so to speak. As Berger puts it, such analysis "bends back upon itself. The relativizers are relativized, the debunkers are debunked."[14]

As an alternative to this circular futility, Sanneh recommends a particularistic methodology that attends carefully to historical exigencies, specific situations, and individual exceptions, rather than sweeping aside such details with a broad broom. By suspending pre-judgments, surprising and useful insights may come into view which may serve to revise stereotypes rather than reinforce preconceived judgments. An interesting example is found in *Piety and Power* where Sanneh discusses the growing hostility of secularists to religion in the modern West. He proposes that religion is not intrinsically incompatible with secularity and, in some instances, might even play a constructive cultural role in "upholding democratic liberalism."[15] To support this proposition, he adduces evidence from what might seem a very unlikely source—an ancient Muslim faith tradition in West Africa.

The Jakhanké (also known as "Suwarians" in some sources), trace their roots to medieval Africa and the teaching of a Muslim cleric called al-Hájj Sálim Suwaré. According to received tradition, he disavowed the use of political or military coercion in religious matters, including the propagation of Islam—an "astonishing position," Sanneh notes, considering the "unambiguous ruling of the Qur'an." The Jakhanké embraced this teaching and formed a society of dedicated (or "professional") clerics to propagate it. They established educational centers (roughly the equivalent of Christian monasteries in medieval Europe) as enclaves, and vigorously asserted their independence from the authority of local or regional kings and chiefs. From these centers, itinerant teachers were sent forth to diverse

---

13. Foucault, *Discipline and Punish*, 27–28.
14. Berger, *Rumor of Angels*, 59.
15. Sanneh, *Piety and Power*, 124.

ethnic groups throughout West Africa to promote Suwaré's pacifist interpretation of Islam. Indeed, the tradition remains alive in pockets today in Guinea, the Gambia, Senegal, and Mali.[16]

The term "Islamic pacifism" might strike contemporary Western ears as an oxymoron in light of violent conflicts with radical Islamists, yet the Jakhanké were committed pacifists in principle and very effective in appealing to West Africans to adopt a pacifist way of life.

> Local populations that had come under the influence of clerical pacifism were so deeply affected that a theocratic dispensation was more disconcerting to them than the prospects of continuing pluralism. . . . The attempt was made many times in the nineteenth and twentieth centuries to create theocratic governments in Muslim West Africa, and each time it failed from the prevailing unfavorable quietist climate of opinion.[17]

Here we begin to see Sanneh's iconoclastic approach. By marshaling African Muslim clerics as supporters of Western liberal values (especially tolerance of religious pluralism), Sanneh demonstrates first of all that not all Muslims interpret Islam in terms of *jihad*. With the same stroke, he challenges the idea that religion *per se* is the cause of all manner of ill in the world, as modern secular critics have vigorously asserted.[18] In so doing, he challenges us to take a closer look at the variable ways that religious convictions are expressed, and also how they are intertwined with social and cultural factors.

## ENCOUNTERING RESISTANCE

It is not always easy to persuade people to take another look, however, especially when they are heavily invested in a certain point of view. Not so long ago, to cite a relevant example, sociologists developed the argument that religion inevitably would decline as modernization advanced, a thesis which came to be known as "secularization theory." In many modernizing countries around the world, however, what sociologists believed would happen simply did not occur as predicted. Instead, in conjunction with national liberation movements and increasing modernization, the Christian faith was embraced by far greater numbers of people in the non-Western world *after* the end of colonialism than during the height of Western imperialism.

---

16. Sanneh, *Piety and Power*, 123–24. For a detailed study, see Sanneh, *Jakhanké Muslim Clerics*.

17. Sanneh, *Piety and Power*, 124.

18. For example, Harris, *End of Faith*; Hitchens, *God Is Not Great*.

Islam and other religions also surged forward in parallel with modernization in many countries. As Peter Berger admits, the sociologists got it wrong.

> The world today, with some exceptions . . . is as furiously religious as it ever was, and in some places more so than ever. This means that a whole body of literature by historians and social scientists loosely labeled "secularization theory" is essentially mistaken. In my early work I contributed to this literature.[19]

In hindsight, secularization theory involved significant methodological missteps. In a revisionist critique, Christian Smith and his colleagues fault secularization theory for having been overly abstract and deterministic, and for focusing on a romanticized intellectual history as the engine of social change. This produced a narrative that portrayed "transformation without protagonists, action without actors, historical process without agents." In short, there was not adequate attention given to human agency or the details of concrete history.[20]

Secularization theory also involved a tacit cultural bias. The modern West was assumed to be the leading edge of human social evolution and the political-economic model other nations aspired to emulate. Religious decline in the West seemed to be a byproduct of an advanced society, so it was assumed that so-called "less developed" cultures also and inevitably would follow the same path as they evolved. The theory seemed so sensible in explaining the decline of religion in the West that sociologists resisted seeing the matter otherwise, until the contradicting reality became too obvious to ignore.

Sanneh reports that he has encountered resistance of a similar type in the academic arena on at least three fronts, and not just among sociologists. First, there is rationalist skepticism about the truth-claims of any and all religions. Second, a negative evaluation of the Christian missionary movement as the religious arm of Western imperialism is widespread and virtually unquestioned among many academics. The third concerns the post-colonial reception of Christianity among non-Western peoples, and how that phenomenon is viewed through Western eyes. Sanneh's own conversion serves to illustrate this latter issue.

In his memoir,[21] Sanneh describes how, growing up as a child, he was rigorously schooled in the knowledge, practices, and attitudes that his instructors said were proper to a Muslim. He took them seriously and adopted

---

19. Berger, *Desecularization of the World*, 2.
20. Smith, *Secular Revolution*, 14.
21. Sanneh, *Summoned from the Margin*.

their view that Islam was superior to other religions, especially Christianity, which they regarded as a "corrupt religion" and the product of "error and blindness." What he observed of Christians largely reinforced this opinion and encouraged him to see himself as "a flag-bearer of Islam."

> When I saw Christians drunk on Christmas Day, the birthday of Jesus son of Mary (peace be upon him), I felt stirring in me the iconoclastic resolve to purge Christians of their sinful habits.... I thought Muslims were right to think that Christianity had lost its right to be considered a religion and should do us the favor of going out of business altogether.... I felt roused to do battle by the belligerent view that someone else's religion was my business, nay, was my mission.... I had reached the point where it was not enough just to be religious; it had to be at the expense of someone else's religion.[22]

Nevertheless, Sanneh goes on to explain how, after extended wrestling with "nagging questions about true knowledge of God," he converted to Christianity.[23] This involved a theological reorientation in regard to Jesus, and a mystical sense of being summoned. "It was as if I heard a solicitous whisper," he writes, "a simple, clear call borne on the wings of infinite forbearance to answer the summons of life: 'Do not be afraid. Jesus surrendered to God. Won't you?'" Responding to this mystical suitor, he yielded to "a providential process that brings one to encounter with unshakeable truth," and found it be a transformative experience.

> Awakened, all sense of struggle, fear, and anxiety vanished. I felt bound and confused no longer. It was a new feeling of release and of freedom, infused with a sense of utter, serene peace. I could speak about it only in terms of new life, of being born again.[24]

In the West African culture of Sanneh's upbringing, it was a matter of honor to openly express one's religious convictions and a dishonor to be insincere in matters of such import. Sanneh, therefore, soon declared his conversion to Christianity to his friends and family members, though not without some trepidation. As he expected, they reacted to his declaration with sheer incredulity and initially some anger. What he did not anticipate was the reluctance of local church leaders to take him seriously as a convert.

---

22. Sanneh, *Summoned from the Margin*, 88–89.

23. Accounts of Sanneh's conversion also may be found in Sanneh, "Christian Missions and the Western Guilt Complex," and in this author's doctoral thesis (Paul, "Towards a Theology of Mission").

24. Sanneh, *Summoned from the Margin*, 102.

Referring to the English Methodist missionary he first approached to request baptism, Sanneh states that "my conversion obviously caused him acute embarrassment, and I was mortified on account of it." It was suggested that he might talk to the Roman Catholics instead, but they were not receptive either. Both groups were constrained, it seems, by a pledge neither to evangelize nor to convert Muslims, which the British colonial government had extracted from the Christian denominations as a concession to Muslim sensibilities, and had established as a condition for operating schools and conducting other religious activities in the region.[25]

Despite these rebuffs, Sanneh persevered in his determination to enter the Christian fold. A year later, he finally persuaded the Methodists to baptize him. As a new convert, he eagerly looked to the church for encouragement and instruction in the faith, but what they offered him was a reading list of mostly liberal theologians and secular philosophers, which seemed designed primarily to cure him of religious enthusiasm. He was "baffled by the apparent determination of [his] church superiors to keep religious subjects from all 'decent' and 'cultured' conversation." Eventually, he realized that the reticence of the missionaries to speak forthrightly with him about his spiritual experiences and religious convictions was not a trait of Christianity as such, but was an attitude "deep-rooted in Western liberal culture."[26]

Sanneh's conversion involved a deep irony, which is instructive to consider for our purposes. In breaking ranks with his Muslim heritage to join the Christian church, he found himself out of step with both communities. His Muslim friends, though perplexed by his decision, understood it in religious terms (albeit negatively, as a falling away from truth into error). West African culture gave credence to religious experience as such, and allowed room for diversity in this regard. Despite some tensions, therefore, these *cultural* values prevailed and Sanneh's social bonds with Muslim friends and family members survived his change of beliefs and his baptism. The Western church leaders in the situation, by contrast, initially saw the voluntary convert as a political problem and were skeptical concerning his professed conversion. Even after they baptized him, they remained uncomfortable with the fervency of his faith. Though he had aligned himself with the Christian religion, and had been accepted into the fold, he was misaligned with the *cultural* sensibilities and social manners that prevailed in that particular Christian community. Theological tutelage was deployed not so much to strengthen his faith as to realign him to the prevailing Western cultural ethos.

25. For more on this, see Sanneh, *Summoned from the Margin*, 94–95.
26. Sanneh, "Christian Missions and the Western Guilt Complex," 330–31.

Returning to Sanneh's comments about resistance in the academic arena, the point to be made is that the negative opinions so widespread among academics—concerning religious truth-claims, the Christian missionary movement, and the growth of Christian faith among non-Western peoples—invite us to interrogate the virtual uniformity of this posture. Does it indicate open-minded and even-handed study of these subjects, or is it merely a social convention rooted in attitudes of cultural superiority and a general discomfort with matters religious? Sanneh leaves no doubt as to how he would answer the question.

> The problem posed by the modernist rejection of God is at heart a cultural problem, that is to say, a problem concerning the claim for the superiority of Caucasian values in being able to explain, interpret and control the world, especially the world of non-white societies.[27]

As Sanneh repeatedly points out, there is no denying that Christianity and its missionary movement deserve criticism. However, the historical association of Christianity with Western imperialism makes it too easy a target for critics in this post-colonial era, and a convenient scapegoat. What critics may overlook is that the problems pinned on Christian missionaries of the colonial era were, arguably, more rooted in their *cultural* biases than in their *religious* convictions. Further, to claim that the missionary message was inseparable from Western culture fails to explain the *post*-colonial embrace of the Christian faith by non-Western peoples. Arguably, the central problem in the colonial era was *cultural* arrogance concerning the superiority of Western civilization, a tendency that persists even in the post-colonial era. In its overwhelming rejection of religion in general, and Christianity in particular, Western academics may have more in common with colonial-era missionaries, in terms of cultural bias and prejudice, than they might care to admit.

## ICONOCLAST AT WORK

In his magisterial study of contemporary Western culture, Charles Taylor contends that people immersed in modern secular society (with all this entails) are rendered virtually incapable of believing in anything beyond an "immanent framework," which means that belief in God "is understood to be one option among others, and frequently not the easiest to embrace."[28] Sanneh describes modern Westerners in similar terms as a "generation of

---

27. Sanneh, *Encountering the West*, 15.
28. Taylor, *Secular Age*, 3.

religiously impaired people."²⁹ He sees this impairment, however, as involving more than intellectual skepticism. Rationalism has a dulling effect on spiritual sensibilities, and the moral demands represented by religion collide with the cultural values of individual freedom and autonomy. Numerous examples could be given concerning the personal and social vices common to humankind and how people may resist the claims of religion on this account, but Sanneh has little to say about such things. Instead, he sees "the most obdurate force we have to contend with" as being nationalism.

> One of the most significant paradigm shifts has been the move from a religious metaphysic to a political metaphysic and the messianic state it fosters. . . . Certainly in the West the transition has been accompanied by an emphatic ethical transformation: to die for one's religion is considered a fanatical act, whereas to die for one's country is considered an act of heroism.³⁰

The paradigm shift to which Sanneh refers here involves the conflation of religion with national ambitions, which in the extreme becomes nationalistic idolatry—the giving of one's ultimate loyalty and devotion to a nation, rather than to God. History is replete with examples where religion has served as a handmaid to nationalistic ambitions, and it clearly is not a problem confined to one particular religion or nation. The example most relevant for our purposes is the entanglement of Christian missions with Western colonialism. As noted earlier, the idea that missionaries were merely religious agents of Western imperialism is regarded by the vast majority of Western-trained academics as a settled fact. Sanneh readily concedes that there is some truth to this view, but he challenges conventional opinion on the subject for stopping short of more careful investigation.

> Modern historiography has established a tradition that mission was the surrogate of Western colonialism, and that . . . these two movements combined to destroy indigenous cultures. In my years of formal training no serious scholar, to my knowledge, took issue with this viewpoint, and I myself conformed unquestioningly to its dictate. . . . I wish in this book to present another point of view, which . . . should help restore some objectivity to the subject and bring it forward once more as part of the active field of scholarly endeavor.³¹

---

29. Sanneh, *Encountering the West*, 163.
30. Sanneh, *Encountering the West*, 173.
31. Sanneh, *Translating the Message*, 4.

The task Sanneh sets for himself is iconoclastic in its intent. His aim is to break up an image of the Christian missionary movement that seems to be as settled as concrete among academics, and to encourage a reconsideration of the matter. He does not go about this by mounting a frontal attack, however. He approaches the task from a more oblique angle. To understand how this serves his purpose, it is helpful to outline his argument in some detail.

The earliest followers of Jesus, according to Sanneh's description, stepped beyond the boundary markers of first-century Judaism and spread the gospel message among Gentiles without insisting that conformity to Jewish culture was a mandatory component of the faith. This became a matter of considerable dispute according to the New Testament record, but the decision to embrace Gentile converts without requiring conformity to Jewish practices prevailed in the end.[32] Even the Jewish practice of male circumcision was ultimately judged as being specific to God's covenant with Israel, not a universal requirement for all mankind.

Furthermore, the apostolic generation viewed the divine revelation received through Jesus as not being bound to an original "sacred" language. Jesus almost certainly spoke Aramaic, but the apostles and evangelists adopted other languages (primarily Greek) in their teaching and writing without qualms. The decision to translate, rather than to regard the divine revelation as dependent upon an original sacred language, contrasts sharply with the status of Arabic in the case of Islam as a point of comparison. In the emerging Christian movement, the impulse was to employ whatever language was needed to communicate the gospel message, and to allow latitude for differences in how it might be assimilated, expressed, and practiced in local situations. This approach was not without controversy, but it prevailed in the end and set the stage for the successive movement of the gospel from one cultural group to another, with considerable variation in Christian practice as the long-term consequence. This is what Sanneh means by the "translatability" of the gospel—the capacity of the Christian message to be transmitted across cultural boundaries and assimilated into new contexts in terms of the local culture.

Sanneh goes on to argue that this pattern was effectively abandoned in European Christendom where the institutions of Church and State joined hands to enforce religious conformity as a political obligation. The medieval European formula *cuius regio eius religio* (whose realm, his religion), meaning that the religion of the king determines the religion of the kingdom, ran counter to the principle of the gospel's inherent translatability. The

---

32. See Acts 15.

European model tied the Christian faith to the territorial interests of monarchs and magistrates, with the corollary that the church's mission existed to serve their ambitions of territorial conquest.

Sanneh goes on, however, to show how the gospel retained its translatable character even during the height of European imperialism. Where missionaries focused on translating the Bible into local vernacular languages, they planted seeds that were subversive to colonialism despite their entanglements with colonial interests. Sanneh, in keeping with the particularistic methodology he promotes, bases this thesis on a careful examination of the work of European missionaries in Africa. His study reveals that the alliance of Christian missionaries with colonialism was never absolute. Some missionaries functioned as religious agents for the colonial project, but other missionaries were a thorn in the side of colonialist authorities and merchants; indeed, many became advocates for Indigenous interests in opposition to colonial authorities. This was especially the case among those missionaries who engaged sympathetically with Indigenous individuals and cultures, as frequently happened among those missionaries who devoted themselves to learning local languages for the sake of translating the Bible.

The careful attention of particular missionaries to vernacular translation not only served the purpose of transmitting the gospel, but also helped to preserve Indigenous languages, histories, and cultural patterns. By developing written forms of vernacular languages that never before had been committed to writing, missionary linguists facilitated the preservation of ancient histories and traditions that otherwise were vulnerable to being lost, which in some instances inspired movements of cultural renewal.

Vernacular translation also aided anti-colonial political movements. Africans, reading "God's book" in their own language, did not find in the Bible a message that justified colonialist oppression. On the contrary, the Bible presented a strong critique of such exploitation and a clear affirmation that God had compassion for the oppressed and was on the side of justice. The application of the translatability principle through vernacular translation projects thus allied many missionaries to Indigenous interests, despite their dubious relationship with colonialism. On the basis of this examination, Sanneh contends that an important distinction can and should be made between missionary actions that accrued to the benefit of Indigenous interests, versus colonial efforts to subdue and control local cultures.

Sanneh extends this line of thinking to characterize the worldwide expansion of the Christian faith as a "vernacular translation movement." In the long-term, he says, vernacular translation projects undertaken by missionaries in Africa and elsewhere demolished the idea that religion is inextricably bound to the "blood and soil" of particular kingdoms and cultures, an idea that can be traced to Émile Durkheim, the putative father of the modern social sciences. Durkheim believed that particular societies (or whole civilizations) take shape in particular ways because of their religious basis, with the corollary that religion is simply a projection of collective social consciousness. As Durkheim famously put it, "God is society, writ large."[33]

Durkheim's theory is akin to the "secularization theory" promoted by sociologists, which saw religion and culture in abstract terms. Secularization theory asserted that religion necessarily would decline in relation to cultural changes, especially modernization, while Durkheim theorized that cultures were fundamentally determined by religion. In both cases, this way of understanding the interaction of religion and culture occludes the critical dimension of human agency, including the possibility of choices and actions that diverge from the general norm. What is clear today is that Christianity, much to the surprise of many in the West, has transformed from a Western religion into a predominantly non-Western, multi-cultural faith—indeed, into multiple "Christianities." Many Western scholars, however, and some church leaders as well, view this development with jaded eyes and more than a hint of condescension.

> A skeptical Western audience, fortified with anthropological theory and with a postcolonial sensitivity, will scarcely budge from its view of Christian mission as cultural imperialism and religious bigotry. Besides, [the idea that] developing societies [are] the new frontier of world Christianity strikes many as far-fetched. If, in the language of nineteenth-century science, the natives consumed themselves in ancestral rites without any measurable effect on their character but instead remained stranded in enchanted jungle haunts, why in heaven's name should the world trust them when they step forward under a Christian banner?[34]

The expansion of Christian faith as a multicultural, worldwide movement in the past one hundred years or so flies in the face of such blatant cultural bias.

While Sanneh credits missionaries with introducing the gospel via vernacular translation, he also insists that missionary contributions alone cannot account for the scale, scope, and diversity of worldwide Christianity today. Missionary "transmitters" of the message certainly have played a role, but he locates the creative dynamism of the movement on the "receptor" side of the process. As Sanneh discovered in his own conversion, the gospel

33. Durkheim, *Elementary Forms of Religious Life*, 351.
34. Sanneh, *Whose Religion Is Christianity?*, 20–21.

message is not merely information, but involves a summons that calls for a personal, existential response. Those who respond in these terms are invited to discern the meaning of the message and to assimilate it concretely into their social context. This occurs most effectively when there is liberty to do so in their own cultural terms. That the growth of Christianity exploded after the demise of the colonial era, with the impulse coming largely from Indigenous leadership, refutes the idea that Christian faith could only make its way in the world thanks to Western imperialism. In fact, the Christian movement seems to be doing quite a bit better without that kind of help.

## CONSTRUCTIVE INTENT

As the Christian movement expanded in the post-colonial non-Western world, receptors of the gospel sometimes perceived its moral implications in ways contrary to the cultural values that strongly influence the Western Church. One example would be the sharp differences in outlook between Western and non-Western leaders in the Anglican Communion, which have become evident in debates concerning human sexuality and same-sex marriage.

Another example is the influence of Latin American evangelical theologians in awakening North American evangelicals to God's concern for the poor. In the 1960s and 1970s, Latin American leaders such as Orlando Costas and René Padilla (among others) began to promote "social responsibility" as integral to the gospel. Their efforts succeeded in widening the theological perspective of North Americans, although initially they ran into stiff resistance.[35]

Many leaders of North American mission agencies interpreted "social responsibility" as a cipher for a liberalist agenda. Remembering the divisive fundamentalist-modernist controversies of the early twentieth century, which resulted in deep fractures in the missionary movement, they seemed to fear that stepping onto the "slippery slope" of liberalism might alarm their conservative donors and undermine their priority focus on evangelization. In hindsight, the controversy around this issue had less to do with theological differences than with the different cultural locations of the respective disputants. If differences are not theological at their base, it is fair to ask if they are part of the continuing effect of Christendom on the Western churches.

Over a long period of time, Western Christianity grew accustomed to the conditions of Christendom in Europe, and by extension in North

---

35. See Padilla and Sugden, *How Evangelicals Endorsed Social Responsibility*.

America. Under this dispensation, the alignment between the church's teaching and predominant cultural values was virtually absolute, in principle if not always in practice. Vestiges of Church-State alliances remain in some countries, but times have changed and the close alignment of Christian and cultural values is no longer the case in the former territories of Christendom. Habits of mind formed under Christendom may still persist, however, which can make it difficult to distinguish between one's religious commitments and one's cultural loyalties. Sanneh suggests that deep conflicts along *cultural* lines are likely to continue within the worldwide church, and he questions whether Western Christians will be able to break free of their cultural commitments in order to join hands with their co-religionists around the world.[36]

Another term for mental habits carried over from Christendom would be Western-centricity. Sanneh illuminates this issue by confronting the crippling psychology of Western guilt vis-à-vis colonialism.[37] He argues that it is a misrepresentation, in the first place, to attribute the growth of Christianity in Africa primarily to the forces of either Western missions or colonial power. Africans, he insists, ultimately played the decisive role in the assimilation of Christianity into African cultures, not missionaries or colonialists. Secondly, the guilt some Westerners continue to express over deeds past suggests that they imagine themselves as being more important than they really are in respect to Africa's religious experience. He is rather circumspect in how he says this, but the point is clear enough. An inflated sense of Western guilt may be deconstructed, paradoxically, as a continuing narrative of Western preeminence—an extension of the idea that the West, even at its worst, remains the central factor in world affairs.

As we have suggested throughout this discussion, Sanneh's analysis and the challenging questions he poses can be interpreted as an iconoclastic effort to break down images of "otherness" that have hardened into stubborn points of view. We also have said that he goes about this with constructive intent. Glimpses of this are evident throughout his work, but it is exemplified most clearly in *Whose Religion Is Christianity?* This diminutive book is unusual among Sanneh's published works, and among academic writings in general, for its form of presentation. In the introduction to the book, he explains how and why he came to adopt an "interview" approach.

> I spoke with profit at many institutions and conferences where, with generous encouragement, I tried the interview approach. The decision to develop that into a book is due to my experience.

---

36. See Sanneh and Carpenter, *Changing Face of Christianity*.
37. Sanneh, "Christian Missions and the Western Guilt Complex," 330–34.

> ... People desire to see connections made between academic ideas and public interest. Academics, too, weary all too easily with hearing lectures, and instead appreciate being an acknowledged part of the audience. I took that as a rebuke of the tendency of talking shop and as a challenge to make conversation a common endeavor. Nothing is more important than making oneself understandable and engaging, and no method is better at that than one that includes the audience in the conversation. In the interview style . . . I became part of the audience, not only lecturing but conversing also, and affirming common ownership of the subject.[38]

In this world we share, it is vital to foster a "common ownership of the subject," as Sanneh says. This requires that we recognize and abandon preconceived constructions of individuals and groups as "other," in the pejorative sense of the term. As we have said, the tendency to construct the "other" as alien, unsafe, unwelcome, or unworthy is not a problem unique to religion or to religious people, nor does it arise purely from religion. Constructions of the "other" that involve a religious point of view inevitably involve an element of cultural values and judgments as well. The same is true when secularists resort to constructions of the "other," including the "religious other," to justify xenophobic outlooks or violent aggression. When non-religious people engage in such constructions, we may safely assume that other ideological and cultural judgments are at play. Colin Gunton has said that the quintessential problem of our age involves "standing apart from each other and the world and treating the other as external, as mere object."[39] If we want to foster a common ownership of the subject, in respect to constructing the "other," we might begin by recognizing that this is a problem that affects us all.

## CONCLUDING REFLECTIONS

Woven throughout Lamin Sanneh's work is the theme that religion and culture are not natural enemies, nor disparate elements of human experience, but are joined at the hip. This is a vital point to grasp, considering the pervasive presence, diversity, and energy of religious movements around the world. The time has passed when social theorists could dismissively assign religion to the trash bin of history. Whether one adheres to a religious tradition of one kind or another, or to no religion at all, we all have a stake in seeing one another as fellow human beings. Non-religious people

---

38. Sanneh, *Whose Religion Is Christianity?*, x.
39. Gunton, *One, the Three, and the Many*, 14.

who view religious people as being infected with the virus of intransigent attitudes and moralistic judgments would do well to look in the mirror and consider their own cultural biases. At the same time, religious people might reflect on those they regard as "other," and consider whether a pejorative attitude is truly a requirement of their faith or might arise from other sources. Honest self-criticism is a good tonic.

Lamin Sanneh's thoughtful and generous engagement with the particularity inherent in human experience reveals that our common tendency to construct fellow human beings as "other" does not arise merely because of one's religion, nor would it cease if all religious traditions suddenly vanished. The problem arises from deeper sources—attitudes of cultural or religious superiority fueled by our individual and group appetite for pride, prestige, and self-interest. In this regard, we are all in the same boat.

We construct the "other," oftentimes, so as to feel justified in disparaging other people, or in simply disregarding them. The challenge we face is to move beyond this destructive habit to a more generous approach. Sanneh helps us by insight and example. By questioning our self-built constructions of the "other," and by offering ourselves to mutual conversation and shared learning, as Sanneh proposes, hardened images may be broken down or at least eroded. By recognizing our commonalities and mutual interests in the midst of objective differences, we may discover ways to work together for the common good. Who knows what could happen? Instead of standing off at a distance, throwing stones of mutual aspersion at one another, we might find ways to build a world that is a bit better for us all. That would be a constructive outcome, indeed.

## BIBLIOGRAPHY

Berger, Peter L., ed. *The Desecularization of the World: Resurgent Religion and World Politics*. Grand Rapids: Eerdmans, 1999.

———. *A Rumor of Angels: Modern Society and the Rediscovery of the Supernatural*. Garden City, NY: Doubleday, 1969.

Berger, Peter L., and Thomas Luckmann. *The Social Construction of Reality*. New York: Doubleday, 1966.

Costas, Orlando E. *The Church and Its Mission: A Shattering Critique from the Third World*. Wheaton, IL: Tyndale, 1974.

Durkheim, Emile. *The Elementary Forms of the Religious Life*. Translated by Karen E. Fields. New York: Free Press, 1995.

Foucault, Michel. *Discipline and Punish: The Birth of the Prison*. Translated by Alan Sheridan. New York: Vintage, 1977.

Gunton, Colin E. *The One, the Three, and the Many: God, Creation, and the Culture of Modernity*. Cambridge: Cambridge University Press, 1993.

Harris, Sam. *The End of Faith: Religion, Terror, and the Future of Reason.* New York: Norton, 2004.
Hitchens, Christopher. *God Is Not Great: How Religion Poisons Everything.* New York: Hachette, 2007.
Niebuhr, H. Richard. *Christ and Culture.* New York: Harper & Row, 1951.
Padilla, René, and Chris Sugden, eds. *How Evangelicals Endorsed Social Responsibility.* Nottingham: Grove, 1985.
Paul, Robert S. "Towards a Theology of Mission in the United States, with Special Reference to Lesslie Newbigin and Lamin Sanneh." PhD Thesis, University of Wales, 2010.
Said, Edward. *Orientalism.* New York: Pantheon, 1978.
Sanneh, Lamin O. *Abolitionists Abroad: American Blacks and the Making of Modern West Africa.* Cambridge, MA: Harvard University Press, 1999.
———. "Christian Mission in the Pluralist Milieu: The African Experience." *International Review of Mission* 74 (1985) 199–211.
———. "Christian Missions and the Western Guilt Complex." *Christian Century* 104 (1987) 330–34.
———. *Disciples of All Nations: Pillars of World Christianity.* Oxford: Oxford University Press, 2007.
———. *Encountering the West: Christianity and the Global Cultural Process; the African Dimension.* Maryknoll, NY: Orbis, 1993.
———. *The Jakhanké Muslim Clerics: A Religious and Historical Study of Islam in Senegambia.* Lanham, MD: University Press of America, 1989.
———. *Piety and Power: Muslims and Christians in West Africa.* Maryknoll, NY: Orbis, 1996.
———. *Summoned from the Margin: Homecoming of an African.* Grand Rapids: Eerdmans, 2012.
———. *Translating the Message: The Missionary Impact on Culture.* Maryknoll, NY: Orbis, 1989.
———. *West African Christianity.* Maryknoll, NY: Orbis, 1983.
———. *Whose Religion Is Christianity? The Gospel Beyond the West.* Grand Rapids: Eerdmans, 2003.
Sanneh, Lamin O., and Joel A. Carpenter, eds. *The Changing Face of Christianity: Africa, the West, and the World.* Oxford: Oxford University Press, 2005.
Smith, Christian, ed. *The Secular Revolution: Power, Interests, and Conflict in the Secularization of American Public Life.* Berkeley: University of California Press, 2003.
Tanner, Kathryn, and Paul Lakeland, eds. *Theories of Culture: A New Agenda for Theology.* Minneapolis: Augsburg Fortress, 1997.
Taylor, Charles. *A Secular Age.* Cambridge, MA: Belknap Press of Harvard University Press, 2007.

# 17

# Light from a Dark Horse
## Karl Barth on Approaching the Religious Other

### Roger Revell

## INTRODUCTION

WHEN IT COMES TO engagement with the "religious other" Karl Barth, one of the twentieth century's leading Protestant theologians, is not on first glance regarded as an apt tutor. Some critics see his theology as yielding little more than a *cul-de-sac* on the road of inter-faith dialogue.[1] Paul Knitter doubts the capacity of "Barthianism" to espouse a "positive approach to other religions."[2] Robert Novak opines that inter-faith exchange under the tutelage of Barth "would seem to be especially hard."[3] In Barth's own time, even Dietrich Bonhoeffer articulated such reservations.[4] Judgments of this sort continue to surface.[5] At a cursory level, this is not altogether surprising given the exclusivism that is sometimes associated with Barth's

---

1. Chung, "Theology of Reconciliation," 212.

2. Knitter, *No Other Name*, 87.

3. Novak, "Before Revelation," 50. For Novak, this owes to Barth's sheer (though arguably inconsistent!) rejection of "nature or being or experience" as an element of divine revelation.

4. Bonhoeffer, *Letters & Papers*, 286, 329.

5. Chung, "Theology of Reconciliation," 211–13.

enterprise.[6] Notwithstanding, the present endeavor petitions for the mitigation—and perhaps even a reversal?—of such views.[7]

The promise of Barth's legacy for fruitful inter-faith dialogue surpasses what first meets the eye. I believe that the capabilities of Barth's legacy beg for further realization; there are promising features yet to be tapped. To this end, I want to argue that Barth's thought stands to positively inform contemporary Christian attitudes towards inter-religious dialogue. This argument derives from consideration of two aspects of Barth's theology. In the first instance, there is Barth's doctrine of religion *vis-à-vis* revelation in *Church Dogmatics* I/2. Connected with this there is Barth's doctrine of little lights, which emerges in his later theology (*Church Dogmatics* III/4). While neither of these discussions unfold with explicit reference to inter-faith dialogue, I believe that they both bear upon Christian attitudes towards inter-religious engagement.[8] Recognition of this—against the aforementioned stereotypes—suggests that Barth is a bit of a "dark horse" with regard to the topic at hand. (A "dark horse" is a colloquial expression for a person who emerges into a place of prominence in a contest in which they otherwise seem unlikely to succeed.) This ramifies in several key senses. First, Barth's outlook in fact serves to *compel* rather than *deter* earnest Christian engagement with the religious other. It does this by infusing Christians with a measure of humility and confidence, both of which are prerequisite for earnest Christian engagement with religious others. Secondly, I will suggest that Barth's perspective also stands to steer the activity of inter-religious dialogue in a promising direction. Along these lines, a Barthian approach aspires to more than just an improved mutual understanding of one another's religious traditions (e.g., enhanced familiarity with distinctive and common doctrines, practices, etc). Further to this, it is oriented towards authentic encounters with the divine.[9]

In advancing these central claims, I will begin by surveying Barth's doctrine of revelation *vis-à-vis* religion. This outline will be immediately followed by a brief presentation of Barth's doctrine of the little lights. With these two doctrines in hand, I will transition to the task of theological appropriation. Herein, I will contend for the salutary influence

---

6. By "exclusivist," I refer to Barth's stalwart commitment to God's revelation in Jesus Christ as the means of all human salvation.

7. My own reassessment of Barth's contribution for inter-faith engagement situates within a wider movement to revisit his potential contributions in this arena. See *Karl Barth Society Newsletter*, 7–11; Chestnutt, *Challenging the Stereotype*.

8. Greggs, "Inter-Faith Table," 77.

9. For more on this type of theological realism or "revelational objectivism," see Charry, *Renewing of Your Minds*, 5–10; Newbigin, *Honest Religion for Secular Man*.

of Barthianism on Christian engagement with the religious other in the twenty-first century. Given that we find ourselves in a period when the need for inter-faith dialogue is ever more pressing, this retrieval of Barth enjoys a certain timeliness.

## BARTH ON DIVINE REVELATION

### *Religion vis-à-vis Revelation (Church Dogmatics I/2)*

Barth's discourse on religion and revelation has been called one of the "most subtle, complex, and compelling sections" in *Church Dogmatics*.[10] It has three parts. Beginning with a splash, Barth critiques conventional characterizations of religion. He takes issue with modernist accounts that situate the idea of revelation *within* the context of religion. Religion is the genus; revelation is the species—this framework makes revelation a "particular instance" of the "universal which is called religion."[11] Barth wishes to turn the tables. Revelation, he argues, must be elevated *above* religion. Revelation is from God; it is not a "human possibility."[12] Accordingly, Barth contends that religion must not interpret revelation. It must be the other way around.[13]

The implications of this Barthian *volte-face* are substantial. In this vein, Barth raises eyebrows by arguing that God's revelation often functions to disrupt Christianity.[14] Here, he depicts Christianity as a *human-constructed* religious system. In many cases, Christian religion is not the bearer of divine truth so much as something which stands to be upbraided by God's revelation! Barth's startling remarks here are a prelude to one of his major points: *religion is a form of unbelief.* Within this exposition, "unbelief" is a translation of the German *Unglaube*. It does not denote the rejection of doctrines so much as "a lack of faith."[15] Barth's outlook situates him "alone among modern interpreters of religion," for it does not begin with the empirical fact of religion but alternatively with "the 'from above' of divine revelation."[16] This does not mean that Barth is anti-empirical. Rather, it means that he refuses to *ground* his theological thought in empirical forms of knowledge. To be sure, Barth is more than willing to give careful attention to the phenomenological aspects of religion; he recognizes the presence

---

10. Webster, "Preface," vi.
11. Barth, *CD* I/2:281.
12. Barth, *CD* I/2:283.
13. Barth, *CD* I/2:284.
14. Barth, *CD* I/2:284.
15. Green, "Introduction," 20.
16. Green, "Introduction," 16.

of "human subjectivity and its machinations" therein.[17] In this sense, he is gladly certifies the evaluations of religion associated with both Durkheim and Feuerbach.[18] Barth even develops a theological account—*via* exegetical argumentation—of religion as a human construct![19] Along these lines, he readily concedes "religion" to be a sophisticated human effort to fabricate God and a path to salvation. This is all part of the phenomenon of "religionism." Yet while Barth acknowledges this phenomenon, he inveighs that it is to be decisively demarcated from revelation.[20]

It is imperative to note that Barth's depiction of religion as a decidedly anthropic affair does not have its sights on non-Christian faith traditions. He is speaking to Christians about Christianity. For Barth, by virtue of God's will, Christianity is intended as a special locus of divine revelation. The church, however, is not always genuinely receptive to such revelation. As a result, the church can be a "feeble but defiant, and arrogant but hopeless, attempt to create something that only God can do."[21] For this reason, Barth cautions against speaking of Christianity as the "fulfilled nature of religion."[22] Apart from God's revelation, Christianity is nothing more than a complex, refined form of unbelief.[23] Moreover, at its worst, Christian religion is not only impervious to God's revelation but even serves to disrupt and obscure it. It can be quite adept at making an image of God that must be discarded when God actually self-reveals.

Notwithstanding this sobering assessment, Barth progresses—in characteristic dialectical form—to an anti-thesis. Christianity can *become* a true religion. God's revelation has the potential to *sublimate* and *fulfill* it. The German term for this transposition is *Aufhebung*. *Aufhebung* has a two-pronged meaning, referring to both the "annulment" and the "lifting up" of something.[24] It is a dialectical term which renders God's revelation as something that issues both a "no" and a "yes" (negative and positive judgments) towards religion. From one vantage, Christian religion is false. From another angle, Christianity becomes true by God's grace. For Barth,

---

17. Hirota, *Shinran, Barth, and Religion*.
18. Greggs, "Inter-Faith Table," 78; cf. Green, "Introduction," 21.
19. Mason, "Christianity and World Religions," 436.
20. Green, "Introduction," 15.
21. Barth, *CD* I/2:303.
22. Barth, *CD* I/2:298.
23. Barth, *CD* I/2:300.
24. Green, "Introduction," 7.

this is analogous to justification; true religion, like a justified sinner, is "a creature of grace."[25]

More than one person has found Barth's variant assertions about the "status" of Christianity to be nonsensical.[26] There is, however, an inner coherence. It is located in the hitherto documented distinction that Barth posits between religion and revelation. This distinction, in turn, rests upon an earnest acknowledgment of God's real, dynamic, free existence.[27] Accordingly, Barth avers that the name of Jesus, as the dynamic revelation of God, is continually needed to create the church anew. True Christianity, as opposed to Christian religion, is a *continual* creation. It must recurrently become the "site and bearer of... true religion" by virtue of God's grace.[28]

In this spirit, Barth's final remarks turn to Christianity as a locus of divine revelation *vis-à-vis* other religions. Barth speaks of the church's favored, though not exclusive, status in this regard. His conclusions are carefully nuanced. Christianity's veracity is not derived from its mere existence, as some sort of *fait accompli*. It does not possess an inalienable "essence" that makes it the "highest religion."[29] Rather, any spiritual merit it possesses is derived from God's on-going, dynamic (non-static) determination to use the church in a special way.[30] Simply put: Christianity is the religion that Christ chooses to sanctify as true religion. This means that the veracity of the church's vocation to proclaim and point to Christ is purely external. In other words, Christian "power and confidence rest utterly on the grace of God" and are incapable of being attributed to "human achievement."[31] In a word, Barth refuses to conflate the reality of Christ with Christianity. By this demarcation, Barth is able to speak of Christianity at one and the same time as both an expression of conventional human religion and yet (potentially) a locus of divine revelation.

### *Little Lights in the World (Church Dogmatics III/4)*

This same demarcation underpins an important aspect of Barth's ensuing thought. Later in his *oeuvre*, Barth speaks about Christ's little lights, or

---

25. Barth, *CD* I/2:326.
26. Green, "Introduction," 18.
27. As noted earlier, this is axiomatic for theological realism.
28. Barth, *On Religion*, 143.
29. Green, "Introduction," 19.
30. Barth, *CD* I/2:358. Christian religion must never rest on its own laurels as the bearer of divine revelation.
31. Green, "Introduction," 25.

"parables of grace," which are small revelations of his truth in the wider world.[32] His remarks at this interval dovetail with his more general account of revelation, doubly affirming God's capacity to self-reveal not only *within* the Christian church but also *well beyond* its boundaries. In this discussion, Barth begins by iterating that God self-reveals through God's Word. In Barth's thought, as depicted back in *Church Dogmatics* I/1, "God's Word" refers to three things: Christ himself, the Scriptures, and the preaching (*kerygma*) of the Scriptures.[33] Now, however, Barth speaks of another form of God's word which is referred to as *extra muros ecclesiae*. He calls such revelations a "third circle of witnesses."[34] They hail from *outside* the church but they function to attest to God's One Word, Christ. In his doctrine of little lights, Barth further actualizes his "previous concept of God's irregular and alien voice."[35] The little lights are "secular parables" and "profane words" which, if they stand in agreement with Scripture, disclose the reality of God and his purposes.

The little lights, says Barth, are marked by common features. Firstly, they must be in the "closest material and substantial conformity and agreement with the One Word of God Himself."[36] Secondly, while they can never be fully equated with the One Word of God (i.e., Jesus the Messiah), they are truthful because they have the truth "indwelling" in them. They reveal God in an "approximating mode."[37] Thirdly, the efficacy and potency of little lights is contingent upon God's action. Put another way: a little light results when it has "pleased the Word of God to allow itself to be in some sense reflected and reproduced" in words or events from the human spectrum.[38] Barth goes on to suggest that God can use *anything* as a little light. By God's power, anything can become a witness to God, including a donkey—remember Balaam's ass, in Numbers 22! In our time, it can include "secular movements or realities unconnected to the church."[39] Again, Barth stresses that such micro-revelations have their source in God's dynamic existence. And their validity, he insists, is tied to their subjugation to Jesus Christ.

32. Barth, *CD* IV/3.1:111–35.
33. Barth, *CD* I/1:88–124.
34. Bloesch, "Finality of Christ," 6.
35. Chung, "Theology of Reconciliation," 212–13.
36. Barth, *CD* IV/3.1:111.
37. Hunsinger, *Theology and Pastoral Counseling*, 124.
38. Barth, *CD* IV/3.1:112.
39. Barth, *CD* IV/3.1:125. See also Hunsinger, *Theology and Pastoral Counseling*, 125–26.

## APPROPRIATION: CHRISTIANS ENGAGING WITH RELIGIOUS OTHERS

### Getting Christians to the Inter-faith Table

With the preceding inventory in mind, I turn to the task of appropriation. How does Barth's construal of the nature of divine revelation bear upon Christian attitudes and practices pertaining to engagement with religious others? There are several key extrapolations I wish to commend. In the first instance, Barth's depiction of divine revelation *vis-à-vis* religion must be seen to *compel*—not *deter*—Christian presence at the inter-faith table. Recall Barth's insistence that Christianity is a human religion like any other. Out of this appraisal, he warns strongly against privileging Christianity as a religious system. In simple terms, this means that Christianity does not have the "corner market" on matters spiritual. *God alone does!* Correlative to this acknowledgement, it is supremely fitting for Christians to stand with a certain creaturely modesty before other faiths. While God does self-reveal through the Bible in the context of the church, such revelation is neither monopolized nor controlled by Christian religion. This recognition necessarily undercuts any form of triumphalism in Christianity. After all, such an attitude would be indicative of spiritual presumption. Holding this in mind, we can recognize that Barth's account of revelation *vis-à-vis* religion is, on the one hand, a doctrine that breeds humility. And humility, I suggest, is a precondition for Christian engagement with religious others.

Barth's construal of divine self-disclosure should empty the Christian of any principled, *a priori* condescension towards different faith traditions. Moreover, as informed by Barth's theology on this front, Christians should approach inter-faith engagement without a privileged mindset.[40] Barth's outlook permits no presumption; indeed, within his thought, such a mentality stands to "invite [divine] condemnation."[41] Proud and triumphant religiosity must therefore be mortified and therein stripped of any power to dissuade Christian presence at the inter-faith table.[42] This theme has been adroitly encapsulated by my friend Richard Topping, who is fond of reminding that to go deep with Christ is to go wide with the world. To the degree that a Christian takes the independent, dynamic revelation of God seriously—as something *distinct* even if *overlapping* with Christian religion—she will not display smug insularity towards other faiths. Rather, when the table is set for inter-faith exchange, she will find her seat.

---

40. Hunsinger, *How to Read Karl Barth*, 244.
41. Mason, "World Religions," 437.
42. Mason, "World Religions," 433–34.

Further elucidating this Barthian theme, Nigel Biggar states that Christians should be people who are eager to "eavesdrop on the world."[43] For in the world and not just the church, Christians anticipate the revelation of God in Christ. This anticipation naturally extends to other religions; they are part of the world in which God operates. This ramification finds ready corroboration in Barth's thought elsewhere. One has but to consider his congenial and receptive study of Pure Land Buddhism.[44] In Buddhism, discerns Barth, one hears the words of Christ.[45] In the context of Barth's program, the intelligibility of this affirmation is grounded in both his theology of revelation and his derivative doctrine of little lights.

In this arena, Paul Cheng classifies Barth's posture as a form of *pluralism*. Such pluralism is the upshot of the "irregular nature of God's . . . communication."[46] It means that Christians are people who know that God can self-reveal anywhere and through anything, including non-Christian religion. At the same time it is essential to perceive that the "pluralistic" ethos of Barth's theology does not equate to spiritual relativism. In other words, the humility which Barth's theology inculcates is not tantamount to a deflation of the church's vocation to confidently bear witness to Jesus the Messiah.[47] This point must be underscored, because the impression that inter-faith dialogue commits one to spiritual relativism is another force which stands to deter Christian engagement therein.[48]

This crucial clarification takes its cue from a fine-tuned balance in Barth's discussion of revelation and religion. Even though Barth chastises Christian religion, he has no intention to undermine proper confidence in the revelation of Christ. One need not be skeptical about the church's witnessing vocation. Barth is clear: the "relativizing of Christian religion does not mean that the Christian faith should become disheartened, insecure, or weak."[49] In short, the church is most certainly called to point to God as God is known Christ. This "pointing" is in no way comparable to Christian triumphalism. As Wessel Bentley explains, what Barth has in mind translates less to "championing" the Christian faith and more to "celebrating" the Christ event.[50] We can even say that Christian confidence in the truth of Christ

---

43. Bigger, *Hastening That Waits*, 150–52.
44. Barth, *CD* I/2:340–44.
45. Chung, "Theology of Reconciliation," 217.
46. Chung, "Theology of Reconciliation," 220.
47. Chung, "Theology of Reconciliation," 218.
48. Greggs, "Inter-Faith Table," 83.
49. Barth, *On Religion*, 119.
50. Bentley, "Karl Barth's Understanding of Mission," 41.

does not demand a preoccupation with converting others to Christianity. In Barth's eyes, the absence of such evangelizing owes not to a lack of faith in Christ, but is actually an outcome of faith.[51] Such faith, he says, knows that conversion is not the child of "religious self-confidence" but rather of God's revelation.[52] Consequently, Christian engagement with the religious other, as with the whole of Christian life, centers on confident *witness* not emphatic *conversion*. For Barth, this is commensurate with the realization that "salvation belongs to the mystery of God" and would, therefore, be possible apart from Christian religion.[53] As this insight connects to the present clarification, it reveals that Barth's thought also buttresses Christian confidence in Jesus the Messiah. For the church, it is appropriate to witness to Christ with boldness, so long as such speech does not supplant God's revelation with reliance on its "own strength and tradition."[54]

By way of summation, Barth shows us that religious humility is not mutually exclusive with confidence in Christ. His thought generously supplies both. In this vein, his legacy is one which encourages earnest Christian engagement with religious others. On the one side, it undercuts forms of triumphalist religious pride which easily deters inter-faith dialogue. On the other side, it assures Christians that serious engagement with religious others does not entail obeisance to the spirit relativism. For Barth, the church should eschew both self-confidence and skepticism.[55] The adoption of such a posture compels Christian presence at the inter-religious table; it also allows Christians to retain the particulars of the faith. In sum, we will *be there* and we will be there *as Christians*.

### *Improving the Conversation at the Inter-faith Table*

I have just reflected on how Barth's paragraphs on divine revelation compel earnest Christian engagement with religious others. This, however, is not all that Barth's theology offers in service of inter-faith dialogue. Herein, my second central claim comes into focus. In a word, Barth's portrayal of divine revelation—and especially his doctrine of little lights—is poised to augment a certain mode of contemporary inter-faith exchange. This modification is salutary. To establish this point, it is first necessary to briefly characterize

---

51. Barth, *On Religion*, 120.

52. Barth, *On Religion*, 120.

53. Chung, "Theology of Reconciliation," 220. See also the story of Elijah and the Sidonian Widow (1 Kgs 17), which Jesus picks up in Luke 4.

54. Bentley, "Karl Barth's Understanding of Mission," 29. See also D'Costa, "Theology of Religions," 630.

55. I am indebted to John Webster for this turn of phrase.

a common—though by no means totalizing—mode of inter-faith dialogue which looks to be unsettled by Barth's theological ethos.

Garret Green observes that modern approaches to the study of religion are heavily informed by 1) social-scientific accounts of religion and 2) the history of religions school.[56] These schools signify a type of "philosophy of religion" which operates to assess variant human religions by a "scientific analysis of religious language," among other factors.[57] To be sure, this approach has been a fruitful one.[58] Among other gains, it displays an adeptness at identifying "the unacknowledged religious . . . bias behind many earlier (and some recent) accounts of religion."[59] Moreover, inasmuch much as the social-scientific ethos prides itself on being neutral, sophisticated, and self-conscious about its assumptions, its interpretations enjoy legitimacy.[60] Notwithstanding, social-scientific accounts of religion can sometimes be insufficiently self-critical. They, too, harbor biases. This is evidenced, for instance, by the fact that certain portrayals of religion—such as that offered by Barth—are excluded from the "religious studies canon." Green suggests that such biases are indicative of "quasi-religious" sensibilities at play in the social-scientific paradigm of religious studies.[61]

To the extent that social-scientific approaches to religion decisively imprint our attitudes towards inter-faith dialogue, a certain form of engagement logically follows. As delineated by Tom Greggs, this equates to a hefty focus on areas of similarity and difference—in terms of doctrine and praxis—between discrete religious traditions.[62] Furthermore, a social-scientific philosophy of religion conduces to what Raimundo Panikkar calls an anthropological model of inter-faith dialogue.[63] This model holds questions about source(s) of religion in abeyance, attending instead to religions as co-extensive phenomena, akin to human languages. Within the anthropological approach, the defining objectives of inter-religion engagement include: gaining familiarity with other religious systems (analogous to learning a new language); refraining from ranking religions (it makes little sense to say that "one language is more perfect than another"[64]); and reflecting on

56. Green, "Religious Studies Canon," 473–74.
57. Panikkar, *Dialogue*, 66–67.
58. Panikkar, *Dialogue*, 66.
59. Green, "Religious Studies Canon," 474.
60. Green, "Religious Studies Canon," 473–74; cf. Green, "Introduction," 29–30.
61. Green, "Religious Studies Canon." 483.
62. Greggs, "Inter-Faith Table," 82–83.
63. Panikkar, *Dialogue*, xxiii–xxvii.
64. Panikkar, *Dialogue*, xxiv.

how different religious traditions stand to supplement and strengthen one another (the task of translational appropriation). Again, there is much benefit to be had through this form of inter-faith activity. At the same time, if one's vision of inter-faith dialogue ventures no further, Barth would be disgruntled. As I see it, his appraisal of religion means that Christianity—or any faith tradition—can certainly be discussed and meaningfully understood within a social-science metric. Yet Barth's stalwart defense of the independent revelation of God in Christ (i.e., "revelational objectivism") means that Christian engagement with religious others should anticipate something *more* than an exchange of religious knowledge. The significance of this critique is not to be missed.[65]

If Barth was a consultant for inter-faith dialogue, I think he would both yearn for and anticipate something greater than an exchange of religious ideas. His sights would be set beyond the horizon of humanity. In a word, he would hope for an *encounter with the divine*. Such an encounter might come through non-Christian religion, though its source would not be that religion *per se* so much as God's sublimation of some feature of said religion in service of self-revealing. To echo Barthian idiom, in such a moment one would witness a little light. Where Christians are invited to set the terms for inter-religious engagement, I think Barth would counsel them to encourage a posture not just of receptivity to other traditions but also, and more importantly, to God himself. After all, it would be a shame for God's voice to be crowded out by our own voices, as they busily transmit and receive data about our religions.

It is important to perceive that the Barthian anticipation of encounter with the divine is *theoretically* excluded from forms of inter-religious engagement that are bound to social-science approaches to human religion.[66] This is because, as Gregg's explains, of the naturalistic/secularistic coloring of such paradigms.[67] As these fundamental traits play out, they show a tendency to steamroll the metaphysical/revelatory claims at the core of ancient religious traditions.[68] This tendentiousness stands in tension with the expectation of divine encounter flowing from Barth's thought. It can germinate an "attitudinal barrier" to the prospect of meeting God in the midst of inter-religious dialogue. For Barth—and for Christians under his tutelage—encounter with God is the highest end of such activity. It does not deny the place of other

---

65. See also Greggs, "Inter-Faith Table," 78; Glasse, "Barth on Feuerbach," 69–96.

66. Green, "Introduction," 27.

67. Greggs, "Inter-Faith Table," 82. See also Sanneh, *Whose Religion Is Christianity?*, 483–85; Smith, *How Not to Be Secular*.

68. Greggs, "Inter-Faith Table," 82. In my evaluation, I am indebted to Sir Roger Scruton's recent discussion at the Cambridge Divinity Faculty on November 10, 2017.

ends (mutual understanding, awareness of points of overlap, etc.[69]), but it does not want to be ultimately constrained by them. The Barthian inter-faith paradigm believes that approaches to religious others which are dismissive of the reality of God will be impoverished. In such an environment, participants are inclined away from true epiphany.

Along these lines, Barth's theology is not opposed to meaningful Christian engagement with religious others. More precisely, it is leery of inter-religious dialogue undertaken upon an essentially secularist pretext. Why? Because such a pretext militates against earnest receptivity to divine revelation. By contrast, Barth's theology gives rise to an attitude of radical openness. At one level, this can manifest as an openness towards other religions. At a more profound level, however, it is an openness towards God, who can and may self-reveal well beyond the bounds of the church. As I see it, Christians who appreciate this Barthian lesson can readily affirm the value of social-scientific metrics used in the context of inter-faith dialogue. At the same time, they will be hesitant towards models of inter-faith engagement that are animated by a thoroughgoing naturalism/secularism. Undoubtedly, such approaches may help people of disparate religions be more open to one another. But if Barth is right, they may not be open God.

Barth's account of religion *vis-à-vis* revelation not only conduces to inter-faith dialogue, but even serves to enrich it.[70] In this sense, Barth is a dark horse in the race towards inter-religious engagement. In defiance of expectation, he shows himself to be a surprisingly useful guide for Christian participation in inter-faith dialogue. His legacy is able to incorporate common conventions surrounding such activity while at the same time pressing for even greater openness in such exchange: *openness towards God*. Going deep with Jesus, after all, means that one is ready to recognize his voice in sometimes unexpected and even strange places.

## BIBLIOGRAPHY

Barth, Karl. *Church Dogmatics*. Translated by G. W. Bromiley, et al. 14 vols. Peabody, MA: Hendrickson, 2010.

———. *On Religion*. Translated by G. Green. London: Bloomsbury, 2013.

———. *The Word of God and the World of Man*. Translated by D. Horton. Boston: Pilgrim, 1928.

Bentley, Wessell. "Karl Barth's Understanding of Mission: The Church in Relationship." *Verbum et Ecclesia* 30 (2009) 25–49.

69. I am indebted to Laura Duhan-Kaplan on this point. See also Mackenzie et al., *Getting to the Heart of Interfaith*.

70. As taught by Prof. Peter Ochs, co-founder of the Scripture Reasoning Movement. For more, see Scriptural Reasoning, "About Scriptural Reasoning."

Bigger, Nigel. *The Hastening That Waits*. Oxford: Clarendon, 1993.
Bloesch, Donald. "The Finality of Christ and Religious Pluralism." *Touchstone* (Summer 1991) 5–9.
Bonhoeffer, Dietrich. *Letters & Papers from Prison*. Translated by Eberhard Bethge. London: SCM, 1971.
Charry, Ellen. *By the Renewing of Your Minds*. Oxford: Oxford University Press, 1997.
Chestnutt, Glenn. *Challenging the Stereotype: The Theology of Karl Barth as a Resource for Inter-Religious Encounter in a European Context*. Bern: Peter Lang, 2010.
Chung, Paul. "Karl Barth's Theology of Reconciliation in Dialogue with a Theology of Religions." *Mission Studies* 25 (2008) 212.
Crisp, Oliver. "'I Do Teach it, but I Also Do Not Teach It': The Universalism of Karl Barth." In *"All Shall Be Well": Explorations in Universalism and Christian Theology from Origen to Moltmann*, edited by Gregory MacDonald, 305–324. Eugene, OR: Cascade, 2011.
D'Costa, Gavin. "Theology of Religions." In *The Modern Theologians: An Introduction to Christian Theology in the Twentieth Century*, edited by David Ford, 625–30. 2nd ed. Oxford: Blackwell, 1997.
Glasse, John. "Barth on Feuerbach." *Harvard Theological Review* 57 (1964) 69–96.
Green, Garrett. "Challenging the Religious Studies Canon: Karl Barth's Theology of Religion." *Journal of Religion* 75 (1995) 473–86.
———. "Introduction." In *On Religion: The Revelation of God as the Sublimation of Religion*, translated by Garrett Green, 1–35. London: Bloomsbury, 2013.
Greggs, Tom. "Bringing Barth's Critique of Religion to the Inter-faith Table." *The Journal of Religion* 88 (2008) 75–94.
Hirota, Dennis. "Shinran, Barth, and Religion: Engagement with Religious Language as an Issue of Comparative Theology." *Shin Dharma Net*, 2003. Online. http://bschawaii.org/shindharmanet/wp-content/uploads/sites/3/2012/04/Hirota-Barth.pdf.
Hunsinger, Deborah. *Theology and Pastoral Counselling*. Grand Rapids: Eerdmans, 1995.
Hunsinger, George. *How to Read Karl Barth*. Oxford: Oxford University Press, 1993.
*Karl Barth Society Newsletter* 54 (2017).
Knitter, Paul. *No Other Name? A Critical Survey of Christian Attitudes towards the World Religions*. Maryknoll, NY: Orbis, 1986.
Mackenzie, Don, et al. *Getting to the Heart of Interfaith: The Eye-Opening, Hope-Filled Friendship of a Pastor, a Rabbi, and an Imam*. Woodstock, VT: SkyLight Paths, 2010.
Mason, David. "Christianity and World Religions: The Contributions of Barth and Tillich." *Anglican Theological Review* 97 (2015) 433–47.
Newbigin, J. E. L. *Honest Religion for Secular Man*. London: SCM, 1966.
Novak, Robert. "Before Revelation: The Rabbis, Paul, and Karl Barth." *The Journal of Religion* 71 (1991) 50–66.
Panikkar, Raimundo. *The Intra-Religious Dialogue*. New York: Paulist, 1978.
Sanneh, Lamin. *Whose Religion Is Christianity? The Gospel Beyond the West*. Grand Rapids: Eerdmans, 2003.
Sawyer, James. *A Survivor's Guide to Theology*. Grand Rapids: Zondervan, 2006.
Scriptural Reasoning. "About Scriptural Reasoning." Online. http://www.scripturalreasoning.org/.html.

Smith, James. *How Not to Be Secular: Reading Charles Taylor*. Grand Rapids: Eerdmans, 2014.
Webster, John. "Preface." In *On Religion: The Revelation of God as the Sublimation of Religion*, translated by Garrett Green, vi–viii. London: Bloomsbury, 2013.

# 18

## From Other to Brother
### Re-interpreting the Canadian Christians' Call as We Stand with the Syrian Muslim Refugee

ALISHA FUNG

### INTRODUCTION

IN OCTOBER 2015, NEWLY appointed Canadian Prime Minister Justin Trudeau promised to relocate twenty-five thousand Syrian refugees into Canada. The majority of Canadians were in favor of this promise, and it helped him win the election. With the accomplishment of this promise, there have come some pressing concerns, e.g., our realistic ability to accommodate this increased population through finance, health, housing, and education. In this paper, however, I would like to highlight the equally pressing issue of our ability to accept, interact with, and respect our new immigrants. The way we do this will determine Canada's way forward in interacting with the *other* among us and within us. I will include insights from the Encountering the Other Conference along with other interfaith sources in order to outline a way forward for Canadian Christians to "go and make disciples" (Matt 28:19) while engaging in authentic interfaith discourse with Muslim refugees.

First, I will discuss Westernization through Christianization in historical Canada and the critical importance of naming and denouncing Christianization before engaging our cultural and religious other. Then I will discuss our present-day context of the Syrian Crisis. Next, I will introduce a theology of interaction through the divine dance: the way Christians are to "dance" and to make room for the "other" in the dance. I use three terms to understand (or redefine) a Christian understanding of inclusivity and right-relationship with our Muslim brothers and sisters: evangelism, the Trinity, and conversion. Evangelism has had negative connotations of Christians yelling on a street corner, sharing good news to believe Jesus has died for the sins of the world. However, I redefine evangelism as the sharing and self-emptying of love Christians have experienced from God unto all those around us. The Trinity represents the Father, Son, and Holy Spirit. This community of three in one shows us a God who self-empties love within Godself and represents the relationship humanity can have with one another through a self-emptying love. Finally, conversion is a word to describe one coming to the belief in Jesus Christ as Savior. Conversion has had negative repercussions in history as well as the present and I use this word to understand these effects. Conversion is also used in this paper to explain how some forms of conversions are inevitable: converting to culture, social norms, and new experiences. Conversion is not just an act by one party, but by two; when refugees come to Canada, Canadians are in a process of converting from "the norm" to a new people and sense of self. I will conclude this paper with, perhaps, a paradoxical way forward for Christians to, "Go and make disciples" without stripping others of their identity through holding, loving, and supporting each other's otherness.

## MARROW AND BONE: HISTORICAL MISSIONAL CONTEXT

Even with its short 150 years of Confederation, Canada has had a rich history of interactions with different cultures and religions. When the European settlers arrived in Canada, their desire to Christianize the land and Indigenous peoples led to horrific ramifications. Today, these still linger as ancestral pain and insufficient care and funding allocation. Unfortunately, Indigenous peoples were not the only ones who were hurt by Westernizing through the name of God: early Chinese, Japanese, South-East Asian, Jewish, Sikh, Hindu, and African settlers felt this xenophobia for many years. It was not until recent decades that apologies were made and legalistic racism was decimated. Thus, "superiority of Christianity was a reflection and a legitimation of the Western striving for domination,"[1] and unfortunately, this Westernizing desire still lingers. This relationship between

---

1. Häring et al., *Learning from Other Faiths*, 125.

religion and culture, "Like marrow to bone," has cast a negative light on the white Christian movement throughout history.[2] If we wish to limit cultural and religious conflict and contempt in the present, we must stay aware of our past: the fact that we are still on Native land, and how Syrian Muslims might perceive us as a Christianizing culture. We must construct new paradigms, in which we desire to understand, help, work, and spiritually live with newly landed immigrants. We must remember that refugees are already converting much of their old realities in simply coming to a new land: a new culture, geography, experience, and societal norms. The leap over the ocean is almost the easy part as opposed to leaping into a new place with new ways of being and living. In our pursuit of interaction with newly landed immigrants, we must remember the desire for conversion (religiously or culturally) is never in our hands, but in God's unique relationship with all individuals, cultures, and religions. "For by grace you have been saved through faith. And this is not your own doing; it is the gift of God" (Eph 2:8). As we learn from our past mistakes, holding respect for the otherness of refugees will do well to start changing the way we subconsciously or consciously yearn for conversion into sameness.

## REALITY: PRESENT-DAY CONTEXT

External forces sometimes perpetuate our Christianizing paradigm. For example, the media is subject to bias, telling stories in a way that captures the most viewers and evokes the most emotion. The terrorist attacks of 2016 in Paris, Brussels, and Orlando were devastating events that shook the world. The events led some to adopt fear and anger towards Muslims as a whole, asserting that Islamic terrorists hate the West and desire to Islamicize the world. The reality, however, is much more complicated. Ironically, the people who are most hurt by terrorism are Muslims. Civil war has displaced millions of Syrians, with an estimate of six thousand people fleeing Syria daily.[3] The borders have started to close up, making it impossible for refugees to find a safe home. Europe has been able to assist the humanitarian effort with three and a half billion Euros but has only accepted 150,000 refugees, most of whom now reside in Germany and Sweden.[4] The six and a half million Syrian refugees displaced within Syria are left with impossible choices: pay smugglers to take them through dangerous waters to Turkey, Egypt, or

---

2. Paul, "Challenging Constructions," 2.
3. "Syria Refugee Crisis FAQ."
4. Abboud, *Syria*.

Libya, or face staying in their highly violent country.[5] The limited amount of aid, education, and health care that can reach Syria cannot support the ever-increasing number of refugees. Since the start of the crisis in 2011, 386,000 Syrians have been killed, including 14,800 children.[6] Ultimately, many Syrians want to return to their home—but a home where there is no violence. In the meantime, by assisting with refugee resettlement, we are given a unique opportunity to forge a new way forward towards friendship and unity between Christians and Muslims in Canada.

## A CHRISTIAN THEOLOGY OF OTHERNESS

Trinitarian theology can be used to support a new paradigm of respect for the other. The Trinity, as I use it in this paper, is meant to understand the generosity (the divine dance) of the Christian God exhibited in the generosity of Godself sharing power and love in three persons: Father, Son, and Holy Spirit. The Trinity as divine dancing is not clear by any means but my defining it in the next section is to offer a glimpse of how wide and overwhelming it is.

The Trinity represents the friendship we see in the unity of God and how we, as humans different in appearance and mind, find unity in one another. In friendship, there is a reality of sacrifice and space required for the other. We know this and see this through the words and life of Jesus in John 15:12–13, "My command is this: Love each other as I have loved you. Greater love has no one than this: to lay down one's life for one's friends." This shows us the love Jesus has for his disciples and the love that ultimately points us back to where it originates from—the Trinity. In this commandment, we can start to see how this love, this divine dance, has inspired God's actions from the Hebrew Bible to present: God emptying Godself to create the world; God pouring Godself into Jesus' life and death to show humanity *the dance*; and the spirit inspiring *our dancing* to make room for our friends, neighbors, and enemies. In the Trinity we start to see the connection that God has with the world that is neither absorbing of one another nor distancing from one another but, rather, radical intimacy and otherness of one another. It is how we come to understand the divine dance of give and take: dying to oneself to make room for the other, being reborn into more fully who we are as individuals made in the Trinity of community.[7] This Trinity shows us not only complete friendship and intimacy but also a deep respect for difference

---

5. Abboud, *Syria*.
6. "Syria Refugee Crisis FAQ."
7. McFague, *Blessed Are the Consumers*.

and distance. In our self-emptying towards our neighbors, or rather, refugees who have found themselves in a new land, a new place, and a new dance, we make room. We make space for their otherness not only so that we will be remade new, but so we will be made new together.

As Christians, we can participate in this divine dance by creating safe spaces for dialogue. Through dialogue, we may discover our commonalities with Muslims: a shared biblical history, respect for the Prophet Jesus, a Day of Judgment, belief in an afterlife, and common religious cores of love and compassion.[8] We may find comfort in knowing Muslims are open to interfaith relationships as they honor this verse in the Qur'an: "You will certainly find the nearest in friendship to those . . . who say: We are Christians; this is because there are priests and monks among them and because they do not behave proudly" (Qur'an 5:82). This type of inclusive faith does not mean we all need to believe the same truth. Rather, it takes us beyond the idiosyncrasies of our specific faith traditions in order to encounter shared values and desires for peace. Christians alone cannot accomplish this task; we need Muslims (as well as everyone else) to heal the hurt of this crisis and work toward a more peaceful, God-permeated world.

When we start to see each other as a non-threat, it can become easy to think this is enough. But the divine dance pushes us to ask whether we are people who are prepared to really hear the other in order to understand and build compassion based on what we hear.[9] In order to do this, we must "not simply . . . [gather] facts about [their] faith tradition. [We must enter] into the depth of relationship between a person and that person's faith."[10] This means leaving our comfort zone of the majority and entering into the "fear" of becoming the minority.[11] If we cannot start learning to cross these lines and make space as God makes space for us, we will remain stuck judging others' faith by the reality of our own and realize we are the ones who have left the divine dance."[12] By creating an inclusive dialogue, we enter into a shared life and existence where we can become people who overcome and end the generational stereotypes of racism and prejudice.[13] This new paradigm shift, this desire to connect with the other is driven by a willingness to put aside a perception of ego, fear, and difference in order to create a

---

8. Mackenzie et al., *Getting to the Heart of Interfaith*.
9. Dwivedi, "Hindu Tradition."
10. Mackenzie et al., *Getting to the Heart of Interfaith*, 16.
11. Gopin, *To Make the Earth Whole*.
12. Mackenzie et al., *Getting to the Heart of Interfaith*, 16.
13. Häring et al., *Learning from Other Faiths*.

space where God's grace can help us die to ourselves and awaken to a new, authentic union with the other.[14]

Refusing to participate in the divine dance can impact our understanding of God and the communities around us. In history we see how negative stereotypes of Judaism and Islam have led to inhumane acts of violence and, unfortunately, still do. In the case of newly landed Muslims, if not careful, we can enter into the same scapegoating and stereotyping of our religious other in order to create an enemy against the Christian West.[15] However, if we look at God's revelation in the Hebrew Scriptures and the New Testament we discover God not taking the side of the superiors, but taking the side of the widow, the orphaned, the poor, or, in this case, the refugee.[16] Unfortunately, Christians often are not known for this type of kindness but are known for what and whom we disagree with; " we . . . seem to know who we are by who we're not"[17] and, in this case, we are not Islamic and we are not wrong. We tend to think we know the way, the truth, and the life because there's a verse in the Bible that gives us the answer.[18] This self-righteousness in "knowing" is detrimental to those around us but especially to ourselves. We tend to let our perception of chosenness or victimhood aid us in our perception of being right but this perception of truth is really a wall separating us from experiencing God through our Muslim brother. When Christians recognize Muslims are on a similar pursuit towards truth as well, we have the opportunity to join hands and journey together towards a, "shared quest for the truth [while] learn[ing] from the other, [so] that in this way both of us, [in] the fruit of our dialogue, can come closer to the [real] truth."[19] To desire this expanded point of view is rooted in being able to understand the Christian and Muslim as part of God's divine dance of revelation, both necessary for God's holy body to work as a whole for all humanity:

> We were all baptized by one Spirit so as to form one body—whether Jews or Gentiles, slave or free—and we were all given the one Spirit to drink. Even so the body is not made up of one part but of many. . . . God has placed the parts in the body, every one of them, just as he wanted them to be. If they were all one part, where would the body be? As it is, there are many parts,

14. Mills, "Searching for the Sacred Other."
15. Burrell, *Towards a Jewish-Christian-Muslim Theology*.
16. Byassee, "Christianity Without Enemies."
17. Byassee, "Christianity Without Enemies," 1.
18. See John 14:16.
19. Häring et al., *Learning from Other Faiths*, 28.

> but one body. . . . God has put the body together . . . so that its parts should have equal concern for each other. If one part suffers, every part suffers with it; if one part is honored, every part rejoices with it. (1 Cor 12:12–26, NIV)

And this is the divine mystery: even within our uniqueness and difference of beliefs, somehow God is working through it all, despite how contradictory they may appear to one another. By entering into this state of submission and humility, we are able to enter into each other's worlds, creating one world where we can enter into God's larger dance of revelation. Laura Duhan-Kaplan expresses this need for revelation through quieting ourselves in order to "experience new religious thought . . . to feel its vibration, and hear its song."[20] This vibration, this song, is not the essence of the person but the presence of God. This act of listening is not only doing a great service to ourselves, but a great service to the world when we respect the presence of God in the people around us.[21] In fact, one important way towards a better world is through listening to the goodness and wisdom in people outside of our religion.[22] When we do this we start to understand that diversity is not God's divine mistake, or even a human-driven mistake, but created and blessed by God.[23] In other words, "It is not . . . particular [truths], particular views or particular forms of behavior, not social or economic success, that bring people close to God, but the simple fact that they form part of a world which is created by God, that they live in the midst of a history which is being guided by God towards its consummation."[24]

Roger L. Revell's paper on Karl Barth's concept of religion versus revelation articulates this vibration of God not just in Christianity, but among other religions as well as outside of religion altogether. He argues that by staying within the confines of Christian doctrine we are limiting our ability to receive God's revelation: "[by] going wide with the world, we simultaneously go deep in Christ."[25] In this act of humbling ourselves before other faiths, God's revelation of Christ can be found (perhaps more dynamically) *outside* the realms of Christianity. However, the uniqueness of our Christian belief should not be discounted. Our desire to call on Jesus Christ and speak of him is something largely in our hearts and is Spirit provoking. But it is not through *our* hard work that Christ can be shared with others, but through

20. Duhan-Kaplan, "Vibration of the Other," 9.
21. Pryce, "'Unitive Being' in the Face of Atrocity."
22. Pryce, "'Unitive Being' in the Face of Atrocity."
23. Mordag, "Rumi's Mindfulness of the 'Other.'"
24. Häring et al., *Learning from Other Faiths*.
25. Revell, "Light from a Dark Horse," 5.

*God's* revelation in us as we bear witness to our Muslim other through our hearts and our hands. It is in this dance that the fullness of God can be recognized in Christians and Muslims alike as we allow the Holy Spirit to work through us and guide us.

## INTER-ACTION: A CHRISTIAN WAY FORWARD

With an awakened compassion for Muslims, Christians actively live out the love Jesus calls us to by, paradoxically, making disciples. Making disciples does not end with Muslims checking the "Jesus is God" box, but begins as a never-ending process of challenging our concept of giving and receiving God's love in unknown, anxiety-ridden territories. In this way, "making disciples" does not come about by a desire for traditional views of evangelism and conversion but rather through acts of love, acceptance, and humbleness. We make disciples through actions that profess the love Jesus has given to our unique religion but we also become disciples by recognizing the power of God and truth God holds in God's dearly loved Muslim. Perhaps the most effective way of holding each other's differences while proclaiming our own truth is by starting small. Lynn Mills insists the best interactions start very small for greatest effectiveness. When we can focus on actively loving one or two Muslims, we can become more attuned to their specific needs and wants by hearing their story and understanding their background.[26] Here, God's grace can enter and create a space for greater respect and understanding.

Specific to our Syrian refugee influx, the way in which we give and serve these one or two sisters or brothers is critical for their self-dignity and progress in their temporary or forever home in Canada. The way Canadian Christians share this type of hospitality with refugees should be with the intention Jesus exemplified throughout the Gospels. When we reach out, provide housing, food, or other support towards refugees, we must do it without any preconceived conditions or strings attached.[27] This type of economy leaves a power imbalance where our refugees are left owing to Canadians. "Instead, we need a theology of hospitality that moves our communities beyond welcome and into a posture of humility, taking our own social situation and that of others very seriously, learning to recognize signs and effects of our privilege and power."[28] Being conscious of this power imbalance will influence the way in which we support these refugees, giving us a greater ability to act with compassion and to treat our

---

26. Mills, "Searching for the Sacred Other."
27. Fast, "For the Love of Strangers."
28. Fast, "For the Love of Strangers," 5.

refugees with the same respect as we treat ourselves. We find this command and understanding through our shared Hebrew Scriptures: "The foreigner residing among you must be treated as your native-born. Love them as yourself, for you were foreigners in Egypt" (Lev 19:34). When submitting ourselves to those in need, we will not only be creating a union with our Muslim brother but experiencing God's Kingdom here and now: "Blessed are you who are poor, for yours is the kingdom of God" (Luke 6:20). Our welcome should not be based on providing help during a desperate time (as important as this is) but on the intention of creating a "mutual covenantal relationship built on reciprocal and intimate love" (Luke 6:20). In this type of relationship we can accomplish networks of peace through the smallest of gestures and place our faith in the ripple effect of love, compassion, and humility.[29] For it is through these gestures we are fulfilling our biblical call and desire for making Jesus known as he became servant to make God known: "In humility count others more significant than yourselves. Let each of you look not only to his own interests, but also to the interests of others. Have this mind among yourselves, [for] . . . Jesus Christ . . . did not count equality with God a thing to be grasped, but made himself nothing, taking the form of a servant" (Phil 2:3–11).

The act of authentic, God-giving hospitality is crucial for our relationship with refugees so that we may begin to work together. When we share life together and work on our shared desires to eliminate poverty, injustice, and climate change, we will find it takes all of us to accomplish these goals.[30] Through our united work, these social, political, and environmental problems will also bridge the gap of our otherness; we can begin to know each other and learn each other's stories from a place of commonality and humanness.[31] Here the act of *converting* comes out of the space we share when we are working together. However, it is not through the intention of changing others' truth or religion, but in making space for them to experience the love we receive by humbly working and living life together as we are faithful to Jesus' revelation in us. In other words, proclamation, dialogue, and action are not separate entities. It is what we do and the stories and lived experience we share that allows God to speak through the bonds we create.

---

29. Gopin, *To Make the Earth Whole*.
30. Mackenzie et al., *Getting to the Heart of Interfaith*.
31. Mackenzie et al., *Getting to the Heart of Interfaith*.

## CONCLUSION

By accepting our Muslim other as our brother or sister, we come to realize religion alone cannot hold the key to salvation; this is God's mysterious business and God is wondrously able to work through anything and anyone, despite their faith or lack thereof. But it is ultimately up to us, the citizens of this world, to participate in *this* type of unity, in God's divine dance, for we are the ones who hold more responsibility than our world leaders for what does and does not occur for peace in our world.[32] This spiritual consciousness allows us to see ourselves in our Muslim other and to understand that when we bring pain to a Muslim, we are bringing pain to God, when we show love to a Muslim, we show love to God, and when we make room for Muslims we enter into God's divine dance.[33] We have entered a devastating time in history where resolution lies far in the future, but God has given us a unique opportunity as Christians and residents in Canada to make room for our Muslim brother and sister so that we can bridge the divide and realize our relatedness in working towards peace together as God's dearly beloved children.

## BIBLIOGRAPHY

Abboud, Samer N. *Syria*. Cambridge: Polity, 2016.

Burrell, David B. *Towards a Jewish-Christian-Muslim Theology*. Chichester: Wiley-Blackwell, 2011.

Byassee, Jason. "Christianity Without Enemies." Paper presented at Encountering the Other: An Inter-Religious Conference, Vancouver School of Theology, May 17, 2016.

Duhan-Kaplan, Laura. "Vibration of the Other: A Kabbalistic Ecumenism." Paper presented at Encountering the Other: An Inter-Religious Conference, Vancouver School of Theology, May 17, 2016.

Dwivedi, A. S. P. "Hindu Traditions Offering Positive Approaches to Others." Paper presented at Encountering the Other: An Inter-Religious Conference, Vancouver School of Theology, May 17, 2016.

Fast, Anita. "For the Love of Strangers: A Theology of Hospitality in Colonial Canada." Paper presented at Encountering the Other: An Inter-Religious Conference, Vancouver School of Theology, May 17, 2016.

Gopin, Marc. *To Make the Earth Whole: The Art of Citizen Diplomacy in an Age of Religious Militancy*. Lanham, MD: Rowman & Littlefield, 2009.

Häring, Hermann, et al., eds. *Learning from Other Faiths*. London: SCM, 2003.

Mackenzie, Don, et al. *Getting to the Heart of Interfaith: The Eye-Opening, Hope-Filled Friendship of a Pastor, a Rabbi & an Imam*. Woodstock, VT: SkyLight Paths, 2012.

McFague, Sallie. *Blessed Are the Consumers: Climate Change and the Practice of Restraint*. Minneapolis: Augsburg Fortress. 2013.

---

32. Gopin, *To Make the Earth Whole*.
33. Mackenzie et al., *Getting to the Heart of Interfaith*.

Migliore, Daniel L. *Faith Seeking Understanding: An Introduction to Christian Theology*. 3rd ed. Grand Rapids: Eerdmans, 2014.

Mills, Lynn. "Searching for the Sacred Other in the Palestinian/Israeli Conflict." Paper presented at Encountering the Other: An Inter-Religious Conference, Vancouver School of Theology, May 17, 2016.

Mordag, Tuveyc. "Rumi's Mindfulness of the 'Other.'" Paper presented at Encountering the Other: An Inter-Religious Conference, Vancouver School of Theology, May 17, 2016.

Paul, R. S. "Challenging Constructions of the 'Religious Other': Introducing the Iconclastic Work of Lamin Sanneh." Paper presented at Encountering the Other: An Inter-Religious Conference, Vancouver School of Theology, May 17, 2016.

Placher, William C. *Essentials of Christianity*. Louisville: Westminster John Knox, 2003.

Pryce, Paula. "'Unitive Being' in the Face of Atrocity: North American Contemplative Christian Responses to Terrorism." Paper presented at Encountering the Other: An Inter-Religious Conference, Vancouver School of Theology, May 17, 2016.

Revell, Roger L. "Light from a Dark Horse: Karl Barth on Approaching the Religious Other." Paper presented at Encountering the Other: An Inter-Religious Conference, Vancouver School of Theology, May 17, 2016.

"Syria Refugee Crisis FAQ: How the War Is Affecting Children." *World Vision*, October 18, 2019. Online. https://www.worldvision.org/wv/news/Syria-war-refugee-crisis-FAQ.

Zaidi, Syed Nasir. "Portrayal of Christianity in the Qur'an." Paper presented at Encountering the Other: An Inter-Religious Conference, Vancouver School of Theology, May 17, 2016.

# 19

# Christianity without Enemies

## Jason Byassee

My title, "Christianity Without Enemies," is meant to be provocative. My teacher, Stanley Hauerwas, has long insisted there is no Christianity without an enemy (for him liberal modernity and the nation-state).[1] To read the New Testament, the job description on Jesus' business card should read "first-century Jewish exorcist." He's barely there before the demons come out. One of the mistakes of mainline liberal Christianity is to speak as if there is no enemy. All that mythological talk of the devil seems intellectually disreputable, so we skip it. We then leave ourselves with no language with which to describe a world coming undone. Is it any wonder our preaching has so little power?

So why the title, if, as Hauerwas argues, there can be no Christianity without enemies?

We Christians, and perhaps people in general, seem to know who we *are* by who we're not. Mainline liberals do this with evangelicals. Sure, we're sort of Christian, but not like those bad ones, who are sexist or racist or fundamentalist. Evangelicals do it with liberals: we have no watered-down faith, unlike those spineless mainliners. The heresy was once called Manicheanism. As a great ancient religion, it had its glories. But St. Augustine realized you can't divide the world up into essentially good and essentially bad. And his

---

1. See, for example, Hauerwas, "Preaching."

theology of evil, as the privation of the good, was the way out.[2] You can't go pick up a handful of evil. Evil is more like a wound. It's an absence, a lack, a distortion, an absurdity. Your enemy is not essentially evil because there is no thing that is essentially evil. Only good *really* exists—God, and the things summoned into existence by God. Evil is a puzzling absence of goodness, not an essential thing, and God will one day heal it.

I'm convinced there is deep wisdom in the history of Christian thought shaped by responding to heresy.[3] One heresy we ruled out was precisely this Manicheanism. It has something true in it of course (to say otherwise would be itself more Manichean!). But the church has been wise to say those who hold this malformed faith ought not to count themselves as Christians or turn up on Sundays. You can't think there are essential evils and essential goods. Creation is good, fallen, and being repaired. Christian orthodoxy's rejection of Manicheanism means we can find good anywhere. Sin too. That combination is what it means for the world to be fallen. What follows is a Christian theology against Manicheanism, *for* a layered view of the world, that says to almost any idea conceivable not altogether yes, or altogether no, but rather yes-and.

I will start with the history of race in my native US, with help from a Nobel Prize Winner and one of the great souls of the world. Toni Morrison wrote about white nervousness about the goodness of black identity decades before the recent Black Lives Matter movement.[4] Why are white people so fragile when we've had it so good for so long? Morrison's view is that if non-white people are not who white people think they are, then white people also aren't who we think we are either. Whiteness is parasitic. It presumes a backdrop of blackness. You only know you're white if there are others who aren't. But if people of color say "No, actually, this is who I am, not the lesser place you assigned to me," then what place is left for whiteness? Our racial categories are Manichean. For me to be good, you have to be bad. African-American theologian Willie Jennings argues that Jesus confuses all of that because Jesus is a Jew. Not black or white, but an identifiable other than both. He calls everybody out of their "natural" identity into borrowing his identity as God in our flesh. Gentiles then have to become part of a Jewish body. Black and white people and any others as well have to leave previous identities behind as we are grafted into the tree of Israel.[5] This paper is a prayer that Christians

---

2. Augustine, *Confessions*.
3. Quash and Ward, *Heresies and How to Avoid Them*.
4. Morrison, *Playing in the Dark*.
5. Jennings, *Christian Imagination*.

would identify ourselves not by who we're not. But by who we are: those trying desperately to follow Jesus in a dangerous world.

One source of our present Manicheanism is our technology. Martin Marty often points out that anytime there is a new media revolution, there's a new outbreak of fundamentalism.[6] Because people can find each other and they're horrified, or horrifying people can collaborate easier. In our day new media outbreaks happen about every ten minutes. And the level of violence we see in the Middle East, North Africa, and elsewhere is horrifying. Even those of us who knew the 2003 American invasion of Iraq was wrong didn't anticipate the level of horror it would unleash in the world. Remember when petty state dictators, relics of the cold war, were bad? Stateless fundamentalism seems potentially worse. In my country, the US, we have a remarkable revival of popular paganism that people often mistake for Christianity. Folks worshiping wealth and power and success and money and thinking it is Christian. I'm tempted to say these two deserve one another—Trump and ISIS. But the gospel is that we *don't* get what we deserve.

The politics of war in the age of terror is one source of our Manicheanism. George W. Bush wanted to rid the world of evil. But as a Christian he should know that only Jesus can do that. Jesus begins his redeeming work with a cross not an invasion. And Jesus is taking his time about completing it—letting evil go for now, being strangely patient with it. ISIS wants to rid the world of moderate Muslims, of Christians, of modernity, to restore an ancient Caliphate. My prayer is for other Muslims to articulate a Muslim theology that's better, more peaceful, more faithful to the Qur'an, than that. I'm struck as a guest in Canada how Canadian worldviews can slip into Manicheanism. Canada at times seems to know who it is by not being American. There are good historical reasons for that, including loyalists coming north after the American Revolution, those opposed to Vietnam fleeing compulsion to fight in an unjust war, Trump. Some of it is moral smugness. In Indigo Books we see this slogan, apparently coined by Bono of U2 fame, "The world needs more Canada." Humble bragging at a national scale.

The church decided that Manicheanism is a heresy. You can't split the world into essentially good and bad. The evil in the world runs through every single human heart. Manicheanism is tempting—we think in a world divided into good and bad we'd be on the good side. But it is not so. God sees a world we all divide into good and bad and God takes the side . . . of the bad. To save. Jesus is the friend of sinners. Dies trying to convert us, God's enemies, into friends with God and one another. For the rest of this paper

---

6. Marty, "News and the Good News."

I'll try to show God undoing our divide into essentially good and bad with a look at the incarnation, the crucifixion, and the resurrection.

First, God's incarnation. This is the Christian revolution for thinking about God: that in Christ *God* has eyelashes and a spleen and a Jewish mom. And like all good sons, Jesus learned everything he knows about God while on his mother's knee. Mary taught him the songs and stories of Israel. And I'm going to tell some of those stories with help of Jonathan Sacks, former chief rabbi of Great Britain, and his book *Not in God's Name*.[7] For Sacks, religious violence comes from a flawed reading of scripture that says God only blesses us and curses others. But the Bible tells its story in a way that subverts any such self-aggrandizing narrative. In Israel's scripture, God blesses Israel in order through Israel to bless the whole world, enemies very much included. When Jesus commands us to love our enemies, he's telling us the Judaism he learned at Mary's knee.

Sacks often argues that most influential person who ever lived on this planet was Abraham. A man who commanded no armies, conquered no territory, performed no miracles, announced no prophecies, yet now 2.4 billion Christians, 1.7 billion Muslims, and 13 million Jews trace their lineage to him. Israel has always been small (Sacks likes to joke that most of the 13 million are in the room he's speaking in at the moment). And Israel has been oppressed by every nearby empire—the Egyptians and the Assyrians and the Babylonians and the Greeks and the Romans, medieval Christendom, the Nazis, the Soviets, and each of whom strode the known world like a colossus and tried to exterminate the Jews and each one of those empires vanished. Guess who's still here? Sacks tells a story from Israel just before statehood. A Jewish settler in Israel named Chaim is arrested by the Brits for running guns. His wife Chava writes him in jail saying "Chaim, I'm proud of you, but you're a farmer, how am I supposed to plant these potatoes alone?" He writes back, "Don't plow the field, I hid the guns there." The Brits intercept the message and pour onto his farm digging up every inch of ground. They find none. Chaim writes to Chava, "Now, my love, you may plant the potatoes." Sacks says, "We Jews are not numerous but we are clever. Maybe we can help figure some things out in a world on fire."

The answer for Sacks is right where the problem is—in the Bible. The book of Genesis is about sibling rivalry. So are our disputes now. Competition between brothers and sisters to be the only one blessed. But the Bible tells a different story. The *second* born always gets blessed. The elder serves the younger. Think of the Bible's greatest stories—Pharaoh tries to stamp out the Jews. But Moses, Israel's liberator, is rescued by Pharaoh's daughter.

---

7. Sacks, *Not in God's Name*.

Raised in his house. In Egypt, Pharaohs were gods. Ramses' name means drawn up from Rah, the sun-god. Moses' name means drawn up from water, or no substantial thing. Pharaoh worshiped power, success, and beauty, like mythic religion always does. But the Exodus story at the heart of the Bible says this—God intervenes in history *to liberate slaves*. And yet Moses doesn't just reverse Pharaoh. The Jews pour a drop of wine when they recount the ten plagues at Passover to this day as a sign of God's tears for his Egyptian children.[8] God's blessings are not just for us. They're *through* us *for* others whom we are to serve and bless, even our enemies. Or in the language of the conference that gave birth to this book, we have to see the humanity even in those whom we call and who call us "other."

Think of Sarah and Hagar, Abraham's wives. Sarah despairs of having a child at 90 so she tells Abraham to take the servant girl Hagar as a wife. Abraham does, Hagar bears Ishmael, and Sarah *despises* Ishmael. Casts him out with the servant girl to die. There we see rivalry. Hagar goes into the wilderness, her water runs out, she leaves the child under a bush to die. And God *hears* the baby's cry. Ishmael means "God hears." God promises a blessing on Ishmael. He will be a great nation. Twelve kingdoms will come from him. Gifts will rain down on him. And Abraham *loves* Ishmael. Weeps over him. When Abraham is told to sacrifice Isaac, he shows no emotion. But Abraham himself blesses Ishmael. The Bible story is told to evoke the reader's sympathy *not* for Sarah. Not for Israel's matriarch, Isaac's mother, bearer of the promise, but for *Ishmael*, Hagar, ancestors of Israel's enemies. When Abraham dies his sons Ishmael and Isaac *together* bury the old man. When Abraham marries another woman after Sarah's death named Keturah, some rabbis imagine this is actually Hagar by another name. Abraham is righting the wrong he previously did. Can you see? God's elect come from Isaac. But the Bible bends over backwards to show a blessing on Ishmael. The two peoples then are not just rivals, but alienated brothers, both recipients of God's blessing. Israel is elect. Distinct. Set apart. And *through* Israel God blesses others. All. Even Israel's enemies. The Bible has blessings not *for* us alone but for us *with* others.

We Christians sometimes fancy that we came up with "love your enemies." *It was God's idea first.* And Jesus got it from somewhere. I'm suggesting he got it from Mary, who got it from the Bible. Marc Gopin tells of speaking to a conservative Jewish audience and hearing one first-row stage whisperer say to another, in critique of his talk, "He sounds like a Christian."[9] No, he sounds like Leviticus. René Girard has revolution-

---

8. Sacks, *Dignity of Difference*.
9. Gopin, "Journey towards Less Violence."

ized the way we Christians have to talk about sacrifice with his notion of scapegoating.[10] Every ancient culture we know practiced the sacrifice of an innocent victim in order to placate the gods. Girard suggests scapegoating gets at something intrinsic to human beings. We are violent. We compete for resources and love. Scapegoating limits the violence. The innocent who suffers calms the violence. Modern people fancy they're not religious and don't sacrifice. Actually, the pile of bodies in the twentieth century and early here in the twenty-first shows otherwise. We still sacrifice, we just don't limit ourselves to one innocent victim. Think back to your own experience in school, when a weaker kid is being bullied, picked on, shunned. That's just humanity, Girard says. We know who we are by who we gang up on and exclude and stereotype and murder.

Girard argues that only the Bible undoes the myth of the scapegoat. Here's how God does it: In Christ, God enters this scapegoating mechanism . . . *as* the scapegoat. What happens on the cross is we all gang up to get rid of the one we can't stand. But then something strange and unprecedented happens. The victim at our hands *returns* to us from beyond the grave not with the vengeance we might expect, as happens in every Hollywood action movie, but with grace. This explodes the entire system of scapegoating. As God undergoes scapegoating we recognize the way we do it and repent of it. Now, when we look at whoever we exclude, we see the face of God, who makes of us a different sort of people who can love the stranger. Girard teaches that salvation comes from the one we would exclude. Jesus shows us what Israel has always taught—love the stranger. You were a stranger in Egypt (Exod 22:21). And our God is always the stranger. Here, the one we crucified. The stranger who saves us.

The final source today is Rowan Williams, former archbishop of Canterbury, and his blazingly beautiful book *Resurrection*.[11] He notes the strangeness of the stories of resurrection in the gospels. Nobody recognizes Jesus. Does he look different? The text never says that. His appearance is just never something they're anticipating. And he toys with them! Hey, why are you all sad? We're just talking about the things that have taken place in Jerusalem. What things? (Luke 24:19). He lets Mary give this little speech, sir, if you, the gardener, have taken him away, tell me where he is (John 20:15–16). And only when they break bread together do they recognize him, and he vanishes. Only when he says her name, Mary, does she see him, really see him, resurrected. And then he says don't hold on to me!? Jesus is always just ahead of us. Just beyond the grasp of what

10. Girard, *Violence and the Sacred*.
11. Williams, *Resurrection*.

we can imagine. Stretching us to go where we don't want to go. He is not an idol in our hands but Lord of the universe.

Think Jesus here with Peter on the beach (John 21:15–18). Do you love me? Yes. Feed my sheep. Do you love me? Yes. Feed my lambs. Do you love me? Peter's hurt now. The Bible never tells us how people feel but it tells us this. Yes. Feed my sheep. His three-time denial is undone, rolled back, with a three-time profession of love. Now, Williams argues, Jesus is teaching us how to engage with our enemies: as surprising friends, even as the resurrected Jesus, trying to convert us. I think of a pastor I knew who said of her antagonist in her parish, "That dang woman is going to make a Christian out of me." Jesus is using our enemies, thorn in the flesh that they are, to teach us forgiveness, patience, love. To make a Christian out of us.

When Williams was archbishop of Canterbury both liberals and conservatives in that communion couldn't believe he didn't kick out their enemies. Both! Have you read his work? He thinks your enemy is Jesus! Trying to convert you! To remove them would only be to remove Jesus. The person you most loathe is actually the surprising presence of Christ trying to convert you.

I preached a sermon recently about the devil. Don't blame me—Jesus talks about the devil a lot. I insisted that the devil isn't a red scaly guy with a pitchfork. A man comes out after and says "It's not a pitchfork. It's a trident." Sure enough, the devil is often presented as a great sea creature, with a trident a sign of that maritime origin. That critic on Sunday is right more often than I like to admit. A sea creature like leviathan, like Jonah's whale, who swallows, destroys. In Christ, the sea creature sees a great treat. A morsel. So good he lets go his grip on Adam and Eve and clamps down on Jesus. He chomps down on the bait, but Jesus' divinity is the hook, who strings the devil up. Now he's done, the sea beast is wounded, thrashing around, harming others sure, but his days are up. Now here's the surprise. As Luther said, "He's God's devil." If you grab the devil by the scruff of the neck, the label on the uniform says "property of the triune God."[12] Christianity doesn't just oppose evil. It uses it for its purposes. Evil has no independent identity. It is simply the shading the artist uses to bring out the light more beautifully. By some sort of divine jujitsu God takes the harm evil would do and works it into God's saving purposes, like an improvisational musician who weaves a false note back into a true melody. Evil is a "happy fault," Augustine says, that brings about so great a savior as Christ.[13]

---

12. Steinmetz, Lectures.
13. Augustine, *Augustine Catechism*.

We creatures cannot not imitate God. That's what it means to be a creature, again, arguing with Augustine here. We can either imitate God's grandeur and majesty, and so be drunk with lust for power and hurt one another. Or we can imitate God's humility, as the incarnate suffering one, and so love one another. There is no space outside where we can avoid imitating God. Even God's enemies accidentally do God the courtesy of mimicking God.[14]

Here is the payoff: we all have enemies. Most of ours are kind of petty. A rival on faculty. An antagonist in church. I don't mean to minimize this. Such folks can keep us up nights and put us on medication. Here's the way to deal with them. It's to give thanks for them. Pray for them. See what in them is right, however hard to see. Any criticism of me as a pastor I tried to ask, ok, what's the one piece of this that's true, that I can learn from. Then the person will think of themselves as heard, listened to, acknowledged. And I might even be a better pastor for it. Rarely worked. But when it did, it *really* worked. Now that I'm an academic I feel the force of the observation that "Faculty fights are so vicious because the stakes are so small." It's true too in church politics. But everyone is trying to do their best, as they see it. A quote so apocryphal it gets attributed to everyone from Plato to the revivalist preacher Alexander McLaren says this: "Be kind. Everyone you see is fighting a mighty battle." And one day we'll kneel together with the demons and angels and all creatures and praise together Jesus' lordship. Why not start now?

## BIBLIOGRAPHY

Augustine. *The Augustine Catechism: The Enchiridion on Faith, Hope, and Charity.* Translated by Bruce Harbert. Edited by Boniface Ramsey. Hyde Park, NY: New City, 2008.

———. *City of God.* Translated by Henry Bettenson. New York: Penguin, 2003.

———. *Confessions.* Translated by Sarah Ruden. New York: Modern Library, 2017.

Girard, René. *Violence and the Sacred.* Translated by Patrick Gregory. New York: Norton, 1979.

Gopin, Marc. "The Journey towards Less Violence and More Empathy: A Scientific and Spiritual Convergence." Paper presented at Encountering the Other Conference, Vancouver School of Theology, May 17, 2016.

Hauerwas, Stanley. "Preaching as Though We Had Enemies." *First Things*, May 1, 1995. Online. https://www.firstthings.com/article/1995/05/003-preaching-as-though-we-had-enemies.

Jennings, Willie James. *The Christian Imagination: Theology and the Origins of Race.* New Haven: Yale University Press, 2011.

Marty, Martin. "The News and the Good News." Paper presented at Conference on Worship, Theology, and the Arts, St. Olaf College, July 19–23, 2010.

---

14. Augustine, *Confessions*; *City of God*.

Morrison, Toni. *Playing in the Dark: Whiteness and the Literary Imagination*. New York: Vintage, 1993.

Quash, Ben, and Michael Ward, eds. *Heresies and How to Avoid Them: Why It Matters What Christians Believe*. Grand Rapids: Baker Academic, 2007.

Sacks, Jonathan. *The Dignity of Difference: How to Avoid the Clash of Civilizations*. London: Bloomsbury Academic, 2003.

———. *Not in God's Name: Confronting Religious Violence*. New York: Schocken, 2017.

Steinmetz, David. "Church History Before the Reformation." Lectures at Duke Divinity School, Durham, North Carolina, Fall 1996.

Williams, Rowan. *Resurrection: Interpreting the Easter Gospel*. London: Darton Longman Todd, 2014.